BENEATH THE SKIN

BENEATH THE SKIN

THE COLLECTED ESSAYS OF

JOHN RECHY

with added commentaries by the author

Carroll & Graf Publishers
New York

BENEATH THE SKIN
The Collected Essays of John Rechy

Carroll & Graf Publishers
An Imprint of Avalon Publishing Group Inc.
245 West 17th Street
New York, NY 10011

AVALON
publishing group incorporated

First Carroll & Graf edition 2004

Some of these essays have appeared, in different form, in the
Los Angeles Times, Evergreen Review, The New York Review of Books,
The San Francisco Chronicle Book Review, The Nation, The Texas Observer,
Village Voice, L. A. Weekly, Viva, The Advocate, and *The Gay and Lesbian Review.*

Library of Congress Cataloging-in-Publication Data are available.

ISBN: 0-7867-1405-0

Printed in the United States of America
Interior design by India Amos
Distributed by Publishers Group West

*This book is dedicated
to the memory of my brother
Roberto Gabriel Rechy.*

ACKNOWLEDGMENTS

THE FOLLOWING AMPLY deserve acknowledgement:

Don Weise for suggesting this collection and following through devotedly and creatively as its editor from beginning to end.

Steve Wasserman for his generous assignments and suggestions that resulted in several of these essays for the *Los Angeles Times Book Review.*

Lucas Crown for suggesting some of these topics and so elegantly designing my Web site on which several of these essays, in different versions, were posted.

Michael Ewing, my partner, whose suggestions and observations have enriched virtually every essay in this book.

CONTENTS

PART III: 1990–2000

PART IV: 2000–2004

CONTENTS

FOREWORD

WHEN JOHN RECHY broke out in 1963 as the bestselling author of *City of Night*, his classic novel about the gay underworld of male prostitution, he became a source of provocative commentary for publications as varied as the *New York Times*, *The Nation*, *The Advocate*, and *The New York Review of Books*. As an openly gay man who was unafraid of addressing sex in print, Rechy used journalism to explore many of the themes that had won him acclaim as a novelist. Yet most of today's readers, including his fans, may be surprised to learn that for more than forty years Rechy has written extensively on a wide array of issues beyond gay sex, including literature, film, politics, religion, and race relations.

Although I have long been an admirer of *City of Night*, *Numbers*, and other novels, finding in these books those rare, dead-on renderings of a radical gay sex life that I identified with closely but seldom saw captured as unapologetically by other gay writers, I myself have been surprised to discover from time to time a marvelous new piece of Rechy's nonfiction writing in the *Los Angeles Times Book Review* or *The Gay and Lesbian Review*. Several of these articles centered on the lives of gay men such as Christopher Isherwood or Liberace, as well as AIDS, drag, body building, and the repeal of sodomy laws. Inspired, I wrote to Rechy, proposing a book of essays, which he generously agreed to do with me.

Of equal note, however, was my realization after some research that Rechy had for decades tackled non-gay subject matter, too—and from a similarly iconoclastic and informed perspective. Whether focusing on the Peace movement of the 1960s or his Latino heritage, commenting on literary giants like Emily Brontë or the films of Sergei Eisenstein, Rechy brought (and continues to bring) the same degree of insight and passion that he's brought to gay issues for years. Indeed, *Beneath the Skin* has been driven in part by my intention of overturning the restrictive, often oversimplified perceptions of his writing being principally about gay sex (about half his body of work—fiction and nonfiction alike—does not focus on gay subject matter). While I embrace, and perhaps even enjoy most, his gay themed essays, I've come to admire his larger body of work so much more through being made aware of his El Paso boyhood, through becoming better acquainted with his battles around the hostilities he faced from the literary establishment after the success of *City of Night*, or simply by being reminded that Rechy has been an outspoken political and literary renegade for well over a generation.

Beneath the Skin collects forty-six articles—some of them reprinted here for the first time, and almost all of which have never before appeared in book form—from the past forty-six years. Beginning with autobiographical accounts of his childhood in Texas and later his birth as a writer in pre-Stonewall Los Angeles, Rechy takes on Anita Bryant, the U.S. Army, Jack Kerouac, Marilyn Monroe, Charles Bukowski, Gore Vidal, the gay Mexican silent film star Ramon Navarro, Tom Cruise, Joyce Carol Oates, the *New York Review of Books*, Pope John Paul II, the U.S. Supreme Court, and George W. Bush. In showcasing the breadth of Rechy's intellectual and artistic gifts, I hope this volume takes readers "beneath the skin" of this pioneering gay novelist, revealing layers of literary accomplishments largely unseen—and therefore unrecognized—until now.

DONALD WEISE
October 2004

PART I: 1958—1980

EL PASO DEL NORTE (1958)

THIS IS ABOUT El Paso (and Juarez: the Southwest), which so long was just a hometown to me and which now is different from any other section in America.

El Paso and Juarez are in the middle of the Texas, New Mexico, and Mexico white, white desert surrounded by that range of mountains jutting unevenly along the border. At sundown the fat sun squats on the horizon like a Mexican lady grandly on her front porch. Appropriately.

Because only geographically the Rio Grande, which in the Southwest is a river only part of the time and usually just a strait of sand along the banks of which sick spiders weave their webs, divides the United States from Mexico. Only geographically. The Mexican people of El Paso, more than half the population—and practically all of Smeltertown, Canutillo, Ysleta—are all and always and completely Mexican, and will be. They speak only Spanish to each other and when they say the Capital they mean Mexico DF.

Oh, but, once it was not so. When the War came, Christ, the Mexicans were American as hell. The young men went to war wearing everything that was authorized, sometimes even more. Huge stars appeared on the Southside tenements and government-project windows. OUR SON IS SERVING AMERICA. My

3

mother wore my brother's Purple Heart to Mass and held it up when the priest gave his blessing.

Outside El Paso City, giant machines dig into the mountains for ores (Smeltertown), and beyond that (where I used to climb poetic as hell) is a tall beautiful mountain.

The Mountain of Cristo Rey.

Huge processions go up this holy mountain. The people of El Paso, Ysleta, Canutillo, of Smeltertown and of Juarez march up climbing for hours, chanting prayers. The procession starts downtown in El Paso, outside the churches, and the groups join each other in the streets, kneeling at intervals on inspiration, carrying placards of the Virgin, Saints in colors. Small bands jazz solemnly, crying dissonant sounds. The shawled ladies of the Order of Saint Something grip rosaries and mumble and feel—as rightly so as anyone in the world—Holy. The priests in bright drag lead them up. They carry sadfaced saints. The small bands stay behind at the foot of the mountain, the musicians wiping the sweat off their dark faces, and drinking cool limonada and mingling with the sellers of Coca-Cola, religious medals. The procession winds up the mountain slowly past the crude weatherbeaten stations of the cross along the path. And at the top, finally—where they say Mass, the people kneeling on the rocks in the blazing white sun—is The Statue.

It is primitive Christ.

Fifty feet tall. And it looks like a Mexican peasant. Mr. Soler made it. I think he was a kind of semi-atheist who didn't believe in God but believed in the Virgin Mary.

But the poor Mexican Christ, what it has to look down on— the line of desperate ants, as the Magazine (I think it was *Time*, or if it wasn't they would have) called it, of mustached, strawhatted men, braceros invading America.

Because the Rio Grande, no matter what you think, is usually dry, as I said, just sand and scrawny spiders and fingery indentations where water should be or was. Sometimes it is very full, though, and beautiful, and then the Rio Grande is like a dirty young black animal full of life rushing along the sand, swallowing the bushy dry banks. And I would walk along its bank, to the mountains. But usually it is so dry that the wetbacks can enter Sacred Country by merely walking across the River.

On their way to Georgia?

Well, I've heard that from I don't know how many people. They say, for some strange reason, that Georgia is a kind of heaven where all good spiks go—some crossing into the country illegally, others standing at the Santa Fe Bridge lined up all rags and cloth bags and wooden and cardboard boxes and holy amulets, whiskers, waiting to be inspected by the Customs-gods. The Magazine also said, well, wasn't it natural, those wetbacks wanting to come into America?—Christ, they heard about sweet-tasting toothpaste. It really said that. And if sweet-tasting American toothpaste ain't enough to make a man face the Border Patrol (as Bad as L.A. fuzz) and the excellent labor conditions in progressive Georgia, well, man, what is? The Magazine said it was sad, all those displaced wetbacks, but all that happened though was that they were sent back, but they tried to come across again and again and again.

(I remember a dead bracero near the bank of the Rio Grande, face down drowned in the shallow water, the water around him red, red, red. Officially he had drowned and was found, of course, by the Border Patrol. And his wife will go on thinking forever he made it with a beautiful blonde Georgia woman—loaded with toothpaste—and so, therefore, never came back to her and the even-dozen kids.)

Which brings me to this—

The hatred in much of Texas for Mexicans. It's fierce. (They used to yell, Mexicangreaser, Mexicangreaser, when I went to Lamar Grammar School, and I thought, well, yes, my mother did do an awful lot of frying but we never put any grease on our hair, and so it bothered me—if God was Mexican, as my mother said, why did He allow this?) Many of them really hate us pathologically, like they hate the Negroes, say, in Arkansas. Here, it's the bragging, blustering bony-framed Texan rangers/ farmers/ranchers with the Cadillacs and the attitude of Me-and-god on My ranch. It has nothing to do with the Alamo any-more. It's just the full-scale really huge (consistent with everything Big in Texas—and Alaska won't change anything) Texan inferiority complex. Dig: the Texas rancher strutting across San Jacinto Plaza, all bones and legs, getting kicks from sitting, later, booted feet propped getting a shine from the bare-foot spik kid, tipping him 50 cents—not just sitting like you and I would get a shine but sitting Grandly, and strutting across the Border owning the streets, I hope he gets rolled. They don't really dislike Mexicans in Texas if they're maids and laborers.

So the Mexicans live concentrated on the Southside of El Paso largely, crowded into tenements, with the walls outside plastered with old Vote-for signs from years back and advertise-ments of Mexican movies at the Colon—the torn clothes just laundered waving on rickety balconies along Paisano Drive held up God knows how. Or if not, in the Government projects, which are clean tenements—a section for the Mexicans, a section for the Negroes. Politely. Row after row of identical boxhouses speck-led with dozens and dozens of children.

So this, the Southside, is of course the area of the Mean gangs. The ones on the other side are not as dangerous, of course, because they are mostly blond and mostly normal Anglo-American kiddies growing up naturally and what can you expect? Like the ones from Kern Place—all pretty clean houses at the foot of Mount Franklin—and if those kiddies carry switchblade knives, at least they keep them clean, and when they wear boots, they are Cowboy Boots.

The Southside gangs—that's a different thing. They're black-haired. And tense. Mean and bad, with Conflict seething. El

Paso's Southside (the Second Ward) gave birth to the internationally famous Pachucos. (Paso—Pacho.) They used to call them boogies, marijuanos, the zoot-suits—and the baggy pants with the pegged ankles were boogiepants, and, man, those tigers walked cool, long graceful bad strides, rhythmic as hell, hands deep into pockets, shoulders hunched. Much heart. They really did wear and still sometimes do those hats that Al Capp draws— and the chains, too, from the belt to the pocket in a long loop.

And sitting talking Mexican jive, *mano*, under the El Paso streetlamps along Hill and Magoffin and Seventh, around Bowie High School and next to the Palace Theater digging Presley and Chuck Berry and Fats Domino, outside the dingy 40-watt-bulb-lighted Southside grocery stores, avoiding *la jura*, the neo-Pachucos with dreamy junk eyes and their chicks in tight skirts and giant pompadours and revealing 1940-style sweaters hang in the steamy El Paso nights, hunched, mean and bad, plotting protest, unconscious of, though they carry it, the burden of the world, and additionally, the burden of Big Texas.

Well, look. In East Texas. In Balmorhea, say. In Balmorhea, with its giant outdoor swimming pool (where that summer the two blond tigers and I went swimming, climbed over the wall and into the rancid-looking night water) there were signs in the two-bit restaurant, in Balmorhea-town then, that said WE DO NOT SERVE MEXICANS, NIGGERS OR DOGS. That night we went to the hick movie, and the man taking the tickets said, You boys be sure and sit on the right side, the left is for spiks. So I said I was on the wrong side and walked out. Later at Kit's aunt's ranch, the aunt waited until the Mexican servant walked out and then said, miserably, Ah jaist cain't even eat when they are around. And because earlier had made me feel suddenly a Crusader and it was easy now, I walked out of the dining room and said well then I shouldn't be here to louse up your dinner, lady.

And you never know it—to look at that magnificent Texas sky.

And something quite something else . . .

Once upon a time in El Paso there was a band of fairies—yes, really, in El Paso, Texas—and this city became a crossroads between the hot East Coast and the cool West Coast (fuzzwise, vicewise) or the hot West Coast and the cool East Coast, depending on where oh where the birls had got Caught Jay-Walking. And soon San Jacinto Plaza (or Alligator Plaza—sleepy crocodiles in a round pond, so tired and sleepy they don't even wake up when little kids grab them by their tails and flip them into the water) was a fairy paradise, rebel. The birls would camp there in that little park—the queens with pinched-in waists, lisps, painted eyes, digging the soldiers from Fort Bliss, proclaiming Too Much. Alas, they went the way of all fairies. The Inevitable Clean-Up came, and the fuzz swooped on them jealously and to jail they went, all fluttering eyelashes justifying gay mother love.

Now it is not the same passing through the park not seeing the queens, not hearing their delighted squeals of approbation floating into the clean summer Texas air. Not the same at all.

At Christmas is when Mexican El Paso is magnificent. I don't mean the jazz at San Jacinto Plaza (trees and lights and Christmas carols and Santa Claus). I mean the Southside Christmas. A lot of them—most of them, in fact—put up trees, of course, but many of them put up nacimientos. My father used to start putting ours up almost a month before Chirstmas when we lived on Wyoming Street. It's a large boxlike thing—ours was, anyway—about six-feet wide, six-feet tall, eight-feet deep, like a room minus the front wall (the minus faces the windows, which are cleaned to sparkle), and inside is a Christmas scene. Ours had the manger and the Virgin of course and St. Joseph, and angels hanging from strings floating on angelhair clouds. To the sides of the manger were modern-looking California miniature houses, with real lights in them—some had swimming pools. And stone mountains. On one was the Devil, red, with a wired neck so that the slightest movement made it twitch, drinking out of a bottle.

Christ was coming, and naturally the Devil would be feeling low. My father painted an elaborate Texas-like sky behind the manger, with clouds, giant moon, the works—lights all over, and he enclosed the boxlike nacimiento with Christmas-tree branches, and then, one year, he had a real lake—that is, real water which we changed daily. The wise men on their way. Christmas lights, bulbs, on top. He moved the wise men each night, closer to the manager. The Christchild wasn't there yet—He wasn't born. Then on Christmas Eve everyone came over. My mother led the rosary. We all knelt. Someone had been chosen to be the padrino—the godfather—of the Christchild to be born that night. He carried the Child in his hands, everyone kissed it ("adored" it), and then finally He was put into the manger, in the hay. We prayed some more. *Dios te salve, Maria, llena eres de Gracia.* . . . At the stroke of midnight, the Child was born. Then there was a party—tamales, buñuelos, liquor.

Most Mexicans are Catholic, of course. My friend Sherman is an intelligent Catholic from Evanston and he said it was bad when Catholics substitute, like the Mexican people he loves so much (Sherman in Chihuahua City that time trying so hard to look like a Mexican peasant, with Indian sandals and muslin shirt—him, six-feet-two and Scandinavian curly blond!—and people staring at him thinking he came probably from the American moon), the image of the Virgin for that of Christ. He loves the Virgin himself, a lot, but still he says Christianity should mean Christ. (He says he would rather see the Mexicans worship the Sun, incidentally, like their Indian ancestors, than become Protestants, because for a while the Baptists especially had a full-scale campaign going, and pretty soon, on the doors of the broken-down Southside houses they tried to invade with irresistible chocolate American candy and bright colors for the shoeless children living in cardboard houses along the Border appeared signs THIS IS A CHRISTIAN HOME PROTESTANT PROPAGANDA WILL NOT BE ALLOWED.)

But that's not what I started to say, which was this—

The Patron of Mexico is the Virgin of Guadalupe. The story says She appeared to Juan Diego, one day, and in order to make the incredulous know that he had indeed seen Her, She stamped Herself on his shawl, and that is the one you see in Mexican churches, all stars and blue robe. Oh, how tenderly they believe in the Virgin of Guadalupe *(even the Priests!)*, and how they love Her, the Mother of all Mexico.

How they Respect mothers because of it. Mothers are a Grand Mexican thing. They belong sacredly in Mexico and the Mexican Southwest.

Dig: a serious Mexican movie. The favorite theme. The son goes away. The little Old Mexican Mother stands at the dingy door with her black shawl sheltering her from the drizzling rain. Christ. The son goes away, and forgets about her. He becomes a Great Matador, lured by women like Maria Bonita before the President's wife—and this is only gossip—chased her out. Wow! The Little Mother in the Black Shawl wanders over Mexico, working for harsh people—like sewing in a factory where, she's so old, poor thing, she can't keep up with the heftier ladies. She comes at last into a very rich home in Mexico City. Of course. It's her son's home. But he doesn't recognize her, and she decides not to tell him who she is so he won't be ashamed of her. She'll just be satisfied to be near him. He is gruff. "Old woman, look how much dust has accumulated on this my favorite table." "Yes, sir." She wipes it. He is cruel, yells at her despite the pitiful black shawl. She takes it, and this is true. Mexican mothers and wives do take it—not Americans, and this is what grips a Mexican audience. Loyalty. One day the Big Corrida comes on. The wife is digging it on television (she can't bear to go it live). The matador is gored. The shawled Mother screams, MI HIJO!!!! The wife knows now, and being Mexican herself and on the way to becoming a Mexican Mother, she hugs the Old Lady. They run out, get a cab, go to the bullring. There he is. Unconscious. Dying. The beautifully dressed wife pulls the shawl off the the little old Mother and proclaims to the dying matador, "Die if God wills it— but not without knowing that—This—Is—Your—Mother!!!!" Everyone is crying, the unnatural son repents (as he must), and all three live happily ever after.

This is real. Mexicans really love Mothers. Americans don't. I don't have a single American acquaintance whose mother faints every time he comes home and again when he leaves. Mine does. The Mexican mother-love has nothing to do with sex, either. You can imagine an American wanting to make it with his mother. She is slick. She looks almost as young and bad as he does. But can you imagine making it with your mother if she wears a black shawl, and even if she doesn't, if she acts all the time like she is wearing one?

How does it follow, then, that a little Mexican kid (as I will tell you later) can say to an ugly big Texan tourist, HEY MEESTER YOU WANT MY MOTHER SHE IS CHERRY? I'll explain it by describing something else. Someone related to me lived with a woman for 25 years. Suddenly they decided to make it permanent. Get married. After 25 years, remember. Not silently, you believe it. They had a real Mexican bash, with canterers and mariachies, and the bride's 26-year-old daughter (from another engagement) crying all over the place—and the bride dressed in WHITE, and the Priest that married them and had been invited over saying well, God was certainly smiling in pleasure to see His laws being obeyed.

There's a Mexican Saint you make bets with. San Calletano, patron of gamblers . . .

Mexican religion is a very real thing, not lukewarm at all, nor forbidding and awesome. Mexican Catholics (and this, again, includes the Priests) believe in a God with two hands, two feet, eyes—the works. The Devil has horns, a tail, and he is most certainly red. Each church in the Mexican sections of the Southwest, and all of them in Juarez have Real patron saints, who guard them. On their days, they have kermesses—this is like a fair. On the really big days (for example, in May, the month of the Virgin Mary), the Indians (who are Catholics although their religion is still magnificently pagan, having room in it for Mayan, Aztec, other legends—witchcraft—right along with the story of Jesus) come into the City. The matachines (they used to scare me, like the beggars I will tell you about later) are Indians dressed in all kinds of feathers, painted all over, making dance marathons, dancing for hours. Some Indians—I think the Tarahumaras—run all the way from somewhere like Chihuahua City to Juarez, offering I suppose that amount of exerted energy to the Virgin. In religious frenzy, they burn an effigy of Satan—a kind of man-shaped catherine wheel. They light him up, and the bastard burns shooting fire straight from hell. The people yell up a storm, and the Politicians and Gangsters shoot real bullets into the air in this tribute to the Virgin Mary.

JUAREZ!

Time and time they try to clean it up. But Juarez is Dirty. And will be dirty long after we are gone.

The same close acquaintance I mentioned before is a gangster in Juarez. They really have bigtimers there, like they used to have in Chicago. You can always tell them by the way they wear Western-type gabardine clothes *à la mejicana,* and hand-tailored boots (NOT square cowboy-type), and always, always, but ALWAYS, sun-glasses, especially blue ones. My relation in question belongs to a very respected Mexican class—the gamblers, the gangsters, the pimps, the politicians.

At night, Juarez is all lights and neon signs. Clip-joints. Cab-drivers pouncing on tourists. This is your chance to find out If It Is True What They Say About Oriental Girls (i.e., does their Snatch slant?). Find out, they say, from Chinese Movie Stars. Get dirty postcards made to order. Peepshows. Men, women, dogs—sometimes a horse. And the little urchin barefoot Mexican boys saying, HEY MEESTER and they really do say meester YOU WANT MY MOTHER SHE IS CHERRY? Bars and cabarets,

Exotic entertainment. The Chinese Palace. The Stork. The 1-2-3. Girls, girls, girls. The thickly painted prostitutes stand in a line openly soliciting at bars—big fat red lips, narrow-waved long hair falling over great big dangling earrings.

At the Taxco they had this magnificent woman who looked like Mopsy of the cartoon. A genius. To wit: She dyed her hair *bright green.* And her costume was a large green powder-puff, same shade, right on her snatch. That started one of the many cleanups. So she had to get decent. She added two tiny green powder-puffs, the color of her dyed hair, to her nipples. . . .

In the early clear-blue Texas-Mexico mornings, the whores, the pimps, the politicians, the gangsters, the gamblers—that is, the upper classes—are all asleep, the rich ones in their grand mosaic houses (sometimes the roof leaks, but, oh, rebel, the luxury of them pads!). And then another group of people takes over the City—the vendors and the invalids and the beggars.

You've never seen anything like it—never so many people lacking legs, eyes, hands—the legless rushing around in their homemade wagons on skate wheels, with padded cloth knuckles rolling themselves along. At almost every corner, outside the market, along the park in front of the Church of Guadalupe, you see the gaunt women sitting draped in black shawls. You can't tell if there is anything wrong with their eyes or if they are just rolling them in a kind of poverty-frenzy. They used to frighten the hell out of me, they reminded me of Death when I used to think of Death as ugly. Around these women there are two or three or more kids, all filthy, mud caking on their legs, and inevitably a baby suckling their withered breasts, where I'm sure nothing is coming. *Madre de Misericordia,* they chant, *virjen sagrada de los dolores, una caridad.* And kids without legs, hobbling along on tree branches. And so much damned ugly poverty.

The market is all sounds and colors—and of course odors and smoke. All along the streets. *Aquí, marchante,* says a seller luring the buyer from a competitor. Prices fall fantastically, and a kind of haywire auction in which the buyer has no part goes on fiercely. Stands of cheap jewelry like broken kaleidoscopes, medallions of Christ and the Virgin, Indian masks, limeade and orchata (drunk by everyone out of the same two glasses), leather whips, hasaderos (like cheese), tacos railroadcar-like restaurants outside, tortillas pounded by the squatting women. And flies all around, always, lord, yes, always flies—especially around the red watermelon slices or pineapple slices where the little girl stands absently with a stick with thin strips of paper tied to it to shoo the flies unsuccessfully to the next stand and fans herself instead. And Mexican toys (always with strings to be pulled and someone kicks someone, or a chicken bites a woman, or a rock falls on an Indian). Paper flowers—different colors, from one stalk, covered with wax to make them look velvety—skirts with gaudy pictures of the Virgin of Guadalupe, of Catholic churches in the City. Boots (purple, yellow, green)—and everyone calling at the same time. Hot "rubies" for a dollar—"emeralds," "diamonds" for pennies. And the flies buzzing.

Outside, in the streets, especially outside the market, the kids in empty parking lots offer to watch tourists' and American shoppers' cars while they're gone—or offer to carry groceries to the streetcar (sometimes running away with them to hungry brothers and sisters—I hope), or offer to show you the City, or take you to a whorehouse.

I forget exactly on what day it is—the 16th of September or the 5th of May—both are important dates in Mexican history, like the 4th of July—the population of the Mexican cities gathers outside the City Hall, the Courthouse, etc., waiting for the President, the Governor, or the Mayor, depending, to give *El Grito*—The Yell. At midnight, it comes. VIVA MEXICO! And they echo, QUE VIVA!!!!

And cockfights!

And witches—lots of them.

They hold a position in the Mexican Southwest almost as respected as that of the priests. There's a kind of hierarchy among them, headed by Don Ben (the Pope of El Paso's witches). A problem too big for an ordinary witch is referred finally to Don

Ben, a root-twisted old, old man. (He won't die—he'll shrink.) I remember when I was a kid, an *espiritu maligno* kept bugging us, misplacing my father's glasses. We ended up going to Don Ben. He fell into a dramatic trance, and when he woke, he said, My *tata Dios* (daddy God) is so busy right now He suggests we call Him later. We called later, and *tata Dios* said to leave the *espiritu* alone and it would go away.

My second-aunt ("she of the blue hair and the deer eyes—ahhh!"—Don Ben's description of her) has had a picture of her husband, inverted in a glass of strange liquid, behind her bedroom door, for years. About 40 years ago, he left her—and this will bring him back someday.

And why should devout Mexican Catholics (as they are) consult witches (as they do)? For the same reason that a man with a sick ear goes to an ear specialist. . . .

And bullfights.

But they don't get the best bullfighters at the Juarez arena, although sometimes they do. The real sight—when the bullfight ain't good—are the Americans in huge Mexican hats being so Mexican, and the inevitable cluster of Mexicans around them, the fawning ones glorifying the grand American—these are the sick ones—and then the opportunists, hoping the money will rub off and willing to see to it that it does.

At dawn, on a lady's birthday—even now and in El Paso—five or six men gather outside her window, singing and playing their guitars. The sun is about to come out. They sing softly,

> *Estas son las mañanitas*
> *Que cantava el Rey David.*
> *A las muchachas bonitas*
> *Se las contava el asi. . . .*

Now the lady comes coyly to the window, standing there until they have finished the soft dawn singing. Now all the neighbors' windows are up and everyone is listening. (No one thinks of calling the police.) Then the lady invites the serenaders inside, and they all have early-morning coffee, *pan de dulce, menudo*. Then the sun is up in the sky.

The Southwest sky. Beautiful and horrifying. And therefore Wonderful.

Because in all the blunder and bluster of Texas about the wrong things, one thing is really so. The sky.

When it is beautiful it is depthless blue. The sky in other places is like an inverted cup, this shade of blue or gray or black or another shade, with limits, like a painted room. Not in the Southwest. The sky is really millions and millions of miles deep of blue—and in summer, clear magic electric blue.

(How many stars are there in the sky? was our favorite six-year-old children riddle. The answer: *cincuenta*. Which means fifty, but also: countless. And it's true, so true.)

Before the summer storms, the clouds mass and roll twisting in the sky clashing fiercely, sweeping grandly across the sky. Then giant mushrooms explode. The sky groans, opens, it pours rain.

But before the windstorms, everything is calm, and then a strange ominous mass of gray gathers in the horizon. Then swiftly, in a moment it seems, blowing with the wind, the steel clouds cover the sky, and you're locked down here, so lonesome suddenly you're cold. The wind comes. The tumbleweeds rush with it.

And always there's the fearful wailing.

POSTSCRIPT: My hometown exists now for me as two cities, the one I wrote about and the one I see when I return periodically, adding new memories, of absences, of people, of places, ghosts now. Some of the words I used here, current at the time, sound strange and amusing to me today: "pad," "dig" and "tiger." The words "fairies" and "birls" jar me, although they are also of the time.

THE CITY OF LOST ANGELS (1959)

S OUTHERN CALIFORNIA, WHICH is shaped somewhat like a coffin, is a giant sanitorium with flowers where people come to be cured of life itself in whatever way. The sign on Crenshaw, surrounded by roses, said: WE TREAT THE SOLES OF YOUR FEET FOR INNER PEACE. . . . This is the last stop before the sun gives up and sinks into the black, black ocean, and night— usually starless here—comes.

You came here to find the wish fulfilled in 3-D among the flowers—the evasive childworld (some figurative something to hold hands with like you used to with Mommie until you discovered Masturbation), the makebelieve among the palmtrees that the legend of the Movies (soda-fountains and stardom and the thousand realized dreams which that alone implies), of perpetual sun (never the lonesomeness of gray . . . lost . . . winter, say, or of the shrieking wind), the legend of The Last Frontier of Glorious Liberty (go barefoot and shirtless along Hollywood Boulevard) have promised us longdistance for oh so long.

You shut the windows, drew the blinds, bolted the doors. Still, life came screaming at you. So you came to Southern California to dash yourself against it.

Like inmates in other sanitoriums, of course, those who came to be cured sometimes die prematurely—but among the roses and the sun: in a swinging haven. So this is why you stay if you stay or come back if you come back: *You can rot here without feeling it* . . . and what more have you been led to expect if you've lived this long? And although you're still separated from the sky, trapped down here by the blanket of smog and haze locking you from Heaven, still there's the sun almost all year round, enough—importantly—to tan you healthy Gold . . . and palmtrees . . . greengrass . . . roses, roses! . . . the cool, cool blessed evenings even when the afternoons are fierce. . . . And the newspaper in its "Forecast of the Stars" omits The Sign of . . . Cancer and replaces it politely with The Sign of the Moonchildren in its gentle Zodiac. . . .

And what you came hoping to be cured with (which is what someone else came to be cured *of*—your sickness being someone else's cure) is certainly here, all here, among the flowers and the grass, the palm-trees, the blessed evenings: sex and religion and cops and nymphs and cults and sex and religion and junk—and these, along with Hollywood Boulevard and Main Street downtown, Laguna Beach, Laurel Canyon, La Jolla in the sun, etc., flowers, palmtrees, smog, Sunset Strip, green-grass all year round, roses, Strip City, all-night movies, fairies, religion, roses, sex, manufactured dreams (and the doctor that can create clouds and stars) . . . and sex and flowers and junk and religion, fairies and sick, sick cops make Southern California The City of Lost Angels as I would like to tell you about it now.

IT'S DAINTY BLUE flowers you think how phony, they're paper—but they're truly real this time, outside the bank on Hill Street off 8th downtown (with the poetic street-names: Hope, Flower, Grand, Spring) where the man put up a sign: WE WILL BE OPEN SUNDAY YOU BUY FLOWERS FOR MOTHER—flowers like white Easter, plants and vines inside the buildings when you go see your attorney—flowers illuminated outside by lights hidden beneath the green tropical-leafed plants across the street, among other places, from The Church of the Open Door over which like in the old college cartoon the sign flashes neonbrightly JESUS SAVES like an advertisement for the bank around the corner. . . .

Oh, yes, flowers . . . flowers from the Garden of the Roses by Exposition Park next to the Dodgers, flowers into the hills— orange and yellow poppies like just-lit matches sputtering in the breeze—carpets of flowers even at places bordering the fre- netic freeways where cars race madly in semicircles—the Harbor Freeway crashes into the Santa Ana Freeway, into the Hollywood Freeway, and when the traffic is clear, cars in long rows in oppo- site lanes, like two armies out for blood, create a *whooooosh!* that repeating itself is like the sound of the windswept ocean, and the cars wind in and out dashing nowhere, somewhere, anywhere. . . . Where?

To for example the golden beaches; Laguna and the Artists and Mamma Gabor; La Jolla and the Elite, set like a jewel in a ring of gleaming sand, next to the mysterious cave—and the sailors nearby flooding San Diego with make-it; Santa Monica and everyone, where pretty girls and boys turn brown in the hazy sun lazily rotting like mangoes but they don't know it, beside the frenzy of Pacific Ocean Park (dig: POP)—"Crystal" Beach—Jack's and the Girls and the would-be kept boys . . . the waves lapping at the sand like frothing tongues—and Long Beach—and the rollercoaster that went hurtling like a rocket and sent the young- man plunging into the ground like a bullet while his girl laughed convulsed at the impossible absurdity . . . the now-ghost of Mus- cle Beach where the men with the balloons for muscles posed for each other, until The Authorities of Santa Monica (Aghast and Indignant) Found Three of Them Shacked with Two Negro Girls, One Twelve, the Other Thirteen, and the city council of Santa Monica, why, it proclaimed: like this is The End. . . . To Venice and the beat generation in stores where the man like a slightly smaller slightly less hairy gorilla encouraged his urine-scented little girl to play in the traffic while he read a swinging Ode to

Allen Ginsberg, amid the beat odor of urine and beer, while away along the Long Beach Pike, teenage girls with painted lips hustled sailors in the park and tough merchant mariners looked for Negro women in San Pedro.

It's more flowers: birds of paradise with long pointed tongues; blue and purple lupin; joshua trees with incredible bunches of flowers held high like torches—along long, long rows of phallic palmtrees everywhere with sunbleached pubic hair. Even downtown if you stand at 9th Street looking up at San-Francisco-like-ascending Grand Avenue (do this on one of those rare Los Angeles mornings that come suddenly like a miracle, when the sky is clear of smog and haze, truly Blue, depthless Blue like a Texas Sky, and you're liberated into it as it were Heaven), you see—magic!—a row of palmtrees! They lead you out, farther, out along Wilshire Boulevard, into Beverly Hills and the jacaranda trees—more flowers (flame-red hibiscus for the rich, rich people—Palm Springs, especially: resort, USA . . .), Amarillo lilies—and Bel Air and Laurel Canyon, Mulholland Drive and Marlon Brando's wife, and into: . . . houses hiding in the trees crouched low (the witch-house out of Hansel and Gretel—and I have to tell you the lady in slacks, shades and calypso hat walking her pink poodle)—houses hiding snobbish or embarrassed, others brazenly shooting up, or trying for clean air, desperately piercing the smog; stooped over like vultures in the hills, wings spread in imitation of Flight.

And I like to think Valentino's falconhouse will make it, soaring away—away . . . to tango-swinging angels.

Los Angeles is Clifton's Cafeteria.

On Olive.

Next to Pershing Square.

And it's draped in verdure outside somehow like a demented Southern plantation in a movie.

But inside!

Inside, to the tune of "Anniversary Waltz" palmtrees burst into lush neonlife! erupt into fourth-of-July-sky-rocket pink! and blue! and green!—phony trees and flowers outlined with neon tubes all over, and the walls of the cafeteria simulate rocks. All around are rainhuts—but surprisingly no rain—draped with lonesome yellow thatch. As you walk upstairs, balancing your all-you-can-eat $1.25 tray—passing the of course American flag, there's the organ, and the man playing (against the sound of waterfalls gushing over phonyrocks and sometimes into your tray) "Anniversary Waltz" for the couple from Kansas here to celebrate their anniversary, who'll write the Cafeteria Folks expressing their Sincere Gratitude (and their letter, thurrillingly, will be printed in the Food for Thot, which is the brochure published weekly by the Cafeteria, full of Inspirational Poetry (Walking, for example, Through the Dark Holding Hands With Thee) and Friendly Thots for the Miseries of the Day). And if you're out and out, you can get for a nickel (or nothing if you ain't got that) a pint of multipurpose food containing every swinging vitamin and necessary mineral to get you through the infernal day, and the Citizens of Skidsville stand hands extended for their box of vitamins and minerals before the lush counters of meats and fruity desserts and gaudy salads that look like they'll bite back—all neonlighted among the simulated caverns and the waterfalls, the thatched huts, strains of "Anniversary Waltz," the American Flag, the tough chick with the camera and the leis about her neck: "Can I take your picture honey for The Folks Back Home?"—and a neonlighted Cross.

Suddenly, that junked-up day, along the serviceline, the cat from New York rubs his pupiled eyes like he can't place the scene: dig the woman in the long flowing drag, man. She was dressed in a kind of robe, with like a turban, green and blue and purple, and sandals, and bright-gleaming anachronistic bifocals which reflected the neonlighted flowers like miniature searchlights.

She had the air about her usually reserved for someone who has just enjoyed A Death In The Family.

Well, she glides through the serviceline with a truly virginal air, sits down, smoothing the folds of her drag—away from the crowd—but benignly, all hushed words and Virginity. Finally she gets up—she ascends. We followed her, like hypnotized, to a place to the right of the entrance—still, remember in the neon cafeteria—where a sign says:

THE GARDEN.

Down the narrow panel of stairs directly under the toilet with many mirrors and Hawaiian scenes in the Lounge. Past the picture of The Founder. Into The Room—where the lady in drag replaces another lady as virginal as herself—like holy sentinels changing the guard.

Now The Room—

And here is The Loom, and the lady is suddenly explaining to us, standing like that picture of Ruth St Denis, that this is a replica of a loom used in the time of Mary. Dig, she drones on like a holy record (we turning her you'll pardon me on), the tables, all genuine replicas, dig the benches; the beautiful parchment books with the Holy words.

Soon, she will allow us to pass into The Garden.

And when we passed into The Garden, through a replica of a wooden door, the bifocaled lady stayed behind like a dream when you wake and it's gone—and we stooped into a kind of cave and sat in the dim murky gray light. I could detect the faintly stagnant odor of probably a phony brook somewhere.

Then a voice booms out from somewhere:

"MILLIONS HAVE PERISHED IN WAR AND TERROR. We survive. . . ."

It tells us how lucky we are. Then The Voice tells us about Christ. It tells us about Sacrifice. Then leading to it I forget just how (the tune of "Anniversary Waltz" kept running persistently through my mind, though you can't really hear the organ down here), The Voice ends with: WHAT SHALL I DO???? Maybe this is not what The Voice had in mind, but what we did was what the bifocaled lady had told us to do—why, we passed into—*lo and behold!*—The Grotto of Meditation. . . .

Under the lush neon jungle erupting upstairs, beyond the tough chick taking pictures with leis around her good-looking neck, under the gushing fountains and the multipurpose vitamin food—under the sad yellow thatch rainhuts and the American flag, and the organ now playing Happy Birthday, directly beneath the head and the mirrors and the South Seas scenes:

There's Christ.

A giant white statute, kneeling before a rock, hands clenched. And then the lights hidden somewhere behind the cavelike rocks (like the lights hidden all over the city to illuminate flowers, or a statute, or a cannon) become brighter, slightly, slowly, then dim—slightly, slightly.

And in the weird light, Christ seems to shift uncomfortably. . . .

As we came out for air like submarines, the lady in blue and green drag and the crazy-gleaming searchlight bifocals, still basking in the radiance of someone whose Dear has just Recently Departed, standing behind the Things For Sale, her wrists touching each other delicately, palms creating a U before her face, said:

O boys why don't you buy some colored slides of our Beautiful Garden—they make Lovely gifts to send home—or just plain old Souvenirs? . . .

MOTIONPICTURE THEATERS DOWNTOWN featuring three movies and hard floors for sleeping when you don't don't care—strung along Broadway and Main Street like a cheap glass necklace—Main Street between say 4th and 6th with jukeboxes rattling rock and roll sexsounds, blinking manycolored, and the Main Street is mean looks and the arcade and magazine stores with hundreds of photographs for sale of chesty faraway nevertobetouched women in black stocking and spiked heels, and the vagrant youngmen trying to score no matter how—along the arcade and the stripmovies, the live New Follies and the flesh-show where the young boy with his hands in his pockets pled with the nymph bumping brutally before him, please, please, *please* honey do it some more, *right here!!* while she Did It on the apron of the stage, snatch crowning the inaccessible V of her spread legs, and he sighed and sank into the seat . . . and even on Main Street: it's Dreamland—Dreamland where the girls in tight reddresses dance for hire in the speckled light and crowded Marty lone-someness extending to Roseland on Spring Street (a title for, say, a musical play by Tennessee Williams), while at the Greyhound station leading everywhere the Vice squad vengefully haunts the head and you can't tell them from the real-life fruits; move to the Waldorf or Harold's on Main Street with the long accusing mirrors where you can hustle the lonely fairies for anywhere from a fin to whatever you can clinch or clip—even, expedi-ently, in the head—very, very quickly—for say a deuce standing before, once, the scrawled message: IN THE BEGINNING GOD CREATED FAIRIES & THEY MADE MEN . . . or Chi-Chi's with the femme queens, the sad young men with sallow painted faces—shadow of the 3-2-6, now closed, downtown on Spring, where out-side, the junkie who looked like Christ asked you right out did you want him to turn you on?

And moved to East Los Angeles where the spade after-hours club seethes with conflict, swings with junk and jazz—black-gleaming faces crying hate the fayboys, not so much in the other largely spade bar farther away on Broadway where outcasts from everything hang, and in the head sweat-gleaming fay and spade faces focus intensely on the dice, cramped bodies in the tiny room exploding with the odor of maryjane smoke more powerful than at Gloria's downstairs when the heat is Off—while the spade chicks with the classic butts squeezed into gold and orange hugging dresses wait outside, and on the dancefloor the bulldikes and the femme-queens dance with each other—the roles of course reversed but legal—broadshouldered women and waist-squeezed youngmen.

The dikes are leading the queens. . . .

Main Street again and the surrounding area to Skid Row: sweaty apartment houses squeezed tightly against each other (but not far from the green ebony trees, the carnations . . .), Spring Street, Los Angeles Street—Skid Row: squeezed hotly protesting against each other, walls greasily containing food from days' cheap cooking, cobwebbed lightbulbs feebly hiding from sweaty plaster peeling in horrendous childhood-nightmare leper shapes snapping at you, windowscreens if any, smooth as velvet with grime—rooms squashed in by lonesomeness where for a buck a night you die that night easily until checkout time—and you can face the day again in that endless Resurrection—among the roses nearby somewhere—the flowered trees before the courthouse on Wall Street, and you step out having paid a fine and see them—lavender and yellow flowers—and a short, short palmtree, with arched leaves shrugging what the hell.

And the Skid-Rowers (now talking about them at night without pad), flying on Thunderbird in this sunny rosy haven—past the owlfaces of the Salvation Army fighting evil with no help from God or the cops, wonder, these citizens of the country of Skids, shall they go to the Mission (and surrender to the owlfaces and the empty uplifting words before the lambstew) or just give up right here, now, on this corner, now on this doorstep, surrender for the night into the pool of their own urine—a surprise to discover—until the heat patrol comes by and makes up their minds, and they wake up hung over in the drunk tank: then out—into the green, green grass, the flowers. . . .

OH, PERSHING SQUARE. They tell me it used to be a jungle of Expression as opposed to now (relative) Repression.

They cut down the bushes.

Gay fountains gush in the midst of the wellkept grass—a stream of colored water, amber, blue. Once, on Christmas (when the Vice Squad couple, a woman and a man, fatherly-motherly spoke to the young vagrants about why don't you go home and get a job—before the bulls took them, the young vags, for a ride in the wagon to the fingerprinting glasshouse)—once, as I say, oh, on Christmas, they had The Dancing Waters on Pershing Square. The bums and the studhustlers and the queens and the vagchicks and the preachers and The Visitors stood on the grass in the middle of the park before the fiercely perspiring man manipulating a set of keys which caused like spurts of water to change colors as it gushed into the air, swaying to the rhythm of the corn-music. . . . Very pretty . . . very, very pretty.

And on Easter, the cops roll eggs for the lonesome children, future, probably, delinquents, whom later they'll spreadeagle against the black and white car with red searchlights like science-fiction eyes—rousting them for mean kicks.

Pershing Square.

It's bordered on the Hill Street corner, at 5th, by a statue of a general, and on the 6th Street side there's a statue of a soldier. They love soldiers and generals in queer parks. On the Olive Street Side, at the corner of 6th, is a tough cannon pointing at Clifton's Cafeteria. And on the 5th Street corner is a statue of— really—Beethoven with a stick, and he is glowering, I mean to tell you, at the Pershing Square menagerie: at, say, Ollie talking sometimes sense, mostly not, mostly rot, and once they threw a firecracker at him which landed on the flowers and sputtered. Ollie was then going to make a Citizen's Arrest, like he says Officer Temple, the fat cop told him he could—but Ollie, oh, he didn't figuring, rightly, the Lord couldn't be on the side of the bulls.

Talking about Citizen's Arrests—whereby anyone can come up to you and say I saw you do such-and-such you are under arrest—once this chick clipped a fat looking score trying to make it with her sweet-boy, and a square caught the scene and marches to the clipping chick and says she is under arrest, he is making a Citizen's Arrest because he pinned her clipping the score. All the swinging hustlers from Pershing Square, oh, they gathered round, while the chick, checking the mean-it faces all with her, said to the square, Like you're going to make a what arrest, man? The Square naturally walks away, leaving the chick with the clipped wallet: a Fine example of Togetherness.

And the statue of Beethoven (getting back) glowers fiercely at the studhustlers coming, coming, and the lonesome fruits coming after them; hears, daily—brutally—Holy Moses strumming a soulful guitar, sees the hungry nymph who haunts the park around the men's head, searching the homeless youngmen, so used to being clipped she leaves her bread on the dresser of the rented room to make it easy; and Beethoven glares at the buck-toothed Jenny Lu, singing spirituals; at the Negro woman sweating quivering in coming-lord-type ecstasy, for sometimes hours, bumping and grinding (lord-*uh!* . . . mercy-*uh!* . . . halleluj-*uh!*) at each *uh!* in a long religious orgasm; at the tough stray teenage chicks making it from night to night with the studhustlers at Cooper's coffee-and-donuts-for-a-dime; at the epileptic young-man thanking God for his infirmity among the roses and the warm sun; and the five white Angel sisters, standing like white candles while their old man preaches, and they hold in turns a picture of Christ crucified. The blood is wax. It gleams in the sun. And the cutest of the angel sisters, my of course favorite, with par-adoxically alive freckles snapping orange in the sun, and alive red sparkling hair, is always giggling in the warm Los Angeles smog-afternoon among the palmtrees—but the oldest is quivering and wailing, and one day, why, the little angel sister, she will see there's nothing to giggle about, her old man having come across at last with the rough Message, and of course she will start to quiver and wail where once she smiled, freckles popping in the sun.

All this to the piped paradox of the Welkian-Lombardian school of corn. . . .

Downstairs, in a little tool hut, hidden in typical sneak-cop fashion, is the baby-joint, like, where the fat bull daily interrogates the new butch-hustlers in the park—and downstairs, like a swollen toad, the bull sits before the pictures of the wanted angels. . . . And Miss Trudi, the swinging queen whose stud husband got busted by this bull, periodically starts rumors about Officer Temple and how she saw him in the mensroom doing you-know-what. . . .

But when the heat is On in Pershing Square, watch out. Like not long ago. The studhustler who used to hang in the park snapping a whip around the water fountain killed the chick like 17 years, who was having such a great time, wheeeeee, and he killed her with an iron. Then he strangled her. Vengefully—vengefully for not having spotted the psyched-up stud before the papers implicated them—the bulls stormed the park. And everyone, hiding out on Main or Spring or Miramar, said, that lousy psycho, man, screwing up for everyone, had to go and kill that chick.

And didn't recognize that the greatwinged bird had merely chosen the guise of Murder to swoop ridiculously upon him.

LONGING FOR A Texas Sky . . .

The sky here is usually a scrambled jigsaw puzzle—all indefinable smears of grayish-blue.

And longing for a Texas Sky, I went to Griffith Park Observatory, made famous by James Dean in *Rebel without a Cause* (and the Lord, oh, He took him away to save the pardon me go-mankind, and left us Marlon Brando in a suit).

It's circular, the planetarium where they reproduce the Sky—shaped like half a womb—like the Hollywood Bowl—and in back of your seat there are headrests so you can look up comfortably. In a moment, they will simulate the most beautiful Sky you'll see in the City of Lost Angels—an imitation Texas Sky. Here it comes! A skyline . . . hint of clouds . . . the black night creeping up . . . the stars appear. . . . You're truly gone—as if the half-womb had opened magically and carried you into the real Sky. But now a Voice announces this is such a planet, such a star, drones on, shattering the illusion—and then there appear Walt-Disney-like cartoons of the figures of the Zodiac on the simulated sky. The illusion is over. You're sitting in a slick shell-shaped auditorium with a voice telling you about distances, etc. They play "Afternoon of a Faun." Now the shellsky turns, spinning, churning you out of the dream. The lights come up. You walk into the smoggy day. . . .

To Forest Lawn, to gloat at the tombs. See the hills all green, the tasteful stones—the marble Depiction of Life (or Love?) in a garden, with benches. Sit in as a fourteenth guest on the duplication of The Last Supper. A super mosaic. Then you go to the actual Crucifixion. A cinemascopic painting presented first in sections, then you see at all—and the sick voice of the ubiquitous announcer (is it the same Voice? . . .) tells you again about Christ like talking about the local boy made good—in such a way I thought this cat's flipped—he's a sadist digging the Crucifixion.

You came to find the dream fulfilled, the evasive childworld.

You go to Disneyland, and you walk through an umbilical tunnel (dig) and you enter the mouth of a whale (Dig) and (Dig!) pass through replicas of nursery dreams! and I don't wonder that when you came out you looked for Mommie and you were stooped over, like curling up. And went to Santa's Village later— and believed in Santa Claus—because there he is, with all his helpers, before your longing eyes. . . . And Knott's Berry Farm, tribute to live TV Westerns (I wanna be a cowboy when I grow up), and they held up the stagecoach, and the chorus girls did a Can-Can, flinging out their garters coyly at the adult tourists shouting with naughty delight. (Their wives thus have an anecdote for The Folks, how the Can-Can girl looked straight at Harry All Through The Show.)

Remembering the swallows, to the Chapel of Capistrano with the giant bell and the sunken gardens where the fruit that day later going to Laguna Beach the long, long way said to hell with the swallows, where's the monks? . . .

And I with my time-obsession stand longingly before the Hollywood Ranch Market watching the clock move backwards. . . .

Dash like a crazy somekind animal on the Hollywood Freeway, into Sunset Boulevard (and remember Gloria Swanson going mad thinking she's playing Salome for Cecil B DeMille in knickers but the flick was shot on Wilshire Boulevard where the slick building now commands attention—a modern act of faith—and Erich Von Stroheim, said Mr. Brackett at USC, insisted there should be a scene of him ironing her panties), to Vine and the recordstore and the TV studio where the visiting ladies in the live studio say oh he's much handsomer on television, and at home say oh he's much handsomer in person—to Hollywood Boulevard, most disappointing street in America—expecting to see The Stars in limousines, and extras in costumes—and see instead the long rows on either side of stores and counter-restaurants and B-girled bars and moviehouses—and, happily, that day, a giant picture of Susan Hayward, the swingingest star in the movies—in a sexpose screaming out against the railroading L.A. cops I WANT TO LIVE!!!!

Toward the end of the stretch of more-or-less activity, before the street turns into softlawned houses and apartment units where starlets live lonesomely wondering will they make it, finding no substitute for stardom in the carefully rationed joints of maryjane for manufactured dreams—there (before the soft-lawned swimmingpooled houses) is a coffeehouse for teenage queers. Inside the mosaicked windows like a church, the dike with pencil and pad, stocked up on bees, writes love poems to the femmetype teenage fairies. After 2 in the morning, they wait in line to come in.

Now here's the Chinese Theater. Your own big foot can rest where The Great Star's tiny one rested, impressed in the cement—though sometimes, tough to say, not quite so tiny, and you're disappointed to find that Marilyn Monroe (sigh) and Jane Russell are represented by their hands, and on premiere days at the Pantages the unenchanted crowd forms early to glimpse the enchanted men and women—and the searchlights screw the sky—while the lady from say Iowa sighs ahhhhh . . . writing mental postcards, and the twin Boswells of the Golden Cinema World—the screeching ladies with the hats and the weird—one of them—personal grudges against *Lolita*—record the phony fable of the Stars, from the dim nightclubs on the Strip—and Chasen's.

While the cafeteria in Beverly Hills serves caviar hors d'oeuvres . . .

Off Las Palmas, along—but on the opposite side—the outdoor newsstand where professional existentialists with or without sandals leaf through a paperback Sartre and the horse-o-manes (going tomorrow to the races where they'll see Lucille Ball) leaf through the racing forms, and the fairies cruise each other by the physique books and the same lady from Iowa staying at the Biltmore for a convention of the PTA buys a moviebook—off Las Palmas on Saturday nights the oldman graduate of Pershing Square writes Bible inscriptions on the street, in chalk, neat, incredibly beautiful letters. The young highschool delinquents with flattops proclaiming their youth heckle him cruelly in merciless teenage fashion while he dashes out his prophecies of not-unlikely doom, and the fairies having crossed the street on their way to the Ivy (where Miss Ana Mae plays her organ coyly) say my dear she is Too Much why doesn't she get a Man and swish on giggling wondering nervously does it show (which ruins a birl) and will they make it tonight and if so will it be someone Nice and early please God so they won't have to add to the shadows on Selma—while the queen who left her telephone number in the toilet at Coffee Dan's waits—this is only conjecture—nervously by her telephone wondering will someone call?

The palmtrees look down apathetically—but green—from the surrounding hills.

Mmmmmrrrrrumph! The motorcycles dash by on the Boulevard—ghosts of the Cinema Bar where the sadists and the masochists, now scattered, used to hang, rubbing leather jackets and staring at belts and boots and exchanging notes with sketched whips across the bar now slowly transferring far out (intentional) to the Satellite and the Jupiter. . . .

Away . . .

Away, beyond the house hidden in the hills where the Doctor of Something Divine stood on the balcony like a fairytale wizard—high-priest of a cult—making clouds and stars appear where there were none—blessing the world from the balcony—and later, inside, preaching love and fraternity, serenity and subsequent contentment, while he padded our legs fraternally, serenely, contentedly—away, away, outside, beyond the spiritualists and the Holy Ghost Services, the maps of Life, dividing life into tiny blocks like beehives—far from the fat Negro woman sprawled like chocolate pudding on Main Street, snoring, the copies of *The Watchtower* falling from her lap to her fat tired feet—beyond MacArthur Park and the little boats where if you ain't got a pad but got a willing fish you rent a boat and screw her on the pond, surrounded by grass, dark-green in the light night, under the stars—the odor of, of course, flowers, and justmown greengrass—beyond the other side of the park where hot mouths lurk in the bushes and the spade cat killed a cop while the ducks shivering out of the water made a noise like laughter—beyond the miles of flowers and greengrass, plants in the downtown buildings, away from the fruit Y where the fairies sunbathe naked with semihardons—beyond the signs on the sidewalks that say LAWD and you think of a religious Negro but it stands for Los Angeles Water Department—far from Strip City on Western and the nymphs with the tantalizing G-strings feeding on hungry yearning eyes—beyond the gossip at Schwab's on the Strip in the afternoons where the beautiful girls and boys go to be Discovered in one way or another (and one of them put a doublepage inside-spread ad in the daily variety film journal, with an almost naked sexpicture of herself, a man's shirt clinging wet to her nipples, open in a V almost revealing her own—and the ad said she's available to Furnish New Blood To Hollywood—she is The Challenge to the movies—call her up and see, and soon after, another ad—another sex picture. HOLLYWOOD HAS ANSWERED!!! And very soon after, why, a young cowboy without shirt, he does the same thing, and he says he too is available to furnish, this time, New Masculine Blood To Hollywood—he also is A Challenge to the movies—and soon, why, Hollywood has answered him too, the ad says, and it shows another picture of the cowboy—and a new phone number) (and the starlet who advertised two months ago now advertises she's back in town again)—and, oh, away, still moving away, from existentialists who used to grace the Unicorn and Cosmo Alley until they became famous as "beats" and now the tourists pay 75 cents for a cup of coffee and stare at each other wondering is he one? beyond Coffee Dan's and the young punks, the bars on the Boulevard and the B-girls looking at their watches, the bar on Cahuenga and the B-boys looking at *their* watches where the male prostitute walked into the women's toilet and the flashy woman followed him . . . far from Chinatown . . . as real as a "hot" Juarez ruby . . . beyond the Men's glamorshop on Sunset, where in a penthouse lavishly decorated the select clientele of gentlemen change the color of their hair subtly, gossiping about the Stars over a cup of Italian coffee in the natural light from the windows overlooking the trees and the flowers—beyond the sirens incessantly screaming—away, beyond the miles of geraniums and grass, past in the summer the stands of youngmen and oldmen selling strawberries and corn at bargain prices—beyond all, all this . . . up there on a hill, threatening heaven, piercing the sky brazenly, all glass and vines, the ocean thrashing beneath it, is The Church of the Wayfarer designed by Frank Lloyd Wright's son.

I am glad to tell you that now at last it has been properly immortalized by Jayne Mansfield when she wed there in kewpiedoll I think pink.

TO SOUTHERN CALIFORNIA everyone comes: to be Discovered and get in the movies, to be loved by the world, to find out if indeed your Brother is your keeper, to find the evasive child-world, or to find God in fruit or vegetables or in the sun or ghosts—or standing on a balcony creating stars and clouds . . . or to bask in the sun—to rot without really knowing it . . . to think you'll be cured, with sex, religion, junk, cool nights, etc. . . . or to cater to personal grudges by joining the Los Angeles Police Force and so attain to holydom and omnipotence and wear the stick like a mighty scepter and the badge like a sort of misplaced halo—and become merely another gang in a many-gang rumble—and brag about it, like the one who said he could keep me 72 hours, for nothing, merely because I was "wise." I had been playing a schizie game to myself, pretending I was a Pachuco, walking cool, past the May Co., on Hope Street, incidentally—walking with long bad strides, shoulders forward, hands outward—a harmless schizie game, you'll agree—and as Badge No. 4118 frisked me on the street, in the afternoon—on the Lord's Day, too—running his hands down my thighs, I asked him was he getting his kicks.

Later, at the station, why, he say I give him a fuck-you finger as he pass me (not true) and it sound so funny even the detective break up and let me go. And when the tough bull go out, with me, I ask him will he give me a ride back where he pick me up, and this, it put him on bad—but he still have his Badge, boy. (And guess what happen now automatically to my middle finger each time a bull car pass? . . .)

And if you're a head or a hype, well it's heaven for you in the L.A. jails. Outside, sometimes, it's not too cool to get. But inside, you take your choice like buying candy bars. Hard or soft. And the junky in the joint died from an overdose.

Dig. Significantly.

Walking along Hollywood Boulevard the other afternoon thinking about how I would end this, I thought I would say: R.I.P., or maybe say that rats in a maze possibly wouldn't know they're lost if they had roses and poppies and sun grass and palmtrees swaying in the cool, cool breeze—and childhood dreams in 3-D: a maze shaped at the same time conveniently like a coffin. And I was thinking about this when I saw her, coming out of Kress's on the Boulevard: a wild gypsy-looking old woman, like a fugitive from a movie set—she was dark, screamingly painted . . . kaleidoscopic earrings . . . a red and orange scarf about her long black hair . . . wide blue skirt, lowcut blouse—an old frantic woman with demented burning eyes, and as she stepped into the bright Hollywood street, almost running into the suntanned platinum blonde getting into a Cadillac, this old flashy woman began a series of the same gestures: her right hand would rise frantically over her eyes, as if tearing some horrible spectacle from her sight. But halfway down toward her breast, the gesture of her hand mellowed, slowed, lost its franticness.

And she seemed now instead to be blessing the terrible spectacle she had first tried to tear from her sight.

I heard a siren scream, dashing along the palmtrees.

POSTSCRIPT: When I read this impressionistic view of Los Angeles now, I'm surprised by how many of the familiar clichés about the city I included—the so-called excesses, "excesses" I have come to view as manifesting unique strengths. As with "El Paso del Norte," this essay contains "hip" words of the time: "bull," "fay," and "swinging." The words that I cringe to read now include "dike," "fruits," "chicks"—and not only because they offend today—but because they reveal a forced, macho "I'm-not-gay" tone. That tone belongs to a time when, even in gay bars, the accusation of being "queer" might result in angry denials, even violent altercations.

"CONDUCT UNBECOMING . . .":
LIEUTENANT ON THE PEACE LINE (1966)

A S THIS IS written, Second Lieut. Henry H. Howe, Jr., 24. of
Boulder, Colo., is locked up in the military prison at Fort
Leavenworth, Kan.—the first soldier to be punished for marching in a peace demonstration against the United States Government's position in Vietnam. He was arrested last November
by civilian police in El Paso, Tex., in a manner which many
contend—and at least one military spokesman for the prosecution asserted—was illegal.

Tried by general court-martial, Lieutenant Howe was
euphemistically charged with using contemptuous language
toward President Johnson and with conduct unbecoming an
officer and a gentleman. A third charge—intention "to promote
disloyalty and disaffection among the troops and civilian populace of the United States"—was dropped.

Although ably defended by his military counsel, Capt.
Thomas C. Bigley of the Judge Advocate General's staff, Lieutenant Howe was found guilty and given a severe sentence: two
years' imprisonment at hard labor, dismissal from the service
(the equivalent of a dishonorable discharge), and forfeiture of
all pay and allowances.

Despite the fact that appeals of his case were pending, Lieutenant Howe was immediately placed in virtual solitary

confinement in the Fort Bliss stockade. He was allowed visits only from his counsel, his family and, on special permission, from his girl friend. He was permitted to receive telephone calls from the same parties, but a call from a Denver reporter was interrupted. His mail and reading material were censored.

Joining the case as civilian counsel, the American Civil Liberties Union quickly announced its intention to appeal Lieutenant Howe's conviction in the civil courts as unconstitutional, being a violation of his right of free speech. The ACLU also charged that holding Lieutenant Howe in the stockade while appeals were pending was a further violation of his rights.

Subsequently, in an automatic review of the case, Maj. Gen. George T. Powers III, commanding general of Fort Bliss, reduced Lieutenant Howe's sentence to one year's imprisonment at hard labor. It was announced belatedly that Lieutenant Howe would be given credit for time served in the Fort Bliss stockade.

In view of the ACLU's announced intentions, General Powers' reduction of the sentence has been interpreted by some as a strategic move whereby the defendant officer may have served his full sentence by the time the case is appealed to other courts. Thus, even if the decision were reversed, the Army seems vindictively determined to punish Lieutenant Howe.

IN AN ADVENTUROUS maneuver (if realized, it would have been the first such instance) the ACLU filed a writ of *habeas corpus* in the U.S. District Court to have Lieutenant Howe released on bail pending appeals. Attorney Melvin L. Wulf of New York, pleading the case as legal director of the ACLU, pointed out that defendant officers in the past have been allowed to remain free or restricted to quarters while appeals are heard—and not imprisoned in the stockade unless the charge involved violence. It was clearly the political nature of the case which resulted in Lieutenant Howe's incarceration, Mr. Wulf implied, and he charged that Major General Powers had acted "capriciously and arbitrarily" in the matter.

General Powers was subpoenaed to answer the charge. A man with three sparse patches of hair and narrow eyes in a face stamped with a stony mirthlessness, attesting to his many years in the Army, General Powers reacted to Mr. Wulf's questioning with the outrage of a man not used to explaining his actions.

He asserted bluntly, almost belligerently, that he had decided to incarcerate Lieutenant Howe because the lieutenant was "not fit to be an officer" and, outside the stockade, he would have had to be treated as one. The general "just knew" that other officers would want to have nothing to do with Howe (although, on Mr. Wulf's prodding, he admitted he had taken no survey, nor asked any officer).

Predictably, General Powers asserted his belief in the infallibility of the Army system ("I have never questioned the constitutionality of a court-martial proceeding"), although, again, Mr. Wulf managed to make him admit that on occasion he had heard that a court-martial decision had been reversed. "I don't think this case will be reversed," General Powers prophesied.

General Suttle, the judge (who had only a month or so earlier ruled against a petition filed by Leon Day asking that the Army be enjoined from discharging him dishonorably for having belonged to the Socialist Workers' Party), left little doubt as to where his own sympathies lay. He pointed out to Mr. Wulf that "we have to think in numbers," implying that Lieutenant Howe's case must be considered in regard not to one individual's rights but to the efficient operation of the Army. He also admonished Mr. Wulf that this was "not a civil rights rally." Almost as predictable as General Powers' testimony was Judge Suttle's ruling that the decision to incarcerate Lieutenant Howe had not been "capricious and arbitrary." He would, however, not act on a motion by Mr. Wulf that the Army be restrained from removing Lieutenant Howe from Fort Bliss pending disposition of his case in the 5th Circuit Court of Appeals. The judge declined to do so on the ground that he had no jurisdiction in the matter, although in ruling at all he had assumed such jurisdiction. No amount of rational explanation by Mr. Wulf concerning this and concerning the fact that Lieutenant Howe's removal would create new difficulties for his defense would sway the judge, who announced his feelings quite succinctly:

"I hope we don't see the day when the federal courts can tell the U.S. Army what to do!"

The next day, Lieutenant Howe was flown to Fort Leavenworth.

Now, his case goes automatically to the Army Board of Review, then, depending on that board's findings and the subsequent decision of the Howe defense, it may be appealed to the three-member civilian Court of Military Appeals, the highest military court. Neither of these two bodies may increase the sentence— only reduce it or allow it to stand. Claiming that Lieutenant Howe's constitutionally guaranteed rights have been violated, his defense will appeal his case in every court available. If it should reach, and be accepted for hearing by the Supreme Court, it will be the first military case heard by the highest court in America.

Recalling that Gen. Edwin Walker was never court-martialed for disseminating Birch Society and similar rightist material to soldiers in his command, one must wonder whether any charges would have been brought against Lieutenant Howe had he been demonstrating, say, for the bombing of Hanoi.

A second trial emerging out of the same demonstration in which Lieutenant Howe participated will be based on charges for libel brought by Dr. Richard C. Trexler, of the History Department at Texas Western College, against the *El Paso Times* for printing a letter exhorting the college authorities to "throw the bum out," and brandishing the wild—and currently popular—charge of "treason."

THE PEACE DEMONSTRATION from which these trials stemmed occurred on an unusually warm, humid November afternoon in El Paso, Tex., when about a dozen young men and women, most of them college students, led by Dr. Trexler, marched in San Jacinto Plaza—the heart of this handsome city—amid jeers and shouts for scorched flesh from a mob of more than 2,000.

The paradox is that El Paso, compared to Texas' pistol-packing large cities like Dallas, or its devil-oriented smaller ones like Lubbock, had appeared, before all this, as the progressive daughter in a wealthy reactionary family. It was the first city in the South to pass an ordinance banning discrimination, and reportedly the first to integrate both its lower schools and college. It accomplished all this without incident, and subsequently one of its previously all-Anglo high schools elected a Negro "most popular boy."

What, then, could have stirred this generally tolerant city into a vortex of hatred? It began like this:

Late in October of last year, Nick Cheshire, a former student at Texas Western College, which is located in El Paso, and Harry Bowen, a graduate student and teaching assistant there, petitioned the city council for a permit to march in protest of the Vietnam war. They had previously been told by a member of the traffic control department that they would need such a permit.

At the hearing of the council, the Mayor, while contending that there was nothing illegal about such a demonstration, called the request for a permit "an exercise in provocation and incitement . . . a further refinement of the tactics of civil disobedience . . . intended to . . . discourage the laws requiring patriotic duty in service of the flag, and impede the conduct of war." An alderman intoned: "I can think of nothing more despicable than a man who will not fight for his country." (It would be interesting to know how the alderman ranked genocide, poverty and lynching in his scale of things despised.)

Although the alderman also admitted that such a demonstration was legal, the council—in what was, for its questionable ends, an idiotic move at best—voted to deny the group permission to march.

Insisting that they would march, the small committee retained J. B. Ochoa, Jr., a man identified with civil liberties cases, as its attorney and found a faculty spokesman in Dr. Trexler, formerly a first lieutenant in the Air Force, now a captain in the inactive reserves.

The hostility began to mount. A branch of a local patriotic club, the Civilians, adopted a resolution asking that Texas Western College professors showing sympathy for students in the protest group be "silenced" (a funny—if scary—echo of gangster movies!) or "separated from the tax-supported salaries they now enjoy."

The Junior Chamber of Commerce drew up a resolution urging El Pasoans to fly the American flag to indicate their "stand against communism." Not to be left out, the local League of United Latin American Citizens (LULACS)—reputedly the only national minority group not represented at the civil rights march on Washington—drew up its resolution opposing the demonstration, perhaps mainly to show that its members are every bit as pseudo-patriotic as the Anglos. It is a compulsion exhibited by certain of El Paso's Latin Americans. (One could call them Uncle Tomáses.)

The intrepid American Legion urged that no permit be given to the demonstrators and, reminding them of the freedoms they enjoyed, inevitably illustrated the most ferocious irony of rampant ersatz "patriotism," its seeking to deny the very freedoms it celebrates.

Germinated by such fever, two threatening telephone calls were made concerning Dr. Trexler, one to his wife, one to the Mayor's secretary. As a result, Dr. Trexler was guarded at the college by a campus policeman.

Shifting from the crowing complacency of the earlier weeks, before the city had revealed that it too contained a group dedicated and brave enough to demonstrate, the *El Paso Herald-Post*, a Scripps-Howard paper, reacted like a wronged wife. Its headlines shrieked, its editorials dealt in innuendo, its news stories inflamed, and its letters-to-the-editor column allowed its readers to denounce, as did that of the *El Paso Times*, an independently owned newspaper. ("Communist-inspired beatniks," the letters shouted, "egghead professors," "malcontents," "anti-American," "seditious," "led by an expert . . . trained for such things," "advocating revolution.") In a typical editorial, while condescendingly upholding the group's right to demonstrate, the *Herald-Post* declared:

"The history of communism has been one of infiltration, subversion and terrorism. . . . In time, unless we stand up to it, it will reach our shores (as indeed it has already in some measure)." After that statement, its thickly rhetorical "caution against tamng advocates of free speech with the brush of treason" (a bow to those "good citizens, who abhor all that the dissident group represents [but who] nevertheless defend its right to be heard") amounted to mere piety. The overall meaning was clear.

Although not known as a "liberal" newspaper, the *Times* at least seemed occasionally to be attempting to sound a rational note. In a stirring move, it printed the Bill of Rights to remind the city of the granted rights which some were attempting to deny the demonstrators.

BEFORE THIS RECENT uproar, the atmosphere at Texas Western had been accurately described as "seething with apathy." A somewhat sleepy college, despite a handful of competent and even talented people on its staff, it had seemed determined to qualify for its nickname—"the high school on the hill." Years ago, a brave instructor had protested the showing, without opposing comment, of the pro-HUAC film *Operation Abolition.* He left shortly thereafter, and apathy again settled on the school like moss.

Lately, however, the college, partly through its Excellence Fund—supported by local private contributions—had managed to bring a more spirited group of teachers to its campus. Among them was Dr. Trexler.

Dr. Trexler's courageous stand caused a roiling questioning of themselves among the complacent members of the faculty who had lulled themselves these many years. A petition, signed by sixty-three faculty members and administrators, urging the city council to reverse its decision—"irrespective of the under-signeds' opinions as to the merits of American policy, or as to the wisdom of the planned protest"—was safely worded, but it was enough to cause great anxiety among some of the faculty.

One later retracted her support. Another explained that he was asking the city to pave a section of land adjoining his property and could not therefore afford to sign. A third questioned the integrity of one of the demonstrators whom she did not like personally. Another contributed—secretly—to the group's legal fund.

The dissenting professors received other support, from the Action Committee of the local chapter of the American Association of University Professors, from 675 students at the college who signed a resolution upholding the decision of professors to speak out, from the Anti-Defamation League of B'nai B'rith, from letters to Dr. Trexler (including one from a woman "in a military home"), and from infrequent letters in the newspapers. But those notes of reason were all but drowned by the cries of lunacy.

At the height of the furor, the city attorney was finally consulted as to the legality of the demonstration. (Incredibly the city officials had not thought of doing this at the start!) The ludicrous result was the revelation that no permit had ever been needed. The city council had acted fatuously on hot air.

ON THE EVE of the demonstration, the Scripps-Howard paper carried an "interview" with Dr. Trexler, featured prominently at the top of its front page. In the only bold-face paragraph of a 20-inch story, the newspaper reported:

"Dr. Trexler said that he believes the welfare state is an ideal situation. He said he does not believe that the individual's control of his own money or property is a basic freedom." In the minds of those already aroused, that was tantamount to making Dr. Trexler a professed Communist.

Protesting that he had been misquoted, Dr. Trexler clarified his views to the editor and the reporter who had written the story. He had said that the "right to own property is not the *only* basic right," he had not mentioned money. He had further said he thought the welfare state was "necessary and desirable" in that "the government has interest in the welfare of its people," and he approved of that interest.

"That's the same as 'ideal,' " said the reporter.

"No, it isn't," the editor admitted.

The paper made no formal retraction, but a clarification appeared about 26 inches down in the body of the story that described the demonstration the next day—too late and too obscure to affect anything. The president of a mortgage company wrote the college president, enclosing a photostat of the questionable interview and encircling the very remarks Dr. Trexler had denied.

"I am encircling a paragraph which certainly distressed me. In view of Dr. Trexler's general attitude, I see no reason for our company to continue to contribute to the Excellence Fund at Texas Western College as long as a man of this type remains on the faculty."

THE ATMOSPHERE HAD grown so ominous that the police department announced it was stocking tear-gas grenades to cope with possible disorders during the demonstration.

At 1 o'clock on that warm Saturday the sad circus finally began.

"Here they come!" a youngish man (hanging from the branch of a tree) shouted to the mob in San Jacinto Plaza. The mood until then had been that of a high-school football rally, young people laughing, vendors doing a good business. But, now, that awful camaraderie which exists among those who have found a mutual scapegoat seemed to embrace the majority of the spectators. Hatred focused on about a dozen young men and women—mostly "A" students at the college—led stoically by Dr. Trexler.

Its dignity further outraging the mob, the small group began its slow, somber, courageous march, outlining a quadrant of the park. They carried signs which read "Have We Asked The Vietnamese?" "End The Bombing," "I Want The Truth About Vietnam," "Would Jesus Carry A Draft Card?"

The only harshly worded sign was carried by a thin, serious-faced young man, clearly not a part of the planned demonstration. His placard read, "End Johnson's Facist Agression in Viet-Nam," and, "Let's Have More Than A Choice Between Petty, Ignorant Facists in 1968." Its two misspelled words perhaps attested to the fury with which they were penned.

This demonstrator, wearing civilian clothes, was Lieutenant Howe, a graduate of the University of Colorado and at the time of the demonstration assigned to the 31st Engineers at Fort Bliss. Not very long ago, he had written his parents that he was proud to serve his country. The escalation of the Vietnam war, despite Johnson's campaign promises to the contrary, had led him to join the demonstration.

"They oughtta turn the boys from Fort Bliss on 'em!," an old man wearing a cap shouted, ignorant that one of "the boys from Fort Bliss" was among the demonstrators. Pitifully he turned (like a child to an adult) for approval from the young people about him. Other sad old men were passing out miniature flags, obviously exulting in the awareness that the crowd was with them. Again a part of an army—this time a heckling, cackling, motley army—they joined in piling insult on insult:

"I'll get the gasoline, you burn yourselves!" "Yellow reds!" "Traitors!" "Commies!" "Cowards!"

An emaciated young counter-demonstrator (paradoxically he looked like the press's caricature of the "peacenik") appeared carrying a sign which read, "Don't worry, the squirrels will gather them up before winter sets in." On the apparent assumption that anyone who carries a picket is against America, the crowd had at first hooted at him as he walked toward the demonstrators, and when he joined the march, an obviously drunk man tried forcibly to remove a tiny American flag which the pasty-faced counter-demonstrator had pinned to his lapel As the crowd read the sign, cries of approval replaced the execration. From the sidelines, the Mayor, sporting sunglasses and a funny small hat, watched with an amused smile as the crowd became surer of itself.

After about half an hour, the demonstrators crossed the street to the garage where their cars were parked. Quickly, Lieutenant Howe was led to one side by the police, who began immediately to question him. The other marchers drove away through a portion of the street cleared by the cops.

Even a howling mob is pitiful; this one hung around for long moments, like those who linger at a party afraid of the isolation they know will grip them once they're alone again. Having acted in unison against a scapegoat that was now gone, they were strangers once more, these outcasts in their own right, so desperate to be incorporated.

WHY LIEUTENANT HOWE was stopped by the cops is still not entirely clear. Several conflicting reasons have been offered, including one that he had called attention to himself on the base by expressing his views against the Vietnam war and was therefore quickly spotted by military police who pointed him out to the civilian police. The fact is that the police knew he was a serviceman (and at the station one cop offered to turn him over to the other prisoners).

Many contend his being held in the first place to be illegal, pointing out that he was stopped and detained ostensibly as a "vagrant" when the police did not have the requisite "reasonable grounds" to suspect him. In a brief filed with the military court, Captain Bigley asserted that the seizure and arrest had been illegal. Angry reaction from the prosecution did not shake its decision to withhold from evidence the placard carried by Lieutenant Howe. (If it had been introduced, the legality of the manner in which it was obtained might have become an issue.) Instead, photographs of Lieutenant Howe carrying the sign were introduced, and the court heard testimony by witnesses as to the wording of the placard.

However, in his review of the case for General Powers, the staff judge advocate, a colonel, admitted that the sign was a product of illegal arrest and subsequent illegal seizure and that for that reason had not been introduced in evidence at the court-martial.

IN THE INTERRUPTED interview by Harry Farrar of the *Denver Post*, Lieutenant Howe is quoted as saying,

> One of the hallmarks of fascism is the suppression of free speech. There is a clear distinction between responsibility to the military and the rights of a citizen. I have never refused to obey an army order. I would go to Vietnam if ordered to do so. On the other hand, I believe I have the right to express my opinions as a citizen. . . . I believe it is my responsibility, as a citizen, to protest against something I think is wrong.

So far, the Army has disagreed; but the case is still to be resolved—perhaps, if all else fails, by the Supreme Court.

And El Paso now? The *Herald-Post* still practices its sometimes subtle, sometimes blatant distortion. Carrying a UPI story on the antiwar demonstration in Washington, it shouted across page 1 "Peace Pickets Wave Red Banners." Any who read beyond that—and many, of course, had not—would discover, buried half a dozen paragraphs beneath the harsh gravestone of the headline, that only six among the more than 15,000 carried the foreign banners. And the *Times* recently chastised twenty-two Presbyterian ministers in San Francisco who, contending that Jesus had taught Christians to pray for their enemies, criticized President Johnson for asking for a day of prayer "exclusively in support of anti-Communist forces" in Vietnam.

Still, there are hopeful indications in this badly shaken city.

The letters to the editor are not as vituperative as before, and one of the city's most sedulous right-wing letter writers recently decried those who deny free speech, no matter of what political leaning.

Also, in numbers exceeding all expectations, hundreds (jammed beyond the doors of the hall), mostly students from "the high school on the hill," attended a pro-and-con discussion on Vietnam, and that discussion was held on the campus of the college where, not too long ago, several instructors had been afraid to sign a petition in support of free speech.

Further, when Harry Bowen, one of the two who petitioned to demonstrate, was informed that he was being fired from his supplementary job as counselor of a privately owned—but college-controlled—dormitory, fifty students threatened to move out of the building, and a group of professors protested the firing to the dean of students. Bowen retained his job.

And greatly significant was the Scripps-Howard paper's grudging editorial after the demonstration. While still denouncing the marchers, it said:

"Perhaps it takes courage of a sort to demonstrate in an unpopular cause."

POSTSCRIPT: This is one of the many articles I wrote for *The Nation* when Carey McWilliams, its great editor, solicited me as a frequent contributor. When the editors changed, even my name was omitted from the roster of past contributors; I asked why but never received an answer.

THE ARMY FIGHTS AN IDEA (1970)

WHILE PUBLICLY SETTING "guidelines" for allowable dissent, the Army is nevertheless moving swiftly and vindictively to squelch legal protest among the GIs for Peace at the Biggs Field and Fort Bliss military installations in El Paso, Tex. The military is employing three primary tactics against this organization of soldiers opposed to the war in Vietnam: intimidation, both physical and psychological; punitive transfers; and trumped-up charges. As the number of soldiers willing to identify themselves as GIs for Peace increases, the Army's tactics are escalating; one of the leaders of the group is facing a possible sentence of six months at hard labor for a very minor infraction, charged under circumstances that look very much like a frame-up.

The group had its formal beginning in August at a meeting in the desert, at the foot of mountains in El Paso's McKelligon Canyon. Several hundred soldiers gathered there, and to the accompaniment of protest songs and speeches, proclaimed their objectives: to promote peace, regain constitutional rights for servicemen, combat racism, provide counseling for GIs, work for bettering living conditions among enlisted men, and extend legal, medical and educational aid to the community—in a city where a very large segment of the citizens are poverty-ridden.

To promote these goals, the dissident soldiers publish *Gigline*, an excellently written periodical whose contents range from clear definitions of allowable dissent to anti-war cartoons. The Army quickly thwarted its distribution on bases by insisting that two copies of each issue must be submitted for prior approval, a provision not applied to *The Army Times*—nor to the two noticeably right-wing city newspapers. This tactic constitutes censorship by delay: by the time an issue is released—if it is released—its news has lost significance, particularly in regard to notices of peace events. Supported by contributions and subscriptions, mostly from GIs, *Gigline* is now distributed in the city.

THE ARMY BEGAN its harassment as soon as it detected GIs for Peace. The group's first chairman, Paul Nevins, drafted out of graduate school while working for his doctorate in political science, was suddenly transferred from an artillery unit to an infantry unit—in Germany. So was Paul Disher, *Gigline's* cartoonist. The editor of the paper's first issue received equally abrupt orders—for Vietnam, although doctors had certified that he was ill. (His orders were later rescinded, after many appeals on medical grounds.) Another GI, originally asked to infiltrate the GI peace organization but won over to its cause, had his occupational specialty changed and was summarily transferred to Korea.

By using its power to transfer personnel, the Army was thus able to try, convict and sentence the dissenters—all without trial. But immediately, other GIs rose to fill the vacuum created by the punitive reassignments. Among them were Jim Nies, a former schoolteacher, and Edward Barresi.

Feeling that the original meaning of Armistice Day, then approaching, was being perverted by a very unsilent "majority," they and other peace GIs applied to the Veterans Day parade organizers for permission to contribute a contingent of dissenters to march in the city. Permission rejected. Since the Army was sending pro-military speakers to grammar schools, the dissenting GIs wrote to the city's school administrations for permission to address the young about peace. Request rejected.

Nevertheless, approximately seventy-five of them gathered with peace placards at one side of the parade reviewing stand on Armistice Day. While not officially joining the demonstrating GIs, the vast majority of spectator soldiers, some in uniform, were clearly sympathetic. As the fat military parade crawled past them, the dissident soldiers flashed peace signs—which were spontaneously answered by other soldiers mounted, apparently against their wishes, on ominous, lethargic weapons. This response to the peace symbol by members of the parade, military and otherwise, would be vehemently denied by a parade organizer, although photographs and newsreel film had captured the flashed "V's."

Obviously as a result of the success of these activities, Nies, Barresi and another GI for Peace were called before an academic review board of the Defense Language Institute, the Army school they attended as students of the Vietnamese language. The reason given for this summons was that their grades had dropped. Failing grade, however, is 70; the lowest average grade of the three was 77. Indeed, Barresi was considered by his instructors to be among the school's outstanding students. The decline in grades was attributable to their refusal to read aloud some of the more highly propagandized and war-oriented lessons in the course.

Normally, a summons before this board—a majority of its five or so members are officers—results in a superficial inquiry into why the student is experiencing difficulty in the course. At worst, a mild reprimand is issued. A failing Green Beret had only recently been recycled into another course. The three peace GIs, however, found themselves the center of an evident politically oriented interrogation. Nies was asked by a major whether he would be able to "search out, contact, and destroy the enemy." He refused to answer on the ground that the matter was irrelevant to his academic standing. With fourteen more weeks to go in their school cycle, all three were suddenly transferred—only hours before the November moratorium activities—two to Fort Ord, the other to Polk. In at least one instance, "disruptive influence" was cited. To date, at least ten transfers can be directly, attributed to activities among the GIs for Peace during its life span of only a few months.

BUT TRANSFERS HAVE not been the only means of intimidation. Other members of the peace group found themselves the objects of intensive scrutiny. During a company inspection, three rooms out of sixteen were singled out—all three belonging to members of GIs for Peace. Students were questioned by the CID, the Army's FBI, about activities of other students. Copies of *Gigline* were seized, later returned. Forbidden to name the peace organization as a beneficiary of his Army insurance policy, Albert Singerman, a veteran of Vietnam, was confronted by an enraged sergeant. "He struck out at me, ranting," says Singerman, "as I was trying to explain to him my right to dissent." Singerman subsequently filed a complaint of assault. Some mail divisions on the posts were ordered to notify security personnel when copies of *Gigline* were being received.

The threat of court-martial began to loom. Papers were drawn against one of the organization members for distributing *Gigline* on post. Although the charges were later reduced, the warning was out. Rumors spread that the information office for the posts was outlining methods on how to proceed against the dissenters.

Sometimes the pressure was insidious. Jerry Magaro, one of the founders of the group and a lawyer who had become the unofficial legal adviser of the peace GIs, suddenly found himself rooming with a soldier who had been busted on pot charges; it was as if the Army were clumsily setting up any possible means of entrapment.

Minor offenses, usually overlooked, became major infractions, and always charged against those known to be members of the

52

peace organization. Two soldiers involved in insignificant parking infractions found themselves without passes, and therefore separated from their families. Says Thomas McNeil, one of the two: "We were charged with having parked our motorcycles in a no-parking area from which two others, not cited, had just driven away. My pass was held over me as blackmail until I accepted company punishment." Accepting such punishment is tantamount to admitting guilt.

One GI, pressing for a reason for the withdrawal of his pass, was told: "Pick your reason." The day before, he had spoken at a peace demonstration in the city. Another soldier, Ron Withem, who had written several letters of complaint against the Army's punitive activities, found that his orders for promotion were the only ones missing among those of his immediate group.

DESPITE THE RAPIDLY escalating pressure, dissenting GIs announced that during the November moratorium they would show their opposition to the war by avoiding the mess halls; they suggested a period of meditation in a chapel. At Biggs Field, they were met in one designated chapel by a menacing group of officers obviously checking name tags.

"The chapel itself was crowded with about a dozen plain-clothes men," says Ralph Skinner, a former student at Occidental College in California and the University of Chicago. "I looked around to see if they were from the press—there were no press signs. They were either Military Intelligence men or men from the Criminal Investigation Division. Riot-helmeted MPs in cars cruised the block."

Even though confronted by such implicit threats, about sixty soldiers had gone through the menacing ranks of plain-clothes men and officers at the chapel; and about three-fourths of the neighboring mess hall was empty at the noon meal—although officers, who ordinarily avoid enlisted men's dining rooms, were that day markedly in attendance.

To ensure a blackout of the Army's shady activities, a man identifying himself as a major from the post information office, had earlier called a television station scheduled to cover the event. "The whole thing has been canceled," the newsman was told. "A colossal flop," an Army officer later croaked about the chapel attendance the Army had systematically, but unsuccessfully, attempted to thwart.

(This was not the first incident, nor would it be the last, involving the chapel, a traditional symbol of refuge. During the October moratorium, the same chapel was closed during the noon hour—for "waxing," a chore ordinarily performed at night; and in December a group of men at Biggs Field were denied permission to hold a service honoring the war dead.)

At Fort Bliss that same day, previously covert intimidation surfaced. Says Magaro: "The word had been passed that those opposing the war avoid the mess halls or report on sick call. Commanders let it be known they would check the mess halls for absentees and obtain names of those on sick call."

FINALLY THE THREAT of court-martial materialized—against Francis Lenski, new chairman of the dissident GIs. His ears ringing loudly from that afternoon's firing on the Army range, Lenski was on his way to the barracks when he became aware of a sergeant yelling and gesturing to him. Realizing that retreat was sounding and that he had not come to attention, Lenski did so quickly.

Although retreat is often ignored except on formal occasions, Lenski is faced with a special court-martial for "failing to render the proper courtesies during 'Retreat Ceremonies,' by not saluting."

The allegations are backed, clumsily, by statements from four second lieutenants, including one who had earlier that day expressed antagonism toward Lenski's peace activities. Laboriously explaining the peculiarly restrictive position of the vehicle they were in, two of the lieutenants stated self-consciously that they themselves did not come to attention during retreat, because, as they explained: (1) "The car was situated in such a way as to prevent us from getting out . . . without interrupting the ceremony"; and (2) "I was unable to exit my car due to the fact that on backing out of my parking place I had been pinned by another car [and] the driver of that car stopped his car during the playing of *Retreat* in such a position as to not allow me to open my doors freely to exit." How both sides of a car were blocked by another car is a mystery of metaphysical proportions.

Stumbling on his own rhetoric, one of the lieutenants added: "To execute the proper measures to free myself enough to open the doors, in my opinion, would have constituted a greater disrespect and disturbance than remaining quiet and in place." In place he, and the other, did remain—and quiet, until the time came to press charges against Lenski. To date, the charges are pending.

MEMBERS OF GIs for Peace are intelligent, dedicated, optimistic. One is immediately struck by their deep belief that things can indeed be better, and by their desire to help make them so. One is also struck by their total lack of Marxist or radical orientation—a fact which, whether good or bad, makes the Army's mutterings of "Commies" a typical absurdity. The peace GIs scrupulously follow the guidelines for allowable dissent enunciated by the Department of the Army itself.

The concerned young men enrolled in the Defense Language Institute are particularly revolted by what they view as the racist attitudes at the school, where some Army regulars have been known to carry as souvenirs plastic-encased ears of alleged Vietcong; these were shown to Vietnamese members of the faculty, who are looked down on by many of the Regular Army personnel.

Not only do some of the officers express contempt for the objectives of the school itself ("First you learn to shine your boots, and then you become affluent [sic] in Vietnamese," said one second lieutenant during a morning formation), but some Regular Army personnel reveal much more dangerous hostility. A sergeant publicly professed his belief that all Vietnamese should be wiped out, nominal allies and avowed enemies alike.

Further, the lessons in the school are themselves propaganda. Says Withem: "They read: 'Come see the villages being burned by incendiary bombs.'" McNeil adds: "In drawings accompanying the lessons, the Vietcong are presented as complete parodies of 'the sneaky Oriental'—treacherous, with grossly overslanted eyes."

"It's *all* unreal, including the transfers," says George Scheurer, vice chairman of GIs for Peace. "The life expectancy of each chairman is ten days," another points out. Scheurer himself has been given abrupt transfer orders to Alaska.

Still the GIs maintain a dedication to their goals. Recently a group of them attempted during visiting hours to investigate an unprovoked tear-gassing at the Fort Bliss stockade. (Recognized by guards as they tried to interview inmates, the soldiers were asked to surrender their notes. They refused, and visiting hours were abruptly terminated. The incident is still sealed in secrecy.) And the weekly meetings continue to draw new members, despite the fact that the soldiers are sure that at least one among them is an Army informer. Since all their activities are legal and open, they easily ignore that fact.

They write letters to Senators. They get in touch with the Inspector General's office. They regularly send releases to the local, and hostile, newspapers. These are buried in the back pages and never deemed of sufficient interest to be sent to the wire services. Thus the soldiers have encountered a "press curtain" about their peace activities.

"You have to stand a great deal of frustration to resist the intimidation," says Scheurer. Apparently many GIs have reached the threshold of resistance. But the Army, threatened, lashes out at them, determined to silence them. A major at a recent command staff meeting is said to have boasted, according to minutes of the meeting, that he will disenroll five students from the language school in the near future and take personal responsibility for doing so. With its awesome power to harass, intimidate and punish, the Army may succeed in squashing the dissident soldiers.

But the GIs for Peace indicate that they too will stand firm. Perhaps, if they manage to do so against the heavy odds, they will supply the answer to the thus far only rhetorical question: What would happen if they gave a war and no one came?

POSTSCRIPT: As a result of the attention this matter generated in *The Nation* publication, then–Defense Secretary McNamara ordered an investigation into the punitive transfers. This group of GIs often met in my home. One of its main purposes was to print flyers opposing the war. Several of those of us in El Paso who supported the GIs drove them to Fort Bliss at night. While we waited in our cars in darkness, the soldiers would "raid" the barracks and spread the flyers among sleeping soldiers. They would then rush out into our cars and be whisked away.

"ALL IT DOES IS MAKE YOU HATE" (1971)

ROM THE MAIN thoroughfare you could almost miss it, a smallish, unremarkable one-story building. Weeping willows afford glimpses of white walls. Closer, you see that the windows are barred. A small wing projects like an angry afterthought. A narrow dirt road, a dead end, proclaims illogically: "One Way— Do Not Enter." If you do nevertheless, you'll see thin mattresses outside piled forlornly; a few feet away, filled garbage cans. Easy to assume the mattresses are part of the garbage; they're not. Mockingly, a golf course nearby is separated by wire. There's a basketball ring a few feet away—but that belongs to the neighboring fire station. In front of the white building are parked official wagons with wire inside separating the front from the rear: mobile cages.

These are some of the voices that emerged recently from that building—El Paso's Juvenile Detention Home—in affidavits given by former inmates to Steven Bercu, a young, long-haired, bearded attorney for the El Paso Legal Assistance Society who has taken up their cause.

A 17-year-old girl, picked up as a "runaway" within her own home: "In my cell I had a window. I could see my parents leaving, I knocked on the window and tried to ask if they had signed papers [committing her to the Texas Youth Council], they just waved and smiled and went away. I was kept in security [solitary confinement]. Then they came to chain us for the ride [to Gainesville, a youth "correctional" institution] with a two-foot-long chain with a leather strap that goes around one leg with metal on it so that you can't cut the strap and then it's connected to the leg of someone else. I was never taken into court at any time about any of this."

A 14-YEAR-OLD girl, a runaway: "I was fingerprinted at the city jail [then taken] to the detention home. The wash lady took me into the bathroom and I had to take all my clothes off. She made me turn around a few times and open my legs and looked at me. I was naked for about ten minutes. I was placed in a cell. They made us take off our clothes before we went to sleep and put them outside the door and they made us sleep in our underwear. You are left with just a sheet, a mattress—an inch and a half thick, real dirty. They wake you up at about 4:45 a.m., you put your clothes on outside the cell. [After breakfast] you go back to the cell. Then you sleep a little while with your clothes on until they come back, tell you to roll your mattress. The matron takes you outside and there is a big police dog standing there and you take your mattress and put it on another. During the day you are not allowed to read, you just sit. Some of the matrons let you sing, but some tell you they will throw you in the security room. [In the cells] there is a coffee can to be used as a toilet. Some of the matrons make you take showers in the dark. If your parents bring you any clothes, you get to change them once a week. Otherwise you can wash your clothes at night right before you go to bed but then they are still wet in the morning and you have to wear them wet."

Another affidavit tells of an incident involving a 14-year-old girl, a runaway. Desperate to get away from the home, if only to the hospital, she cut her wrists with the glass from the light in her cell. The matron couldn't open the door because they were not allowed to after 9 p.m. She got two men from the office.

Bleeding—"grabbed by the hair and dragged out," according to another statement—the girl was taken out of the cell, alcohol was poured on her arms and they were wrapped in a towel. One man reportedly said, "Do you want to go do a better job?" She was returned to her cell and threatened with "security." Denied blankets, her brassiere taken away—so she couldn't choke herself—she slept nude, without even a sheet. Some of the matrons allowed her another mattress so she could cover herself. She was never taken to court.

A 15-year-old girl, in the detention home on three different occasions: "The first time, I was ten and I was picked up by the police for shoplifting, taken to the city jail, fingerprinted, taken to the detention home. When I was 15 years old, I was picked up [again], a runaway. [Later that year] I was picked up at a friend's house. After I had been [at the detention home] two hours someone came in and read what they called our rights. . . . The dishes were always greasy, the sheets always dirty. A girl who was having her period could only have one Kotex a day. I was embarrassed by being strip-searched in front of a lot of other girls, and the matrons made snide remarks. I was never in court at any time."

ANOTHER VOICE—that of a girl whose mother had her picked up as a runaway: The mother had brain cancer and had only recently been hospitalized. Despite her physical condition, her presence was required when she decided to get her daughter out. She went to the home with a lady companion. Even so, the girl was not released—pending further "investigation." The friend asked to see the girl, or to leave a note explaining that it would require a few more days before they could pick her up. He would inform her himself, the man she spoke to told her. Finally out, the girl sobbed that no one had told her of their presence, she had not known what was happening. She told of being awakened at night and taken into a bright room "to make a confession"—and of a girl, an epileptic, who had seizures because her drugs were removed. She told of another girl who asked for toilet paper and was told by a matron, "Use your finger."

Another affidavit, from a teenage girl: "My first night there one of the girls in my cell tried to make advances to me, I hit her. I was called in and reprimanded for causing a fight. I saw lots of bugs all over the place, roaches. Another girl told the matron she had gotten her period. The matron refused to do anything. So the girl stole paper towels and sneaked them back into her cell to use as a sanitary napkin. No one advised me of any rights, and at no time was I taken to any court."

A boy, black: "I was in my room alone when a guard walked in and said, 'I'm getting tired of your shit.' Then he kicked me on the knee. At room check another guard asked, 'What's the trouble with you?' Then he hit me in the stomach. He was always teasing me about my knee. He would say, 'How's your knee?' and laugh, called me 'Smokey,' 'Whitey,' and 'Snowball.' Also as he turned off the lights at night he would say, 'Don't smile' and laugh. I don't understand why I was left alone in solitary all the time and why they called me names about my race."

Another boy, first picked up—in his own home—as a "run-away" and "incorrigible" when he was 14: "I asked how I could be a runaway when I was at home and how I was an incorrigible." He was told his mother said so. He remembers his mother telling him she was confused, she thought she could get him out any time she wanted. "I asked if I could make a phone call, I was told no phone calls could be made unless approved." He remembers "guards banging boys into the wall." Back in the home two years later, "I cut my wrists. There was blood all over. The guard said to me, 'You stupid son of a bitch. Next time borrow my knife and slit your neck.' Then he told me that if I pulled another stunt like that I would be handcuffed and locked up in solitary. The guard then went to get medical aid, I washed my cuts and put on Band-Aids he brought me. Next morning I saw the wounds were still open, I was afraid there might be an infection, I asked for a doctor, I was completely ignored. The following day a guard came and I asked him for a doctor. I was taken to Thomason General Hospital, given a tetanus shot. The doctor told me my cuts had needed stitches but now it was too late. One week later I was sent to Gatesville [a Texas "correctional" institution for boys]." He was not told where he was going until he arrived there. "I spent five months. I was never in any court at any time for any of this."

IN LATE OCTOBER a series of excellent articles written by reporter Bill Payne exposing alleged irregularities at the detention home appeared, with editorial support, in the *El Paso Times*. He reported that the avowed purpose of the home at its dedication was the ending of imprisonment of juveniles and providing them with vocational training. The home soon became nothing more than a jail; and in 1966 two members of the Juvenile Patrol, assigned to apprehend youths, were charged with forcible rape. Although no conviction resulted, the patrol was abolished. The articles described the shattered intentions of the home, the unsanitary conditions, the oppressive atmosphere of prison.

Payne revealed that among employees there, one formerly was a truck driver, two had been investigated for alleged neglect or abuse of their own children, another was a retired military policeman and still another was hired after committing her own child to the Texas Youth Council without court hearing. About his own qualifications, the head of the home was quoted: "I'm not going to go into it."

Simultaneously with the appearance of Payne's series, Steven Bercu was raising grave questions of due process in juvenile cases. The juveniles' refrain—"I was never in court"—revealed doubts about the constitutionality of the detentions and committals.

Though a large percentage of such committals to the Texas Youth Council are made on "agreed judgments" supposedly heard by the one-judge Juvenile Court of El Paso County, actually no court hearing ever takes place, Bercu revealed. Parents merely sign the necessary papers at the detention home, declaring a child "uncontrollable" and asking the court to commit him to the Texas Youth Council. The judge then signs the papers naming the child "delinquent." Such judgments are then recorded on a standard form that indicates that the child appeared at a formal court hearing.

At meetings of the El Paso County Juvenile Board and the Texas State House of Representatives Criminal Law Study, then holding hearings throughout the state, Bercu read into the record parts of the affidavits obtained from the youths. He labeled the detention and arrest of juveniles illegal—often without warrants and without notification of parents; he alleged that children are detained for indefinite periods without appearing before a judge as provided by law. He pointed out that judgments in court records state that the juvenile admitted allegations in the petition for committal when children are actually not present at the signing of the papers on "agreed judgments" to the Texas Youth Council, and that petitions containing the allegations to which the juvenile purportedly pled guilty are not served.

He decounced all this as being in violation of Section 7B of the Texas Juvenile Court Act. That section makes it mandatory that the youth be represented by counsel, appointed by the court when the minor and his parents cannot afford counsel. (Attorney General Crawford Martin has enunciated the minor's right, through counsel, to cross-examine state's witnesses and to present witnesses of his own and other evidence for his defense. The state must prove delinquency.)

Bercu further scored the policy of the probation department in not defining their rights to juveniles and added that hearsay evidence is often admitted and that counsel is denied them. Calling the home "completely mismanaged," he decried the absence of educational, psychological and rehabilitative facilities. He described unsanitary conditions and the beating of children.

He pointed to the absence of a physician at the home and the lack of cooperation toward agencies volunteering their services in the best interests of the children.

He also revealed that although in one year the El Paso Center for Mental Health and Mental Retardation had granted the El Paso Probation Department $10,604 for in-service training for workers and psychological counseling for juveniles, only $220 had been used.

After Bercu's presentation, approximately 20 witnesses appeared in support of the handling of the home. A significant number were parents who had committed their own children. Testifying on the home's behalf, one youth stated that no court hearing had been held in his case. One woman even defended the cans used for toilets: "The coffee can is no stranger to lower-income groups." One parent who had committed her own daughter said she didn't see the need for court hearings: "We adult people decided it would be better for her to go."

REACTION TO BERCU'S allegations and Payne's articles was swift—if notably belated in some instances. The assistant county attorney admitted being "shocked." "I never knew this was going on." A sergeant of the police department was quoted as saying: "I thought they'd cut out that kind of stuff."

About health conditions in the home, an assistant city attorney upheld that the "situation is certainly one that should be looked into." (Because it does not sell food, the home is not governed by health ordinances. Perhaps as a result of this lack of emphasis on health, one Juarez, Mexico, youth with tuberculosis was held in the home two or three weeks, Payne revealed. There is no evidence that the parents of the exposed children were notified.)

State Sen. Joe Christie announced his intention to introduce a bill creating a full-time juvenile court and to "run with" whatever legislation might be necessary to effect change. "From what I have read and from the statements of Texas Attorney General Crawford Martin reprinted in the *Times* series, [the procedures involved] certainly do not appear to meet constitutional Requirements." He was supported by State Rep. H. Tati Santiesteban.

A sergeant of the El Paso Police Department was further quoted: "The kids are getting the short end of the stick. And when it's all over and we put [them] back on the street, in many cases there's no way ever to put the pieces back together again."

A judge of the juvenile board reacted. (In charge of operations at the home, the board is composed of seven judges paid $325 a month in addition to their regular salaries.) He was quoted: "If the juvenile court records show there was a hearing in cases where there wasn't one, that sounds bad." He said that on a recent visit to the home he had seen a child with a puffy, inch-long cut which might have been infected; only mercurochrome or iodine had been applied to it.

Already, some effects of Payne's and Bercu's disclosures have been felt: The cans which were used for toilets at the home are gone. Orders have been given that court forms will now accurately reflect what happens in each case.

But too much remains the same. Importantly, the efforts of attorney Bercu to release two youths on writs of habeas corpus, alleging violation of due process, have been denied. The matter is under appeal.

An eminent local psychiatrist specializing in children and adolescents offers the following enlightened guidelines for correction of the dire situation: The setting up of a full-time juvenile court presided over by a judge familiar with juvenile problems; the need for recreational activities in the home and its maintenance by fully qualified personnel in an atmosphere that does not suggest the crippling ambience of a prison.

In an imaginative and bold proposal that would cost the county nothing, he recommends that qualified psychology majors from the University of Texas at El Paso, on a volunteer basis—and perhaps for college credit—provide psychological testing to juveniles in trouble, while sociology students, in conjunction with existing social agencies, work with the parents involved. Thus the juvenile court judge would have at his disposal a psychological and sociological evaluation to enable him to handle each case individually.

To this might be added the need of a psychiatrist available to the youths.

Will all—or any of these conditions be changed? Will the furor fade into familiar apathy? Though neither Bercu nor Payne have retreated, the *El Paso Times*, which bravely and prominently presented Payne's series and Bercu's allegations, now sadly gives indications of withdrawing.

A young girl, an ex-inmate of the home, makes the following forthright point: "I'd rather be dead than go back to the detention home. The way they treat you, all it does is make you hate."

POSTSCRIPT: A flurry of investigations into abusive conditions soon faded from the news.

THE SUNSHINE GIRL'S HOMOPHOBIC PITCH (1977)

O N JUNE 7, in Dade County, Fla., the rights of a minority will actually be put on the ballot. In a special election that will cost thousands of dollars, voters of metropolitan Miami well be asked whether to repeal an ordinance that merely reaffirms basic guarantees, such as the right to be employed without bias and the right to live where one chooses.

Suppose that the rights of Jews, blacks, women or Chicanos were being put to a vote. Civil rights advocates would march on Dade County, editorials full of outrage would appear in every major newspaper, celebrities would rush to volunteer for fund raising and we would be hearing from a President committed to human rights. It could hardly be otherwise—except when one is confronted by the real instance: that the minority involved is the only one discriminated against by law, the homosexual minority.

"Kill a Queer for Christ," proclaim sacrilegious bumper stickers in Florida, where an advertisement in the leading newspaper, the *Miami Herald*, stated that "cultures throughout history . . . have dealt with homosexuals almost universally with disdain, abhorrence, disgust—even death." Is this a call for murder? Yes, and it is underscored every time Anita Bryant or some homophobic public official rants in hatred against homosexuals, legitimizing violence. Savage attacks on homosexuals follow.

Blueboy magazine, a gay publication, carries this chilling news item in its new issue: "A gay man was beaten to death by a teenager outside a bar in Tucson, Ariz. When asked what moved him to attack the man, the 17-year-old confessed murderer said, 'That's the way I was taught.'"

Taught where? In the very schools in which Anita Bryant is trying to "protect" children from homosexuals.

At a time when President Carter concerns himself—correctly—with human rights in Russia and elsewhere, at a time when the *Los Angeles Times* and the *New York Times* decry the injustices of apartheid, there is little but silence about the frightening developments in Florida.

A new kind of gentleman's agreement—a frightened gentleman's agreement—exists even in the "liberal" heterosexual establishment. It is an agreement to ignore the daily wreckage of lives by arbitrary sex arrests and the subsequent suicides, to ignore the daily violation of homosexuals' civil rights; to systematically shun gay subject matter; to never mention the marauders inevitably unleashed and legitimized by public campaigns against homosexuals.

With the help of the news media, the Anita Bryants of the world repeat a whole litany of ugly myths; that homosexuals are child molesters, although many studies have shown that most molesters come from the ranks of heterosexuals; that homosexuals are to blame for "prison rape," when in fact such attacks almost invariably are on the slightly built young men, often homosexuals, by heterosexual men deprived of women.

Already two states, Arkansas and Idaho, have revived archaic laws against private homosexuality. The Supreme Court has moved to deprive homosexuals of rights granted to others. In a Virginia case, the High Court upheld the right of a state to regulate homosexual acts. In another decision, the Court let stand a ruling that a high school newspaper could refuse to print the meeting notices of gay organizations.

If for no other than selfish reasons, those who support other minorities should feel personally threatened by this escalating bigotry against homosexuals. Historically, oppression begins with this sort of persecution. Heterosexuals also ought to be concerned about the huge amounts of money poured into police harassment of homosexuals. True law and order would protect old people and others increasingly threatened by raging violence, by muggings, rape, murder; a compassionate society would use its money to help people; it would build better schools, housing, and hospitals.

Even in these barbaric times it is difficult to imagine a popular exhortation to "Kill a Nigger"—or a kike or a broad. Yet in Dade County, Fla.—in America!—bumper stickers publicly cry for blood: "Kill a Queer for Christ."

POSTSCRIPT: So much has changed, so much remains the same. The proposal to amend the Constitution to curtail gay rights indicates the antipathy to homosexuality that is still deeply entrenched, and easily aroused, in the American psyche.

COMMON BONDS AND BATTLES (1978)

THERE EXISTS A dangerous silence about the tensions between homosexual men and heterosexual women. As we enter the worst era of threatened human rights since the McCarthy fifties, this ugly truth demands exploration. Its implications contribute to the erosion of homosexual rights and the denial of women's rights.

(I am speaking throughout as a homosexual male, and I am avoiding the word "gay" because I believe that just as blacks shed the derogatory euphemism "colored," so homosexuals must shed the equally derogatory word "gay." "Homosexual" is on a par with "heterosexual"; "gay" and "straight" are not equal terms.)

What are the causes of this ancestral tension? How may they be dissipated?

The factors that make up the causes are too complex for full exploration here, but the antagonism that heterosexual women feel probably arises from the resentment stirred by the cultural shock of "competing" with a homosexual man: the woman's sexual power is denied. The homosexual man's resentment may emerge from his having been taught, even forced, to respond to someone he does not desire sexually and from the imposed guilt for not doing so.

How to resolve the animosity is more important than its historical origin. The realization that we are mutually threatened by enemies in common is essential. We have similar obstacles to overcome.

The babbling Los Angeles ex-police chief who initiated savage pogroms against homosexuals is the same man who attributed the rising crime rate to women's liberation. The sponsors of referendums that are accumulating against homosexuals are equally opposed to the Equal Rights Amendment. The comedian who crowed about the defeat of human rights in Dade County also called women "bitches." The bully who hounds young "sissies" often literally or metaphorically rapes women to prove his "masculinity." The Florida-orange-juice queen upholds the notion that women who perform fellatio are "worse" than the homosexuals she despises. Los Angeles police keep under surveillance not only the Gay Community Services Center, but the Women's Resource Center as well. Hate-pocked young men with their "chickies" invade homosexual turfs to scream "Faggots!"

Both women and male homosexuals have equally loathsome myths to debunk—the myth of the female inviting rape, the myth of homosexuals as child molestors.

And homosexuals and women share still another enemy in common: the enemy within, the masochistic saboteur. Many women deride "libbers" and blindly support "our men." Some homosexuals are unconcerned so long as they can dance nightly on a sequined grave to disco music pounding a dirge.

We share a fear of difference. Women's groups still war about accepting lesbians, and "straight" homosexuals decry the transvestite—who is, paradoxically, often heterosexual. (I do not agree with the point of view shared by some women and some homosexuals that the homosexual transvestite is a mocking parody; to me "she" has become, in our time, a courageous star in the important theater of sexual shock therapy.) Increasingly, it is difference itself that is assaulted. Witness the Kinsey Institute survey's blessing homosexuals as "well adjusted" in proportion to how closely they conform to heterosexual standards of monogamy!

An ease in "passing"—in the sense of what is conventionally acceptable for "good ladies" and "nice fairies"—allows the saboteur to reign. The result is a wounding conservatism. A group of homosexuals at a rights rally sings not "We Shall Overcome" but "God Bless America." With Phyllis Schlafly as cheerleader, conservative women equate patriotism with sexual repression. The woman who sees her financial security as "housewife" threatened by the women's movement is like a rich homosexual who, to protect his real-estate interests, cooperates in sweeps against "undesirable" homosexuals in their cruising areas. Instead of questioning the total network of exploitive attitudes, both groups too often accept the tenets of their oppressors.

Understanding that sexism that exploits women exploits homosexuals, acceptance that the erosion of all rights is implicit in antihomosexual legislation (the progression from "queers" to "broads" to "niggers" to "spics" to "kikes" is easy), would result in a unity and a release of energy that could sweep away all anti-human-rights movements.

That unity will come, too, in large measure through the discovery that a unique closeness can, and already very often does, occur between a homosexual man and a heterosexual woman. While accepting and honoring each other's sexual choice, unthreatened, each acknowledges and respects the specialness, power, and beauty of a woman and the specialness, power, and beauty of a man.

POSTSCRIPT: I'm baffled now with what seems to me to be an incorrect implication in my essay, that the rift between heterosexual women and gay men is considerable. That isn't generally true, especially among intelligent younger women. I think that this implication arose from my consulting a woman I had a very close friendship with about her attitudes; those are largely her views and I accepted and developed them. I do like some of the more relevant observations in this essay.

During the AIDS crisis—and this article was written long before that—lesbians rushed to the defense of stricken men, contributing hours to provide care, food, transportation. Their dedication was truly awe-inspiring. I would hope that gay men would rally with equal devotion to the causes of lesbians—and all women—especially in the battle against breast cancer.

Today I increasingly believe that at least a significant part of the widespread hostility toward gay men has its roots in an enduring disdain toward women within the heterosexual culture. In the view of too many "straight" men (and some women, usually their wives or "girls"), the gay male demeans himself when, by desiring men, he becomes "like a woman," a lesser being. The heterosexual male's own assumed "superior" status as a man is thus questioned, shaken.

MASTERS AND JOHNSON
FOCUS ON HOMOSEXUALITY (1979)

THE IMPACT OF this mighty book will be major, but it abounds in
fallacies and aims an implied judgment at homosexuals and
heterosexuals.

Pioneers in the field of heterosexual sex therapy, Masters
and Johnson courageously broke barriers. Now they say they
intend to do so for homosexuals—and a blessing for them for
largely avoiding the barbarous term "gay."

They find homosexuals "not physiologically different" in sexual response. They vow to shun judgments. But judgments
beyond physiological aspects abound throughout.

Of 94 males studied, 84 comprised 42 couples, and of 82
females, 76 comprised 38 couples. Of the coupled men, only five
"cruised the local gay bars." Yet in the real world the number of
homosexual couples is minuscule compared to that of "uncommitted" homosexuals crowding bars. Conclusions from this
unrepresentative segment result in major fallacies.

This portion of the study ended in 1968, one year before the
launching of homosexual liberation at the Stonewall Inn protest
in New York City. Profound ramifications of that event are not
reflected.

Subjects were recruited using Kinsey's sexuality scale of
0 to 6, "0" designating those with no homosexual contacts;

"6" those with no heterosexual contacts. An astonishing 20 of the men and 20 of the women came from Kinsey 3—smack in the middle of the spectrum—and 37.3% of the men and 41.4% of the women came from Kinsey 1-3. Conclusions about homosexuals then, were apparently based on a high sample of bisexuals.

These coupled, "socially stable," educated (approximately 80% college-trained), white (no black males) homosexuals comprised a culturally "heterosexual" and sexually bisexual-oriented group. That might account for the findings that heterosexual fantasies abound in homosexual encounters.

Judgments are made. "Committed" is bequeathed on acceptable couples, and "uncommitted" homosexuals—the vast majority—are described as "not infrequently . . . defying rather than living with prejudice."

The doctors assert having "no point of contention with the well-defined position of theology on the subject of homosexuality." An avoidance of judgment?

The most controversial element deals with "conversions" (homosexuality to heterosexuality) and "reversions" (heterosexuality to homosexuality and back) in a study of 54 "dissatisfied" homosexual males and 13 women—most in both groups married—treated between 1967 and 1977. No indication is given whether the doctors would extend complimentary therapy to "dissatisfied" heterosexuals. Now "conversion," with its evocation of singing angels, is wedded to "commitment."

Results of "conversion" and "reversion" therapy are presented in terms of failure. The authors claim success is subjective. Thus they warn that a 20% "treatment failure rate" does not—the mind reels—imply 80% success. The therapist might be overly optimistic, and "if the client wants the moon and the stars," like Bette Davis in *Now, Voyager*, and "gets only the moon," like Paul Henreid in the same film, he or she may be only half-satisfied. This borrowed flight of poetry adds clouds in defining "moon" and "stars" in terms of sexuality.

Conclusions are shoved farther into the land of Alice when we learn that 16 of the 43 male "non-failures" were lost to follow-up studies. The doctors estimate that only two or three of them "reversed." Others flew to heterosexual bliss and handed them an "overall failure rate" of only 33%. With additional "adjustments," they project that "an overall treatment failure of more than 45% is unlikely."

There it is. "Conversion" to heterosexuality is possible—more than half the time. You could change if you wanted to. You already have heterosexual fantasies.

While ostensibly extending the demarcation of the sexually acceptable, this study merely shifts it to include those found alike by a selective process that begins with acceptable "alikeness." Implications leap to exclude "uncommitted" heterosexuals. Difference itself is undesirable.

The time has come to say: Let us breathe. Stop categorizing us. We have come out of the closets, don't thrust us into laboratories. Let us create from our own individual perspectives. Proust, Woolf, Michelangelo, have illumined more of mankind than the mountainous graphs and tables of scientists seeking to contain us all in sameness.

POSTSCRIPT: I found this book hilarious, much more than I conveyed here. The doctors' studies convinced me of a position I hold steadfast: that the question about what "creates" homosexuals will be relevant only when we ask what "creates" heterosexuals. These studies are very often ludicrous. I knew a man, a self-avowed heterosexual, who was writing a sociological book about hustlers. Standing on one of the hustling corners of Selma Boulevard in Los Angeles, I saw him driving by. Another hustler near me pointed him out and said: "That guy's a talk freak. He pays you to hear stories about hustling. So I made up some real good ones for him." Those ended up as "sociological finds."

A CASE FOR *CRUISING* (1979)

I SHARE IN the homosexual rage sweeping New York—a rage too long dormant—against the centuries-old abuse of homosexuals. That anger is now directed at stopping the filming of Gerald Walker's novel *Cruising* by William Friedkin.

Two main arguments have emerged for stopping the film. The first is that it may unleash a wave of violence against homosexuals. The second is that its concentration on the elements of cruising, leather bars, and sadomasochism may result in a distortion of all homosexuals by focusing on a small segment.

My thoughts on violence and censorship—the issues involved here—are shaped by intimate encounters with each. As a homosexual, I have seen "queer bashers" with chains ready to lash in cruising turfs; have seen the faces of homosexuals branded by lead pipes by hate-pocked "straight" attackers; have heard the curdling epithet "Queers!" and the accompanying crash of glass; have experienced the frustration of failing to get cops to move into assaulted areas they invade only to arrest homosexuals.

As a writer, I have experienced censorship, too. Last year in England an anti-homosexual group effectively banned a nonfiction book by me, *The Sexual Outlaw*, by threatening the publisher with a suit before publication, thus intimidating booksellers into not carrying it. That book, the group claimed, would pervert by presenting homosexuality in a "positive" light.

I do not question the homosexual anger in New York. It is the particular nuances of this matter, and possible hidden ramifications, that I believe should be explored further.

Now, it would be naïve to deny the special impact of films. It is also risky to predict that impact; and it may prove dangerous, based on such prediction, to move into the quagmire of prior censorship. Censorship continues to be a major factor in the oppression of homosexuals. For years, the motion picture code forbade any treatment of homosexuality. Showing of Genet's *Un chant d'amour* and Kenneth Anger's *Fireworks*—groundbreaking homosexual films—resulted in raided theaters. Until recently, photographic and verbal presentations of homosexuality were *ipso facto* causes for censorship. Confiscation of homosexual magazines and books was routine, and jail sentences resulted. Gore Vidal's *The City and the Pillar* was denied advertising space. Only last year, the *New Yorker* rejected advertising space to a staid homosexual publication.

Where shall the line now be drawn, and by whom? Is *Roots* offensive for showing violence against blacks? *Holocaust* against Jews? Shall television news clips exposing war atrocities—factors in ending the Vietnam war—be censored? And news stories of murders and kidnappings? What about *Looking for Mr. Goodbar* and *Hard Core*, both of which contain gross scenes of heterosexual brutality rendered even more offensive by posturings of morality and gratuitous anti-homosexual implications? And Kubrick's *A Clockwork Orange*?

Granted that Friedkin's intentions may not be noble; remarks attributed to him from years back sound at best archaic today. (One should point out, however, that his film of Mart Crowley's *The Boys in the Band* was very daring and sympathetic for its time.) Undeniably, the producer of *Cruising*, Jerry Weintraub, has been vulgarly offensive, insensitive to real issues. But can one determine from a script a film's full meaning, which is also shaped by essential elements of performance, editing, even music? It is not only *Cruising* that is involved here: The precedent set by preventing its production will reach out to all other films—and may ricochet.

What are the long-terms effects? Will any group demand to see a script in advance? May the same argument be used against a film made by homosexuals and opposed by heterosexuals? Shall we determine artistic expression by popular consent? May we not inadvertently be assuring that no director, no producer—not even homosexual ones—will dare to deal with homosexuality onscreen at all? Anita Bryant attempted to silence our voices before it could be known what we would say. Our mere presence in schools, she asserted, would pervert children, even bring violence on them. She interpreted the impact of our behavior and, prejudging it, moved to ban it.

Thomas Paine saw the trap of selected censorship: "He that would make his own liberty secure must guard even his enemy from oppression ... if he violates this duty, he establishes a precedent that will reach to himself."

If this film turns out to be odious, might we not turn it to our advantage, clarifying the elements it has, even if distortedly, exposed? Might we not point out that the violence against us is a result of sexual repression and other outside pressures inflicted on us—that the seamy places shown are those we have been shoved into by those societal strictures? Might we not use it to expose the indifference to violence against homosexuals, and the fact that one of the major outrages we face is the latent homosexuality of cops who stalk us and even turn into "queer bashers"?

Might we not, further, encourage powerful but uncommitted homosexual directors and producers to counter the Friedkin film's purported distortions by dealing with our realities instead of hiding, as those producers and directors often do, in musical inanities and films brimful of social conscience toward everyone except homosexuals? At present, the troubling subject of violence toward homosexuals dealt with in *Cruising*, however sensationalized its treatment may turn out to be, is virtually unknown to others than the victims of that violence.

It is exposure, not secrecy, that precedes the solution of a problem. When, a few years back, a cruising park in Los Angeles was ravaged by a wave of "bashings," it was media silence and police apathy—no exposure—that allowed the attacks to continue unabated night after bloody night until murder inevitably occurred.

The second reason proffered against the filming of *Cruising*—that it presents a negative view of the homosexual world—also needs close examination. I firmly believe that not even implicit criticism of the homosexual world may be made that does not contain a greater criticism of heterosexual totalitarianism. But once that is emphasized, it is dishonest to deny that many homosexuals prefer certain subjects of homosexual life to remain hidden—especially that of sadomasochism.

Understandably, in view of the rabid homophobia, some of us want to conceal all that can be possibly determined as "ugly," even when that ugliness is implanted by heterosexual bigotry. The result is that we often become the only minority intent on showing our oppressors how happy they have made us. We assert that by insisting doggedly on presenting a so-called "positive" image—often a euphemism for heterosexual imitation—even to the point of denying the enriching spectrum of our experience, including an abundant sexuality, which needs no apology.

Beyond the immediate context of what *Cruising* may or may not show, some questions should be asked. Would we allow any other film to deal with some of the elements we are objecting to in Friedkin's? Or should we banish them totally from exploration? Only from heterosexuals or even from our own? Will there be a leap to demand to see advance galley proofs of magazine articles and books?

Is there, in fact, an increasing fascination with sadomasochism and leather, especially in our proliferating orgy rooms? Are the orgy rooms altering the pattern of homosexual behavior? Do those who frequent them comprise a small "freaky" segment, or a growing faction on the homosexual landscape? And if it is a disturbing faction, does it not require exploration?

And, finally, why does every homosexual film or book—unlike heterosexual films or books—have to represent our entire world, each and every one of us, when we have so many rich and diverse voices?

We homosexuals cannot improve our world for ourselves and for those who follow us—and improving is a duty we should all feel—if we ban the exploration of our problems. They will not go away if we shove them into the closets from which we have ourselves emerged. The homosexual energy now crackling in New York and elsewhere against oppression has been too long unreleased. Now that we homosexuals have rediscovered the spirit of the Stonewall Inn protest, the power must be used strongly. But critically. For the fight still clearly looms.

POSTSCRIPT: After this article came out, Friedkin, a director I continue to admire highly, called to thank me. I clarified that I was not defending his film, only the right to make it. When the film was finished and both of us were in Los Angeles, he called to ask me whether I would see the film, privately, before its release, for my reaction. After meeting him in his office, a friend of mine and I were whisked in a black limousine to a studio theater, where we sat, alone, watching. The original first images of the film were these: On a graffiti-scrawled wall was splashed the slogan of gay liberation at the time: WE ARE EVERY-WHERE. There then occurred a quick-cut to the murdered homosexual, being pulled out of the river. The film was opening in New York the following week, and there was no time for any major editing. This much was possible: On the telephone I told Friedkin that the juxtaposition was appalling; I suggested the shot of the wall be deleted, and a disclaimer inserted to indicate that what was depicted was a small segment of a vast world. He deleted the offensive shot and included a revision of the disclaimer I had dictated. I felt that at the very least an edge of the predicted violence might have been defused. But I was called a "traitor" by the planners of a gay protest against the film for just that, attempting to defuse the violent message; I had weakened their demonstrations. Later, Friedkin felt I had betrayed him when I wrote an essay, included later here, in which I described *Cruising* as one of several heterosexual films in drag. Today, I feel Friedkin might have made a powerful film of *Cruising* if he had contacted people sensitive to and knowledgeable of the subject, and if he had not been constricted by the attempts at pre-censorship.

PART II: 1980—1990

HOLLYWOOD AND HOMOSEXUALITY: HETEROSEXUAL FILMS IN DRAG (1980)

✦ A beautiful figure with long blonde hair, pinched waist, devil-angel face, swings along a dark street. She wears a black leather cap, leather skirt, leather jacket. The woman is really a man dressed as a woman dressed as a man in leather.

✦ In a flimsy dress which allows us to see his carved pectorals, a handsome young man wearing makeup is involved in a violent fracas with other males. Muscles strain sensually.

✦ A lithe man moves through a twisted concrete tunnel. At its opening semi-nude men, sweating, form a chorus line, writhing with chains twined around their bodies.

✦ Panting, a woman listens to a tape recording of another woman being raped; she peers through a telescope at the object of her desire in an apartment across the street—the woman she herself has paid a man to rape.

✦ Effeminate men wave colored ostrich feathers as they dance with tuxedoed men who are equally effeminate and whose pants turn out to be slit skirts.

✦ Wearing only a cowboy hat, boots and a jockstrap, a huge black man appears out of nowhere in a police station and begins beating up a man who blurts out—Who is that?

W HAT IS ALL that?

These are scenes from recent movies purporting to deal with homosexuality and aimed mainly at heterosexual audiences. Virtually all the directors, writers and lead actors involved are heterosexuals. None of these films—or their originators—understands their subject, a fact which doesn't stop them from speaking with fake authority about homosexuality.

There are three main genres in this trend, typified by: (1) William Friedkin's *Cruising,* which palms off heterosexual fantasies as homosexual realities. (2) Paul Schrader's "closet film" *American Gigolo,* in which the protagonist, though clearly a homosexual type, loudly proclaims his heterosexuality while being manipulated into a homosexual milieu that he can then nobly reject—the director denying homosexuality by dressing it in heterosexual drag. (3) Edouard Molinaro's *Birds of a Feather (La Cage Aux Folles),* a pseudo-liberal picture in which derision of homosexuals mascarades as sophisticated, accepting wit.

Not too long ago all suggestions of homosexuality were outlawed by the Motion Picture Code. When homosexuality managed to squeeze in overtly, it did so only in the form of villainy and/or insanity. Some grimly unforgettable examples:

In *The Fox,* poor neurotic Sandy Dennis is crushed by a falling tree for her love of another woman. Ernest Borgnine in *The Sergeant* kills himself in humiliation for having kissed John Phillip Law—one hot kiss is all it took.

Marlon Brando, after combing his hair neatly, shoots the object of his warm affections because his loved one prefers the captain's wife in *Reflections in a Golden Eye.* The film based on the famous song "Ode to Billy Joe" reveals that the mysterious object which sank into the river was the body of a cute kid who threw himself into the muddy waters rather than face being homosexual. Ironically, William Friedkin's version of Mart Crowley's *The Boys in the Band* remains the most truthful and compassionate of the films of those times. Richard Benner's Canadian film *Outrageous,* about a flagrant transvestite who flaunts his difference, proudly remains by far the best of the recent lot.

CRUISING AND CREDIBILITY

Pointing out only the obvious mistakes in *Cruising* will show that Friedkin knew very little about the subtle, difficult subject he plunged into, saddening those of us who highly regard his other work. One can grant him the freedom to deal with any subject he chooses—and oppose those who attempted to precensor him— but he must be faulted for exposing sadomasochism, an acknowledged wound in a part of the homosexual world—without exploring its causes which clearly lie in heterosexual oppression.

The film is trashily littered with untruths. Friedkin went for sensationalism—and the truth be damned. The blonde transvestite in leather would be banished from macho turf. Her world of femme hustling does not intersect with the leather world. Another example: Totally out of context, a car license plate is shown bearing the identification FFA69. No practitioner of the ugly sexual act known as "fist fucking" would advertise mutual oral copulation. And it's anybody's guess what the mysterious black man in the jockstrap represents.

Friedkin has no idea of the nuances of homosexual sex. Yet in *Cruising* he is still puzzling over what men "do together." One man says to another that he "doesn't do anything, just wants to be worshipped." In the next frame, this very man does *everything.* A man asks how "big" he is. In an impossible line of dialogue that would send any self-respecting homosexual away laughing, the other man answers, "party size," whereupon the first man announces that he, too, "does nothing" in which case the other's party size, or small-gathering size, organ would not matter one millimeter.

Confronted with these absurdities, Friedkin amazed a New York press conference by stating that the killer or killers in

Cruising are heterosexuals. How, then, does he account for the semen found in the anus of one of the victims? He'd have to think that one over, said the unabashed director.

Friedkin may have been mesmerized by visions of homosexual flesh because undeniably *Cruising* conveys spectacular bar scenes saturated with male sensuality—masculine, muscular bodies twist and churn in mass permutations, semi-stripped bodies cruise shadowy streets and parks. Dark sex radiates from the screen.

HOSTILITY IN DRAG

In the same genre, Gordon Willis' *Windows* is a heterosexual man's fantasy answer to the following question: Why, at a crucial time of woman's sexual emancipation, would a woman turn away from men and toward women? Why? Because an evil psychotic lesbian has paid to have the object of her desire brutally raped by a man so she'll turn to her for comfort and whatnot. *That's* why. Equally offensive, despite his posturing liberalism and insipid intellectualism, is Woody Allen's depiction of two lesbians in his recent much-celebrated film *Manhattan*.

Paul Schrader, of *American Gigolo* fame, epitomizes a director whose films are rampant with hatred for and fascination with homosexuality. This conflict results in a need to dress his film in heterosexual high drag. He's also much less honest than Friedkin, who at least tried to neither disguise his subject nor his fascination—nor did he assume a fake moral posture. Schrader claims his research for *American Gigolo* was "internal." But, when one knows nothing of an external subject, internal research exposes only fantasies, not reality.

Julian, played by Richard Gere, could easily be a homosexual. He even parodies a "femme homosexual" expertly while he helps a woman choose art objects to adorn her home. But he draws the line at "fag tricks." This is meant to arouse our respect for his basic morality.

To prove Julian's assertion, Schrader constantly has him eyeing every woman around—old, young, plain, beautiful. They in turn are swept away by this sexual tornado, and Schrader's camera, in a sex tizzy, is thus able to ogle Gere in every state of undress, sinew for sinew, even upside down. All from the women's point of view, of course. One might say that through the use of his camera, the director is able to have his cake but not eat it.

Still, Schrader insists on asserting the overt "gay" background, so called, as Julian goes hunting for Leon, his evil black pimp-hustler-pusher-homosexual. Julian moves through what looks like a twisted tunnel. Is he in Hell? Worse, he's in a homosexual disco.

In contrast to Julian's well-kept body—he only turns heterosexual tricks, remember, and that keeps a man fit—we are shown only the sleaziest street-type hustlers who resort to "fag tricks" in an area of Hollywood abandoned years ago as hustling turf because of constant police raids. But it looks depraved and who cares about reality in these films, anyhow?

When Julian is framed by the evil black man in the sadomasochistic murder of a "kinky" woman, he offers to turn fag tricks in exchange for an alibi from the dastardly pimp Leon. Magically Julian is saved from this fate. In one of the most unintentionally hilarious sequences on film, Julian shoves bad ole Leon half way over a balcony railing, quickly repents, tries to pull him back, only to have clumsy Leon slip from his shiny pimp boots and plummet onto the sidewalk. One damn thing after another. But racism comes to Julian's rescue. A white detective tells Julian to forget the black pimp—everyone saw him trying to save Leon.

Unreal, you say? Schrader isn't bothered by such considerations. Remember *Hardcore*? That film, which included one of the grossest scenes in film history, took numerous swipes at homosexuals while adopting a hypocritical moral posture. Originally framed as a father's dream about his runaway daughter, *Hardcore* later dropped that frame completely but let the dream stand as "reality." (*American Gigolo* is Schrader's nightmare based on "inner research.")

Also in the "closet" genre are: Hal Ashby's *Shampoo*—the least offensive—*Midnight Express* and *Looking for Mr. Goodbar.* In *Midnight Express* a ménage à trois occurs with the camera—a lyrical nude scene in which dreamy yoga poses are struck in a grimy dungeon shower, and surrounded by shafts of sunlight through the prison bars our hero rejects the advances of another man. But wistfully.

Looking for Mr. Goodbar is Richard Brooks' indictment of a woman who is promiscuous and cruises bars, like many homosexuals. Vengefully, he consigns her to homosexual turf (which he does not understand) where she will encounter her murderer, the muscular young man we first saw in makeup and flimsy drag. He's been goaded into that unspeakable attire by an overtly effeminate man who loves him for his masculinity. Then why the drag? Don't ask! Brooks doesn't know any more than Friedkin does about the mysterious semen in *Cruising* or Schrader about hustling.

Despite its silliness, *Cruising* has some merit, though tainted. One doesn't have to approve of it in order to acknowledge the visual assault that Friedkin's masculine tough homosexual men will make on the heterosexual consciousness. Audiences cannot easily laugh away the stark new image of men who would clearly take exception to being called "sissies."

BIG LAUGHS: ZERO TRUTH

Audiences *can*, however, and *do*, roar with laughter at Molinaro's *Birds of a Feather,* a huge hit which represents the third genre of closet films. In its final ramifications, *Birds of a Feather* is more deeply damaging than *Cruising*. By representing two nice, middle-class, middle-aged men living together in a facsimile of heterosexual marriage, this film makes it easy for its audience to think they are accepting these cute fairies who, in their cunning domesticity, pose absolutely no threat.

To reinforce heterosexual views and give heterosexuals more laughs but little truth, *Birds of a Feather* depicts not one but both of the coupled men as campily effeminate. Even the men dancing with the transvestites in the nightclub of which the two stars are proprietors are madly, rampantly femme. Even the black "butler," though muscular, wears costumes straight out of Frederick's of Hollywood.

At one point, the more effeminate of the main characters refers to himself bitterly as a "freak, a laughingstock." The audience agrees, and cracks up. Out of compassion? Certainly not.

Incredibly, the less effeminate man has a son. Abandoned by his mother, raised by his father and his effeminate lover, the son, now grown, asks his father to "act like a man," remove his makeup, send his kind male surrogate mother away, and convert their resplendently ornate apartment into an austere "home" where he can bring his girlfriend's conservative parents. The son's treacherous ingratitude is never dealt with, but we hardly notice, we're laughing so damn hard at those cute fairies.

Now let me say that I have been a longtime champion of the so-called "drag queen" and her courage. And, I have cautioned homosexuals not to get caught in the trap of imitating our oppressors with rigid machismo. I long to see the transvestite depicted in film in all her valiant glory. After all, it was her breed who rioted at the Stonewall Inn in 1969, thus beginning "gay" liberation—and, ironically, the emergence of the new macho homosexuals who often ungratefully ostracize her. So, I'm not objecting to the spectacle of drag and effeminacy.

What's offensive about *Birds of a Feather* is the deliberate courtship of prejudice. The heterosexual audience laughs, thus rendering the objects of their prejudice acceptable when ludicrous. What passes for compassion is at best pitying contempt. Nor am I upholding a rigorous machismo.

It's a fact of Hollywood life that the many powerful homosexual directors and producers there remain notoriously closeted—

meanwhile heterosexual directors go gayly along misrepresenting a subject they know nothing about. Understandably, homosexuals are calling for a halt to grotesque distortions of our world. For "positive images." But there's an implicit danger in the demand for films which present only such figures as are currently deemed "politically correct." All too often that desired image is one of the conforming, middle-class masculine man in a "loving" relationship with only one man—a "heterosexual" marriage.

This could turn into another kind of misrepresentation—by homosexuals who shove into a closet those they now call our stereotypes, but who are probably our heroes, like the rioting transvestites of the Stonewall era. We may mistake liberation for surrender to what heterosexuals restrict us to—all in the name of that so-called "positive" image.

Patricia Nell Warren has written a popular and much-optioned novel called *The Front Runner* which many homosexuals believe would project just such a "positive image." But that book depicts one of the most romantic of all homosexual myths: the macho coach who falls in love with his athletic student. It too is pure fantasy evoking adolescent longing, this time a woman's fantasy of a male homosexual's fantasy.

What we need—heterosexual and homosexual alike—is a presentation of homosexual reality that doesn't apologize for its rich sexuality or splendid variety—from musclemen to transvestites. Truths will emerge only through a spectrum of films which show what is beautiful as well as ugly, what is good as well as bad, what is comforting as well as troubled.

That homosexual landscape is populated not only by coaches and masculine lovers any more than by only leathermen. It is populated by queens, daring promiscuous outlaws, hustlers, young people, old, happy and sad homosexuals. They are found in the bars, on the streets, at quiet candlelit dinners or marching for human rights.

The film world musn't be reticent to explore, through its wonderfully powerful images, our variegated homosexual world. That exploration should be allowed to deal honestly with the causes for the fascination with S & M—in that faction of our world. Denying its existence is untruthful, too. Nor must we neglect to deal with our very real and abundant capacity for happiness and love. And portray it truthfully.

POSTSCRIPT: The published title for this essay in *Forum* magazine was "How Hollywood Straights Picture Gays," whereas my title was the one included here. I dislike the references to heterosexuals as "straight." I still don't care for the word "gay." I often suggest a much more glamorous designation for male homosexuals: Trojans.

TWENTY YEARS OF GORE VIDAL:
A CANDIDATE FOR CANONIZATION? (1980)

THE JACKET OF *Views from a Window: Conversations with Gore Vidal* suggests the dwelling place of God, lacy clouds, ethereal blue. The reason becomes clear in Robert J. Stanton's introduction to this collage of the "best" of the Vidal interviews in the past twenty years.

"We laugh nervously as he intelligently exposes stupidity and hypocrisy in American politics, religion, education, the arts and even our life styles," Stanton writes about Vidal. Although "we are hurt that he doesn't forgive us our sins," we continue to "embrace him" even as he "quite frankly tells us . . . he does not love us." Yet, "deep within us," we know that his "just and demanding" criticism is "for our own good."

The meaning of the heavenly jacket is clear. Stanton is proposing Vidal for canonization. Four miracles, a Holy Life and martyrdom are requirements.

Vidal's creation of "Myra Breckinridge" is one miracle, a work of satirical art challenged, in our time, only by Nabokov's own grand lady, "Lolita." Some of Vidal's essays shine like the star he claims—with hyperbole, one assumes—led "quaking shepherds" to his birthplace. Another miracle may gleam among works one has not read, including "Washington, D.C." and "Burr." "Julian" is a "contender," in the boxing metaphor of a writer not dear to Vidal. For insurrectionary power, *The City and the Pillar* may qualify.

On to the Holy Life. A wounded army of *advocati diaboli* protests Vidal's often brutal wit—Mailer, Capote, Mrs. Onassis, the Jagger family. Ghosts clutch their way out of graves to testify—Hemingway, Kerouac, Moby Dick. Vidal makes even ghosts and whales weep.

He won't forgive Anaïs Nin myriad mysterious trespasses, including her use of the word "ensorcel." Not without reason, he detests the literary "desultory autopsies" of academics—but when his own academic, Stanton, does a dizzying interpretation of "The Judgment of Paris," Vidal grants absolution: "One way of seeing it."

Excoriating writers who turn to book reviewing, journalism or teaching, he finds "less compromising" his writing for television. Those of us who write, review books, turn to journalism—and even walk the streets—are reminded, in Butler's words, of those who "Compound for sins they are inclined to/By damning those they have no mind to."

Still, Vidal does not hesitate to side with justice in dangerous causes, and he has honorably helped to rescue writers shoved into limbo—John Horne Burns, Calder Willingham. He shattered literary restrictions on sexual subjects with *The City and the Pillar*—and for his pioneering courage was ignored for a decade by a host of critics.

If being the object of petty manifestations of envy makes martyrs, Vidal is a candidate. Admirably unhumble about his blessings—famous, talented, on television often enough to qualify as a series, he confounds the Furies who lurk behind the *National Enquirer* waiting for "stars" to fall, preferably by aging fatly and surrendering pride. A stylish survivor, Vidal will not become a mess.

Yet he attributes too much to envy. After all, his books rule best-seller lists. The *Boston Globe* called him "our greatest living writer." If villainous English departments still shun him, he is now—cruel fate of proud heretics!—a member of the literary establishment.

Noble aspiration and enlightenment enhance a Holy Life. Vidal wants to be "the person who wrote the best sentences in his time." Two dazzlers open "Myra Breckenridge." His advice to young writers has the sweet, sagacious economy of a Zen master's: "STAY AWAY!" But he slips: "The use of language appalls me," he says, meaning "the misuse of language."

In generalized discussions of sex, especially in a doggedly civil exchange with Lord Longford, Vidal's views shine like virtue itself. But his attitudes on contemporary sexuality are at times dated. He insists that everyone be bisexual, advises a fiery "gay liberationist" to "go to the polls," and upholds that homosexual is not a noun, although for almost two decades dictionaries have defined it as such. "Boys are looking more feminine," he claims, having avoided West Hollywood.

In a messianic tizzy, he proposes combating overpopulation by allowing an "Authority," through an "intelligent program of eugenics," to decide "which genetic types should be . . . allowed to die off. Later he clarifies he never really favored this—it was only a "possible notion."

Vidal is not ready for canonization. But he is a writer who dares to be intelligent, original, challenging. At his best he can be superb. Whatever he thinks of the profession, he is a grand teacher.

In this splendid collection—thank you Mr. Stanton—Vidal asks: "Does one mellow or does one rot?"

One is delighted to report that Vidal shows no indication of doing either.

POSTSCRIPT: My first encounter with Vidal's work was in El Paso when as a teenager I went to pick up *The City and the Pillar* from a rental library I frequented. The librarian looked at me and shook her head. "And you're such a sweet boy," she said ruefully. I like my essay here very much, it's funny and respectful of a man and writer I admire highly.

BURROUGHS STROKES AGAIN (1981)

HE EFFECT OF *Cities of the Red Night* is not unlike a television set gone lucidly mad—splicing news clips, cartoons, commercials and movies into a nightmarish vision of a barbaric, doomed, hilarious world. Or: It is as if Robinson Crusoe joined Terry and the Pirates; the Katzenjammer Kids raided Joyce's "Nighttown"; Sade's perfervid hallucinations melded into the contrived "tortures" of Flash Gordon.

Few important, contemporary writers have been so mistreated as Burroughs, his recent books ignored or damned. Like Orson Welles, he seems to have been offered up to posterity, which is too often wrong; it merely has the last word. Yet Burroughs' work has influenced a whole generation. His voice has remained bold amid the mewling of many of today's cowed—but East Coast–consecrated—writers.

Why excoriated or ignored? There is the troublesome legend of the man—drugs, exile, shootings. There is his ridiculed, misunderstood "cut-up" method of writing, with reliance on "accidental" juxtapositions—but of selected material—for its startling effects. It is not to attribute cosmic overtones to Burroughs to point out that the orderly universe is thought by many to have derived from "accidental" fission.

Too, there are the sly "put-ons" he obviously relishes, to catch critics. In the straight-faced foreword to this book he leads us to believe the idealistic pirate Captain Mission and his socialist utopia really existed. Defoe (who invented the captain), Swift, Gertrude Stein, Nabokov, Picasso also "play" with their audiences.

Threatening to some is the undeniably steely center of Burroughs' mad world. He does not love humanity, often courts the demonic—in the tradition of Baudelaire, Sade, Genet.

True, Burroughs sometimes writes flat, ugly sentences, to mar otherwise grand passages. He is perhaps in too much of a rush to reach his structural ends to bother always with handsome syntax. After all, he is shattering conventional forms to achieve his "accidental" architecture.

"Unless writing has the danger and immediacy, the urgency of bullfighting, it is nowhere to my way of thinking," wrote Burroughs years ago. "I must reach the Front." In *Cities of the Red Night,* he reaches that Front.

In 1923, a health officer journeys to find the origin of a mysterious plague. In 1702, Noah—Burroughs never shuns the obvious—joins a ship as mate. In the near future, Clem, a private detective, is hired by parents to locate a missing son. In narrative and language, this picaresque novel deliberately sets out to evoke a series of boys' adventure stories—except that the health officer is an opium addict, the virus is a "Doomsday bug," its symptoms being sexual ecstasies and/or death; Noah's ship is attacked by transvestite pirates and Clem uncovers body-transplants to perform a sexual exorcism.

At first, Burroughs' indulgences exasperate. The clichés—deliberate, one hopes—private parodies, dogged repetitions and schoolboyish humor apparently send Burroughs into peals of laughter—and his admirers to the abyss of despair.

Even so, wild magic works. Like an assertive drug taking time to act, the book grasps us. We are thrust into a savage comic apocalypse in "Ba'dan," one of the Cities of the Red Night, decayed "Fun City . . . afterbirth of a dream . . . arena for deadly sexual games." Riots rage. "All the bad characters of history gather for a last-ditch stand . . . bravos from 17th-Century Venice, old western shootists, Indian Thuggees," assassins, samurai, gladiators, hatchet men, pistoleros, the CIA, the KGB—all the noble heroes of man's glorious history.

Then Burroughs smashes his own anarchy. Like a crazy movie, the book "unwinds," retells itself in rapid motion. "Audience reactions" are inserted; riots are absorbed into a nightmare, sliding into a dream swallowed by—perhaps—drug-withdrawal hallucinations; and *Cities of the Red Night* itself becomes a high-school play, a child's lurid tale of "pirates from other planets"; and even a live etching. "Just the basic mystery of life," Burroughs shrugs. "Now you see it, now you don't."

In the midst of this exploding reality comes a lament from Noah: "I remember a dream of my childhood. I am in a beautiful garden. As I reach out to touch the flowers they wither under my hands. A nightmare feeling of foreboding and desolation comes over me as a great mushroom-shaped cloud darkens the earth. A few may get through the gate in time."

Through the most familiar symbol of modern destruction has Burroughs stumbled on despair? And even . . . shed a tear?

I recall the only time I met Burroughs, in a tacky suite at West Hollywood's Tropicana Motel. Types out of *Rolling Stone* magazine lounged, while Burroughs, on a barstool, watched the television screen. The color picture broke into jagged patterns of "accidental" perfection. Then the "realistic" picture returned. I think I remember a look of dark seriousness on Burroughs' face. But I'm not sure. What I do remember definitely is that, after the ambiguous moment, the corners of his lips tilted, upward.

Cities of the Red Night is Burroughs' masterpiece. In it, the world ends with a bang—and a barely perceived whimper, disguised by the wicked smile of one of the most dazzling magicians of our time.

MEMORY BABE (1983)

A N ARTIST MAY be destroyed by his legend, especially one created beyond him; it may also lock him in a vise of misinter-
pretation. Even those who have not read Thomas Wolfe exile
him to adolescence; Djuna Barnes is an exotic literary orchid;
Gertrude Stein, an influence. No assault on Hemingway will ever
push over his hairy pedestal.

Gerald Nicosia dedicated 10 years to *Memory Babe: A Critical
Biography of Jack Kerouac*—in major part to convince us that Jack
Kerouac is more than a catalyst for better writers.

Fiction carries more truth than biography; the former does
not pretend to tell "the" truth, the latter does and so dissembles.
Biography is at best a *possible* approximation of a life. Nicosia
reconstructs this particular life in minute detail, from hundreds of witnesses. The result is a splendid work illuminating the
pathos of a beautiful young novelist who, like Elvis Presley,
became an object of derision when he dared to age.

The book sprawls like an epic novel with a vest cast of characters, including a busy creation named Allen Ginsberg; a black
beauty, Mardou Fox; a rebellious angel, Neal Cassidy; a mad
genius, Bill Burroughs.

In his early New York days, as a student at Columbia, Kerouac
played a game with Burroughs, Ginsberg and others, squaring

off as "Rimbaudians"—beautiful, seduceable innocents—and "Baudelairians"—jaded seducers. Kerouac was a Rimbaudian.

Nicosia follows Kerouac into the labyrinthine madness known as book publishing as *On the Road* collected insults from publishers until a valiant female editor proclaimed it "a classic of our time." Heavy promotion, plus the author's combination of physical beauty, athletic prowess, talent and sudden fame, prepared a mine field of jealousy that exploded into malice. How else to account for the literary mugging on a book in the adventurous tradition of *Huckleberry Finn*?

Norman Podhoretz, the Joe McCarthy of literary conspiracies, insisted the book's message was: "Kill these intellectuals who can talk coherently . . . kill those capable of getting seriously involved with a woman, a job, a cause." He even claimed Kerouac's work influenced the scrapping of the B-1 bomber. Other critics sank to the occasion, proving again that posterity is often more easily satisfied than the Sunday book reviewer.

Myth burgeoned: Kerouac simply "typed"; he was a primitive, a "know-nothing" extolling violence . . . Stanley Kowalski as poet.

Yet *On the Road* was much revised—once rewritten in pencil— while Kerouac attempted to absorb the style of Swift. He admired Shakespeare, Joyce, Proust, Melville, Lewis Carroll. He took writing courses with fabled teachers. Refusing to allow his books to become violent films, he upheld that his reference to "beat" artists meant "beatific."

His constant return to his mother provided another area of unfair assaults. (Poignantly, she answered a *Confidential* magazine attack on her son by writing a rambling letter denying he was a "mamma's boy.")

Nicosia becomes reckless about Kerouac's sexuality. He rakes exhausted gossip, sexual braggadocio from men and women. Kerouac "went for almost a year without intercourse," he blithely tells us. In an unintentionally hilarious passage, he reconstructs the time Kerouac first saw Cassady's genitalia—and corroborates that historical moment in a footnote citing two authorities.

He does not avoid Kerouac's dark side. Kerouac denied having fathered a girl, almost certainly his. Toward the last—isolated, his work increasingly derided, then ignored—he ranted against Jews, blacks, homosexuals, echoing his parents' bigotries. Yet the same man had gloried in the black men's jazz, fallen in love with a black woman, cherished Jewish friends, had sex with men. That surprising, ugly shift remains disturbing.

The Kerouac character in *Desolation Angels* declares, "Every night I still ask the Lord, 'Why?' and haven't heard a decent answer yet." He never did. He grew heavy and flushed form liquor, his physical perfection gone. He accosted strangers and proclaimed his identity. "Is it a good book?" he asked a girl on the beach reading *On the Road*. Ignored, he frantically insisted he was the famous author. She called the police; he was arrested. The tattered Rimbaudian now required proof of his own identity.

Whether or not a reader agrees with Nicosia's evaluation of Kerouac as a "great" writer, he persuades the reader to return to Kerouac's work. And there, one finds evidence of the promised "inner order," color symbolism, religious allegory, refined form, genuine innovation—and passages of beauty. Nicosia has written a grand book about a haunting, haunted writer who may yet overcome the burden of his largely imposed reputation.

POSTSCRIPT: I'm glad that Kerouac has deservedly become a vital figure in American literature, despite the fact that toward the end he was being shoved aside in the "academies." I think his books would have been terrific with much more editing. My editor, Don Allen, was also Kerouac's editor on some books. In a magazine interview Kerouac referred to Don Allen as "the best editor." Don's reaction, when I mentioned that, was: "Oh, he said that because I let him do whatever he wanted."

I like Kerouac for another reason: He went back home to live with his mother, just like I did with mine until she died.

AIDS: MYSTERIES AND HIDDEN DANGERS (1983)

T HE ONLY FACT about AIDS is that it exists. It is probably fatal, but not enough time has elapsed to determine that, extending needed hope to patients. Beyond that fact, assertions range from reasonable conjecture to cruel fabrication. Suspected, even invented horrors pour out as facts from a hostile press in gloating obituaries on our sexuality; some of our own publications borrow these assumptions; too many homosexuals accept them. Caught in this rampage of conjecture, we are endangered by another illness, the exhumation of guilts and self-hatreds we insisted were buried forever. This may go on killing us even after a cure for the diagnosed illness is found.

A homosexual in a Hollywood store cackles, "Know what gay stands for?—'Got AIDS Yet?'" In a New York bar one man screeches at another, "Bitch! I bet you've got AIDS!" Accusing him of being "responsible" for present dangers, a heavyset man savagely pummels and kicks a slender, shirtless homosexual cruising the Silver Lake turf of Las Angeles. But this time the attacker is not a heterosexual thug— he too is homosexual.

AIDS commands our lives. Every homosexual has contracted a form of it, in fear, suspicion . . . and accusation.

Cruelly, viciously, a homosexual writer asserts in the *Village Voice* that AIDS patients lurk in darkened doorways. However genuinely motivated, a homosexual reporter in San Francisco provides two journalists of doubtful credentials the flimsy basis for *California* magazine's violent accusation that homosexuals are hiding the danger of AIDS. Instead of questioning the spurious allegations, several homosexual newspapers carry those spewings as facts. In the boredom-of-it-all tone that afflicts that magazine, a *Christopher Street* columnist writes: "And so the recent comparison of the behavior of pigs infected with African Swine Fever Virus—pigs observed to lick sperm up from the floor, to fornicate with each other—and male homosexuals is not merely darkly amusing, it is quite accurate."

Time magazine crows: "The flag of gay liberation has been lowered . . . and many do not regret it." Even "good heterosexuals" find bonds with Jerry Falwell. In one of the meanest articles—its prejudices are masked as "intellectual concern"—Jonathan Lieberson in the *New York Review of Books* applauds homosexuals who have "become 'twice born,' despising their former promiscuous selves." *The New Republic* finds in AIDS a "metaphor" symbolizing "the identity between contagion and a kind of desire."

Chilling in their lack of compassion, these journalistic assaults have in common the rancid stench of repression, a note of harrowing triumph in the authentication of bigotry. They attempt to make AIDS patients accountable for their illness—much as blacks have been blamed for their poverty, women for rape, Jews for the Holocaust. AIDS affirms Susan Sontag's powerful observation: "Nothing is more punitive than to give disease . . . a moralistic meaning."

On a hot afternoon in Beverly Hills a slightly effeminate man waits for a bus in the shade of a park. A man identifying himself as a cop orders him out: "We don't want queer disease." A few miles away, in Santa Monica, a homosexual gets knifed by a man screaming: "Diseased pervert!"

Hidden dangers: namely, the emergence of a pressurized generation of once-healthy homosexuals branded by assumptions of mutual contagion—murderous lovers. Impotence, alcoholism, addiction, suicide. If old guilts are entrenched as new ones, there will be a return to institutions of our oppression: religion, psychiatry, the tenets of repressive politics. Darker closets more difficult to break out of because we are helping to shut the doors.

What outlet for a young man just coming out, what of him, with eager yearnings, when his first contact may be fatal? As the projected period of incubation is extended without evidence— from months to years—how will living under a lingering sentence of death affect every single area of endeavor among homosexuals?

A psychological time bomb, its forms of implosion and explosion another unpredictable aspect of AIDS.

"Sure, we had raids, arrests, jailings, but we kept on living, and fully—and having sex; if nothing else, that got us through," says a middle-aged man. "What now?"

Because our sex was forbidden harshly and early by admonitions of damnation, criminality, and sickness, sexual profligacy became—not for all of us but for many more than we claim—an essential, even central, part of our lives, our richest form of contact, at times the only one. Because our profligacy questioned their often-gray values, the enemies of desire supported our persecution. With AIDS their sexual envy was avenged: The illness was "created" by promiscuity! they exulted.

But was it? Promiscuity occurred virtually as often before the late sixties as after; the literature of those times confirms that unequivocally. It merely shifted to safer locations, and there was wider knowledge of it. Then why now?

Two men go home together. They strip. Cocks rise in ready desire. (Will he be the one who kills me, the one I kill?) They press sealed lips, trying to awaken softening cocks.

We prevailed over torturing inquisitions, concentration camps, jailings, registration as "deviants," aversion therapy. Then in 1969 a few courageous transvestites, male and female, resisted arrest at the Stonewall Inn, other homosexuals rioted, and gay liberation was officially born. Then it all changed! Instantly! We paraded, chanted prideful slogans, linked hands! *And left the unjustified, heterosexually imposed, but now powerfully absorbed guilts in the darkest closets of ourselves.* Mean bars proliferated. We ritualized fantasies of punishment without exploring origins. Discarded: "fats, femmes, trolls!" Banished: defiant "stereotypes!" The young exiled the now-old fighters—and cut themselves off from a heritage of endurance. Older homosexuals who qualified as "hunks" were granted extensions on their sexual passports— too often to act as punishing "daddies," instead of as needed, experienced guides through still-mined territory.

Yes, there was courage, abundant courage. We vanquished Anita Bryant, crushed the Briggs Initiative. In prideful triumph, we thrust our vast energy outward as anger, and we overcame again.

Why—now—the threatening chaos, the blind meanness turned against our own? Because the rallying crises of our immediate past had demanded no introspection. The enemy was outside, identifiable. AIDS, with its mysteries, tapped our unjustly inherited guilts where we had left them unexplored:

Inside.

POSTSCRIPT: "It was the best of times, it was the worst of times." The erotic years halted, and death loomed over all active gay men. There were startling moments of grim discovery, like learning of the deaths of friends only upon finding their names embroidered into the AIDS quilt. Soon, gay men of a certain age and generation, shared a graveyard of memories, of intimate strangers gone.

THE DEAN FROM DUBLIN: A TRULY CIVILIZED MAN (1984)

> "Here is layed the body of Jonathan Swift, Doctor of sacrosanct Theology, Dean of this cathedral church where savage indignation can no longer tear his heart . . . a man who to his utmost strenuously championed liberty."

> "I have and detest the animal called man."

THE FIRST QUOTATION is Swift's epitaph, written by himself; the second is a declaration by the same man. The two provide possibly the only undisputed consistency in the great dean's life and work—the seeming contradiction, paradoxes that followed even after death: *Gulliver's Travels,* his masterful and bitter view of mankind, was bowdlerized into a benign children's adventure. Born into poverty in Dublin, he was well educated in London. At first a Whig, he became a Tory whose devotion to the Anglican Church allowed him to accept its demand of allegiance from public servants. Yet he upheld the right of private dissent, and he raged against censorship.

He was a dean of the Church of England—and he wrote the most damning allegory against religion. In *A Tale of a Tub,* while professing to side with the Anglican Church, he did not allow it escape his scorn. In *The Battle of the Books* he vaunted the ancients over the moderns, but his own work is markedly innovative, influencing modern writers from Sterne to Joyce, Nobokov, Burroughs—and the films of Bunuel.

This Tory, who moved in genteel society among the elite, wrote the most powerful indictment of the rich and their exploitation of the poor. In *A Modest Proposal,* he uncovered barbarity in the so-called "voice of reason" when it purports to argue for the "common good" in order to disguise cruel self-privilege. Assuming a tone of cunning "civility," Swift proposes the slaughtering and dressing of the infants of the Irish peasantry, predominantly Catholics, for the dinner tables of wealthy English landlords. His "modest proposal" exposed the prevailing conditions allowing starvation in Ireland.

That enraged essay and other created what came to be known as "boycott." The man who professed to detest the land of his birth became its national hero.

Yet his view of humankind was bleak. He hated war. In the heart of man was a trove of "vileness and baseness." Hell *must* exist if only to accommodate "damn'd poets, damn'd critics, damn'd blockheads"—and senators , lawyers, judges, lords, squires, priests, prelates, parsons."

"Ecstatic mysticism" aroused him to splenetic anger, and that led to one of the most hilarious feuds in literary history. In *The Bickerstaff Papers* he parodied the banal predictions of astrologer John Partridge, then went on to foretell the "instant" of Partridge's death, on which date he delivered the astrologer's "elegy": "Strange, an astrologer should die / without one wonder in the sky!" A much-alive Partridge raged into disrepute.

At times, Swift's dark vision is stripped of satire. He saw "love of Life" as an exception to God's intention that reason prevail over passion, because "from the dictates of reason" every man would "despise" life, and "and wish it at an end, or that it never had a beginning." Here he leaps centuries to link with Sartre, Beckett.

There is a clear point where all Swiftian "contradictions" intersect. His consistent target was hypocrisy. He found it in the many masquerades of tyranny and oppression. His was a severely wounded "idealism," and satire was blood pouring from the unhealed wound. He could take no side without seeing ludicrous elements. What had been called Swift's "misanthropic" indictment of humankind is, more, a clarity of vision.

The power of his satire at times overwhelms the fact that Swift was also a masterful stylist. He wove suspense into the very syntax of sentence, sculpting a precise, clear, yet complex prose.

Angus Ross and David Woolley, editors of this splendid collection of Swift's work, pay respect to the author with intelligent choices and approach. Their introduction melds biography and history for interconnections. The chronological arrangement of Swift's letters, essays, poems, allegories and sermons allows a view of the man's work as it evolved. Lavish notes—at the end so that they do not obtrude—are enlightening and relevant, at times scholarly, at times commendably jaunty, never interjecting arcane interpretations that would have sent the Dean to his savaging pen.

This essential volume allows full resonance to the mighty voice of one of the world's greatest writers—and one of its most truly civilized men.

POSTSCRIPT: After this essay appeared, a gentleman angrily wrote the editor of the *Los Angeles Times Book Review* asking what qualified the author of a book titled *The Sexual Outlaw* to review the work of Jonathan Swift.

CITY OF NIGHT REMEMBERED (1984)

ITY OF NIGHT began as a letter to a friend in Evanston, Illinois. It was written in El Paso the day following my return to my hometown in Texas after an eternity in New Orleans. That "eternity"—a few weeks—ended on Ash Wednesday, the day after Mardi Gras. The letter began:

> "Do you realize that a year ago in December I left New York and came to El Paso and went to Los Angeles and Pershing Square then went to San Diego and La Jolla in the sun and returned to Los Angeles and went to Laguna Beach to a bar on the sand and San Francisco and came back to Los Angeles and went back to the Orange Gate and returned to Los Angeles and Pershing Square and went to El Paso . . . and stopped in Phoenix one night and went back to Pershing Square and on to San Francisco again, and Monterey and the shadow of James Dean because of the movie, and Carmel where there's a house like a bird, and back to Los Angeles and on to El Paso where I was born, then Dallas with Culture and Houston with A Million Population—and on to New

Orleans where the world collapsed, and back, now, to
El Paso grasping for God knows what?"

The letter went on to evoke crowded memories of that Mardi
Gras season, a culmination of the years I had spent traveling
back and forth across the country—carrying all my belongings in an army duffel bag; moving in and out of lives, sometimes glimpsed briefly but always felt intensely. In that
Carnival city of old cemeteries and tolling church bells, I slept
only when fatigue demanded, carried along by "bennies" and
on dissonant waves of voices, music, sad and happy laughter.
The sudden quiet of Ash Wednesday, the mourning of Lent,
jarred me as if a shout to which I had become accustomed had
been throttled. I was awakened by silence, a questioning
silence I had to flee.

I walked into the Delta Airlines office and told a pretty youngwoman there that I *had* to return to El Paso immediately. Though
I had left money with my belongings scattered about the city in
the several places where I had been "living," I didn't have enough
with me for the fare, and a plane would depart within an hour or
so. Out of her purse, the young woman gave me the money I
lacked, and added more, for the cab. I thanked her and asked her
name so I might return the money. "Miss Wingfield," she said in
a moment of poetry not included in this novel because it is too
"unreal" for fiction.

I thought I had ripped up the letter I had written about that
Carnival season; I knew I had not mailed it. A week later I found
it, crumpled. I rewrote it, trying to shape its disorder. I titled it
"Mardi Gras" and sent it out as a short story to the literary quarterly *Evergreen Review*.

From childhood, I had wanted to be a writer. My mother was
Mexican, a beloved, beautiful woman with truly green eyes and
flawless fair skin; my father was Scottish, a confusing, passionate,
angry man with blue eyes, which, in my memories, seem always

about to shed tears. I learned Spanish first and spoke only it until I entered school. At the age of eight I began writing stories, all titled "Long Ago." At about thirteen, I started a novel called *Time on Wings*—about the French Revolution, which I researched diligently. The great enlightenment that comes only in midteens led me to "deeper" subjects, and I began an autobiographical novel titled—oh, yes—*The Bitter Roots*. It was about a half-Mexican, half-Scottish boy, doubly exiled in many ways: by his "mixed" blood (especially significant in Texas), by his present poverty contrasted with his parents' memories of wealth and gentility; he was "popular" only during school hours, after which he rushed home to secret poverty.

At sixteen, my "works" included many poems, among them two "epics" about angels at war in Heaven, more than 500 pages of *Time on Wings*, about 200 pages of *The Bitter Roots*, both started in pencil, continued on a portable typewriter my father, in one of his many moods of kindness within anger, bought me. I abandoned both books and went on to finish a short, strange novel titled *Pablo!* Set in contemporary Mexico and the jungles of the Yucatán, it was framed about the Mayan legend of doomed love between the moon and the sun, who saw each other at the dawn of time. The main character in this "realistic fantasy"—in which animals talk, witches incite grave violence—is a youngman who tells the story of a "beautiful woman who died."

On scholarship given by the newspaper I worked for as copyboy, and with the financial help of my brother Roberto, I went to college in El Paso. After classes, I often climbed the nearby Cristo Rey Mountains, bordered by the Rio Grande, usually waterless here. I read a lot, eclectically; my favorite writers included Euripides, Faulkner, Poe, Margaret Mitchell, Lorca, Melville, Jeffers, Hawthorne, Camus, Milton, Ben Ames Williams, Dickens, Emily Brontë, Nietzsche, Dostoyevsky, Chekhov, Donne, Gide, Henry Bellamann, Giraudoux, Pope, Djuna Barnes, Tennessee Williams, Proust, Joyce, Frank Yerby, Dos Passos, Thomas Wolfe, Capote,

Mailer, James Jones, Henry James, Gertrude Stein, Beckett, Farrell, Nabokov, Kathleen Winsor, Swift. I saw many, many movies.

An English teacher offered to recommend me for a scholarship to Harvard, his school. But I went into the army. I didn't tell anyone except my immediate family—and I burned most of what I had written, except for *Pablo!* I had been gone only a few weeks when my father died and I returned to El Paso.

The rest of that time of my life in the army is as "unreal" as an attached memory, with the exception of "leave time" in Paris. I went in a private and came out a private. Released, I went to New York to enroll in Columbia University. Instead, I discovered the world of Times Square.

My life assumed this pattern: I would invade the streets and live within their world eagerly; then I would flee, get a job, walk out of it—and return to the waiting streets like a repentant lover eager to make up, with added intensity, for lost moments. At the New School for Social Research, I began another novel, unfinished, *The Witch of El Paso,* about my dear great-aunt, *Tía* Ana, who had "deer eyes" and magical powers. Soon I extended my "streetworld" across the country.

In El Paso, a letter arrived from Don Allen, one of the editors of *Evergreen Review,* in response to my story-letter, "Mardi Gras"; he admired it and indicated it was being strongly considered for publication. Was it, perhaps, a part of a novel? he asked.

I had never intended to write about the world I had found first on Times Square. "Mardi Gras" for me remained a letter. But thinking this might assure publication of the story, I answered, oh, yes, indeed, it was part of a novel and "close to half" finished.

By then, I was back in Los Angeles under the warm colorless sun over ubiquitous palm trees. But the epiphany of questioning silence which had occurred in New Orleans made me experience the streetworld with a clarity the fierceness of the first journey had not allowed. I could "see"—face—its unique turbulence, unique beauty, and, yes, unique "ugliness."

"Mardi Gras" appeared in Issue No. 6 of the famous quarterly that was publishing Beckett, Sartre, Kerouac, Camus, Robbe-Grillet, Ionesco, Artaud. Don Allen wrote that he would be in Los Angeles on business and looked forward to seeing the finished portion of my book.

Instead, I showed him part of the setting of the novel I still had no intention of writing. I took this elegantly attired slender New York editor into one of the most "dangerous" bars of the time ("Ji-Ji's" in this book). Pushers hovered outside like tattered paparazzi greeting the queens. Inside the bar, the toughest "male-hustlers" asserted rough poses among the men who sought them or the queens. Don Allen said he thought perhaps the bar was a bit too crowded. As we drove away, the police raided it.

Later, Don—he became Don—would confess that he suspected there was no book. So he encouraged me to write other short pieces, which appeared in *Evergreen Review*; a lyrical evocation of El Paso and a Technicolor portrait of Los Angeles. Then Carey McWilliams, editor of *The Nation*, asked me to write for the magazine. For *Evergreen Review* and *The Texas Quarterly*, I translated into English short works by some young Mexican authors. The writing was yanking me from the streetworld, the "streets" pulled as powerfully. To connect both—and with sudden urgency—I wrote a story about Miss Destiny—a rebellious drag-queen who longed for "a fabulous wedding"—and about others in "our" world of bars, Pershing Square, streets. The story was very "literal"; I felt that to deliberately alter a "real" detail would violate the lives in that world. I sent the story to Don. He admired it a lot, but some in the growing staff of Grove Press, publishers of *Evergreen Review*, did not, and the story was turned down. That day, when I saw the people I had written about, Chuck the Cowboy, Skipper, Darling Dolly Dane, Miss Destiny, it seemed that not only my story but their lives and mine among them had been rejected: exiled exiles.

Alone smoking grass on the roof of the building where I rented a room, I looked in the direction of Pershing Square just blocks away. Nearby church bells tolled their last for the night. Everything seemed frozen in darkness. As children, we had played a game called "statues": Someone swung us round and round, released us unexpectedly, and we had to "freeze" in the position we fell (always—and this would assume importance for me later—adjusting for effect). Now the image occurred of a treacherous entrapping angel as the "spinner" in a life-game of "statues." It was that imagery which was needed—and had been there behind the reality—to convey Miss Destiny's crushed romanticism. I rewrote "The Fabulous Wedding of Miss Destiny," imbuing it with a discovered "meaning." I had begun my "ordering" of the chaotic reality I was experiencing and witnessing.

I had been asked by one of its editors to contribute to an adventurous short-lived quarterly, *Big Table,* which had broken away from *The Chicago Review* in a dispute over censorship. Soon, Miss Destiny debuted there, among Creeley, Mailer, Burroughs.

As sections from the growing book continued to appear in *Evergreen Review,* I began getting encouraging letters from readers, agents, and other writers, including Norman Mailer and James Baldwin. When several editors—at Dial, Random House, others—expressed interest in the book and there were two offers of an advance, I telephoned Don; I could not conceive of this book's appearing other than through Grove Press. Not only was Barney Rosset, its president, publishing the best of the modern authors—and battling literary censorship—but *Evergreen Review* had largely created the interest in my writing that others were responding to. As my now-editor, Don came to Los Angeles with a contract and a small advance for the book I had begun to call *Storm Heaven and Protest.*

But I still didn't write it.

I plunged back into my "streetworld." Hitchhiking I met a man who would become instrumental in my finishing this book.

I saw him regularly, but I kept my "literary" identity secret; I had learned early—but not entirely correctly—that being smart on the streets included pretending not to be. Not knowing that I had graduated from college and had already published sections from a novel I had a contract for—but concerned that I might be trapped in one of the many possible deadends of the streets— he offered (we were having breakfast in Malibu, the ocean was azure) to send me to school. I was touched by his unique concern, and when he drove me back to my rented room on Hope Street, I asked him to wait. I went inside and autographed a copy of "The Fabulous Wedding of Miss Destiny" and gave it to him. He looked at it, and then at me, a stranger.

Then I needed to flee the closeness increased, perhaps, by the fusion of my two "identities." Consistent with another pattern, a letter arrived from a man who had read my writing: he would be happy to have me visit him on an island near Chicago. A plane ticket followed. Painfully trying to explain to my good friend who had picked me up hitchhiking that I *had* to leave Los Angeles, I left and spent the summer on a private island. When summer was ending, I migrated to Chicago, quickly finding its own Times Square.

But I was pulled back to Los Angeles. Extending the understanding that makes him, always, deeply cherished and special in my life, my friend who had wanted to put me through school— and whose "voice" is heard in part in the character of Jeremy in this book—now offered to help me out while I went to El Paso to finish—where it had begun—the book I again longed to write.

I returned to my mother's small house and wrote every day on a rented Underwood typewriter. My mother kept the house quiet while I worked. After dinner, I would translate into Spanish and read to her (she never learned English) certain passages I considered appropriate. "You're writing a beautiful book, my son." she told me.

It was difficult to write that book. Guilt recurred as I evoked those haunting lives. Oh, *was* I betraying that anarchic world by writing about it—or even more deeply so if I kept to myself those exiled lives? I increasingly found "meaning" in structure: In "Between Two Lions," I wanted to create out of the reality of Times Square a modern jungle in which two of its powerful denizens connect momentarily, but because of their very natures inevitably wound each other. The story of Miss Destiny found fuller meaning in the childhood game of "statues." I attempted to tell the story of Lance O'Hara as a Greek tragedy, the chorus of bar-voices warning of the imminent fall of the demi-god, the almost-moviestar on the brink of aging, the whispering Furies conspiring to assure the fall. From my early fascination with mathematics, I "plotted" the chapter on Jeremy as an algebraic equation drawn on a graph, the point of intersecting lines revealing the "unknown factor"—here, the unmasking of the narrator. Memory itself, being selective, provides form; each portrait-chapter found its own "frame." (The most difficult chapter to write was Sylvia's.) My rejected Catholicism was bringing to the narrator's journey a sense of ritual—and the bright colors of garish Catholic churches are splashed in descriptions throughout this book. As I wrote, stirred memories rushed the "stilled" present, and to convey that fusion I shifted verb tenses within sentences. The irregularly capitalized words I hoped would bring a visual emphasis that italics could not.

Before writing, I often listened to music: Presley, Chuck Berry, Fats Domino, Beethoven, Tchaikovsky, Richard Strauss, Stravinsky, Bartok—to absorb the dark, moody sexuality of rock, the formal structure of classical music, the "ordered" dissonance of modern composers.

Each chapter went through about twelve drafts, some passages through more than that—often, paradoxically, to create a sense of "spontaneity." The first four paragraphs that open this book were compressed from about twenty pages. The first chapter was written last, the last one came first. Although four years elapsed between the time I began this book—with the unsent letter—and the time it was finished, most of it was written during one intense year in El Paso.

Three titles had been announced with published excerpts: *Storm Heaven and Protest, Hey, World!* and *It Begins in the Wind.* The intertwining chapters that connect the portraits were called "City of Night" from the start. But I did not conceive of that as the book's title. I did consider: *Ash Wednesday, Shrove Tuesday, The Fabulous Wedding of Miss Destiny, Masquerade.* Finally, I decided: *Storm Heaven and Protest.* Then Don Allen—always a superb editor—suggested the obvious: *City of Night.*

The book was finished. That night—and this is one of the most cherished memories of my life—my mother, my oldest brother, Roberto, and I were weaving about my mother's living room, bumping into each other, each with great stacks of the almost-700-page typescript, collating it—I had made three or four carbon copies.

The manuscript was mailed. I went to return the rented typewriter, but I couldn't part with it. I bought it; I still have the elegant old Underwood, now comfortably "retired."

Proofs came. As I read, I panicked. In print, it was all "different"—wrong! About a third of the way through, I began changing a word here and there, a phrase, a sentence, a paragraph; then I started back at the beginning. By the time I had gone through the galley proofs, the book was virtually rewritten on the margins and on pasted typewritten inserts. But *now*—I knew—it was "right." I called Don, then in San Francisco, to "prepare" him. He was startled but agreed with the alterations. Despite Don's preparation, others at Grove reacted in shock at the rewritten galleys. Knowing how expensive the resetting would be, I had offered out of my royalties to pay for it—a contractual provision. But Barney Rosset made no objection to changes, and he did not charge me. Publication was rescheduled, and the book was reset.

I had no doubt that *City of Night* would be an enormous success. I was right. In a reversed way. I had thought it would sell modestly and that the book would be greeted with critical raves. The opposite occurred, dramatically.

Before the official publication date, my book appeared in the No. 8 slot of *Time*'s national bestseller list. Also before publication, I saw my first review. Even for the dark ages of the early 1960's the title of the review in *The New York Review of Books* was vicious in its overt bigotry. What followed matched its headline. The book climbed quickly to the No. 1 spot on bestseller lists in New York, California. Nationally on all lists it reached third place. In a review featured on its cover, *The New Republic* attempted to surpass the attack of *The New York Review of Books*; it was a draw. The book went into a second, third, fourth, fifth, sixth, seventh printing and remained on the bestseller lists for almost seven months. In its assault of about eight lines, *The New Yorker* made one factual mistake and one grammatical error.

Only the book's subject seemed to be receiving outraged attention; its careful structure, whether successful or not, was virtually ignored. I was being viewed and written about as a hustler who had somehow managed to write, rather than as a writer who was writing intimately about hustling—and many other subjects. That persisting view would affect the critical reception of every one of my following books, and still does, to this day.

I remained in El Paso. Once again, a letter came with a plane ticket, to New York. A man who had read my book and was outraged by its treatment in *The New York Review of Books* invited me to attend the American premiere of Benjamin Britten's *War Requiem* in Tanglewood. But I was waiting for an answer to a request I had made of Grove; and it arrived, a further advance on royalties so I could make the down-payment on a house for my mother.

I flew to New York to meet another major figure in my life, the man who had invited me to Tanglewood; and I spent the following months with him in a fourteenth-storey apartment overlooking the Hudson River (an enormous eagle appeared on the balcony one day and peered in through a glass wall), then in

Tanglewood; and then we went to Puerto Rico, the Caribbean Islands. On a beach I read in a New York gossip column that I was a guest of Mr. So-and-so on Fire Island, a place I have never visited. That was the first I would learn of several men claiming to be me, impostures made possible by the fact that I had decided not to promote this book, to retain my private life; only my publishers knew I was in New York, in Riverdale.

In late September I returned to El Paso, to another of the most cherished memories of all my life, of my mother joyfully showing me the house I had bought for her, her new furnishings. She had a dinner-reception for me, with my brothers and sisters and my special great-aunt.

Strangers appeared at my house, creating ruses to be let in. One youngwoman came to the door, claiming to be the "Barbara" of this book. In school, in the army, and on the streets, I had been what is called a loner—very much so. These incidents increased my isolation. But it seemed appropriate to me, this period of "austerity": I did not want my life to change radically while the lives of the people I had written about remained the same. In El Paso I began the transition from "youngman" to "man." I created my own gym in my mother's new home, and I began working out fiercely with weights.

Some excellent reviews began appearing, and eventually the book would be translated into more than a dozen languages. Letters arrived daily—moving letters, from men, women, young ones, older ones, homosexual, heterosexual. I answered every one. When I went out, it was usually to drive into the Texas desert. I had only two or three friends. With the exception of brief trips to Los Angeles and one to New York, I remained in El Paso in relative isolation until my mother died and I left the city perhaps forever.

More than twenty years and seven books later, how do I feel about *City of Night*? It thrills me—not only for myself but for the many lives it contains, those always remembered faces and voices—that within my lifetime this book, so excoriated when it first appeared, has come to be referred to frequently as a "modern classic." And I no longer feel the guilt I battled so long, about the "real people" I thought I would "leave behind." No— they are a permanent part of my life, of that part of me—the writer—who tells of his journey as a "youngman."

POSTSCRIPT: The real "Fabulous Miss Destiny," who is the model for one of the main characters in *City of Night,* was one of the few people who conveyed to me that they had recognized themselves in— and me as the author of—that novel; there were others, but none conveyed that recognition as dramatically as "Miss Destiny." After the section titled "The Fabulous Wedding of Miss Destiny" appeared in the literary quarterly *Big Table,* I ran into her on Hollywood Boulevard. She gushed, "I want to thank you, my dear, for making me even more famous." Later she gave a mean interview about me to *One* magazine, which featured her on the cover. Still, I was glad she was getting attention. I don't know how she managed to get my telephone number; but for years, she called me ebulliently, often late at night and groggy with liquor, asking that I assure whomever she was with—"a husband"— that indeed she was Miss Destiny in my novel. I always did that, gladly. A year or so ago, the calls stopped. I assume she's gone to Heaven, where she shines among queenly angels.

LESS THAN ZERO (1985)

THE 20-YEAR-OLD author of this pruriently violent book is being widely vaunted as the voice of his generation. The voice is one of traumatized self-pity, passivity and blind self-absorption as heard in this chilly novel about teenage males.

It is certainly the first MTV novel—rampant with aimless rage and symptomatic images and attitudes that it does not quite understand, symbols of fascism, women crawling as slaves, homosexuality derided while courted by imitation.

At age 18, Clay, the narrator, returns from an Eastern college for Christmas in Los Angeles. He dines with ridiculed parents at exclusive restaurants, attends parties, snorts mountains of cocaine, plays video games, watches MTV. He witnesses an anorexic girl photographed as a "pinup" while she shoots up. He samples a vile $15,000 "snuff movie." He learns that a friend is pushing drugs to junior-high students and that another keeps a young girl hallucinating on LSD so he can pass her around as a sex toy. He goes with others to view the body of a teenager in an alley. He visits a friend who keeps a chained 12-year-old girl clogged with drugs for his friends to abuse. From another friend, he hears a credo of fascistic privilege: "If you want to do something, you have the right." Clay takes no action against any of these outrages, none.

Yet he screams to his expensive psychiatrist: "What about me?"

Authenticity is essential in a novel purporting to illuminate unexplored territory. Ellis knows the world of ample wealth. But in certain essential areas, the book suggests the possibility of sensationalized distortion. Some incidents are staples of "creep chic," horrible rumors spread by a few morbid college students swearing to know "someone who saw" the snuff movie, other ugly outrages.

The only plot line is blatantly contrived, involving the mysterious activities of Clay's best friend. Julian becomes a homosexual prostitute because he has an expensive drug habit—and his family has canceled his bank account and credit cards, and it would be a "bummer" to sell his gorgeous Porsche! Julian takes Clay to meet his pimp at a most propitious time. "You bringing your friend here might be a good thing," says the pimp, because a client "wants two guys, one just to watch. Of course." Of course. This artificial device allows Clay to witness what he considers "the very worst"—an act of male prostitution that he watches, for money he does not need.

Beyond sensational content, what of literary quality? As a first novel, it is exceptional, exhibiting notable potential. The best writing describes violence—the tortured death of a coyote under the wheels of a car, every twist rendered in detail. Expertly, Ellis captures the banality in the speech of teenagers. His cool, languid prose is impressive but slides into self-parody: "Angel was supposed to go with us tonight, but earlier today she got caught in the drain of her Jacuzzi and almost drowned." There are more desultory cigarette lightings than perhaps in any other book ever published. "Suddenly," "and then," "for some reason," "missing a beat"—these occur singly or together with dogged persistence.

In a recent essay, Joyce Carol Oates takes exception to the growing notion that sanity lies in "the capacity to assimilate horrors without comment." One might infer that Ellis intends to present objectively for indictment by the reader this world of opulent decay, except that Clay chooses his lacerating judgments and exonerations too carefully. They are delivered in the book's last paragraph:

Los Angeles: Guilty! People are "driven mad by living in the city." Parents: Guilty! They are "so hungry and unfulfilled they ate their children." And Clay and the teenagers preying on those younger than they? Not guilty: They are merely "looking up from the asphalt and being blinded by the sun." With that lofty, vague phrase, Clay releases himself and his malicious friends from all responsibility. Corrupt as the parents may be, nothing conveyed about them here approaches the ancient depravity of these male teenagers. They arouse not pity but an extending fear, because they will inherit the power and wealth of the parents they despise.

POSTSCRIPT: I admire this novel now even more than at first. Originally my admiration was compromised by the fact that I was sure the author was gay—from the content, the images—but he was claiming otherwise; I was also dismayed that a scene in the book seemed to have been "inspired" by one in mine, though misunderstood. So when an advertisement for his novel appeared in the *L.A. Weekly,* and used a quote from this review, I called the publicity man and asked that my supportive quote be removed. I do regret that.

A HIGH COURT DECISION
AND A SENSE OF BETRAYAL (1986)

OR HOMOSEXUALS THROUGHOUT the land, the Supreme Court's 5-4 ruling that the Constitution does not protect private homosexual relations has eroded much trust in their country's system of justice. A sense of "betrayal" is reiterated among younger homosexuals, while older homosexuals see a potential return to the violent repression of years past. There is a further, subtle cruelty in the timing of the decision, coming as it does on the eve of Independence Day, the honoring of American liberties—now excluding homosexuals.

A young New York producer expresses "disillusionment at years of believing that whatever the President or Congress might do, the Supreme Court would protect our freedoms." A young Los Angeles performance artist describes himself as "suddenly cut adrift from freedom in my country." A director of youth services predicts a time when homosexuals may have "to look state-by-state to find acceptance as non-criminals."

Older homosexuals recall a similar climate that allowed years of invisible outrages: prison sentences of up to life; suicides; blackmail resulting from arrests; roundups out of gay bars and into waiting police vans. Policemen were known to shadow men leaving bars and to break into private residences.

Are reactions of betrayal and fears of burgeoning repression justified? I strongly believe so.

Not since the Supreme Court declared in the Dred Scott case that slavery was legal and blacks were not citizens has there been a High Court ruling as seeped in prejudice as this one. In a cold, almost mocking tone, the decision reads at times like a biased tract. Ignoring any separation of church and state, it quickly asserts its basis in "moral teaching," the "ancient roots" of "Judeo-Christian moral and ethical standards." From Roman courts to "the King's courts," "ecclesiastical courts," it roams over centuries of bloody history to pluck out selective indictments of homosexuality in accusing language: "heinous . . . abominable." It reminds, chillingly, that homosexuality was once a capital crime.

It asserts a sophistry that banishes fairness: For centuries homosexual acts have been considered criminal; therefore they remain criminal acts to be condemned today. If longevity of prejudice is an antecedent for legal rulings, the same argument would hold against blacks, Latinos, Jews, Asians, women—all objects of historical persecution. The same religious and historical sources cited throughout allowed for slavery, burnings at the stake, torture, religious persecution—the punishment of adultery by death, the stoning of disobedient children. Shall the court enforce these?

In a separate concurring opinion, Chief Justice Warren E. Burger feels the need to "underscore" the view that "in constitutional terms there is no such thing as a fundamental right to commit homosexual sodomy." Substitute the inflammatory phrase "homosexual sodomy" with "heterosexual sex acts," and the impact of the law is clear. Indeed, the Georgia statue here upheld extends its malice to acts by married heterosexual couples, allowing the government to pry into all private lives.

In an eloquent dissent from this violent invasion of "houses, hearts, and minds," Justice Harry A. Blackmun affirms true "values most deeply rooted in our nation's history." He then enunciates the precise attitude being expressed by individual homosexuals throughout the country: "I think the court today betrays those values."

The onslaught of prejudice unleashed by the Supreme Court is a cause for deep shame in this country.

POSTSCRIPT: Years later, Justice Kennedy would regret his decision upholding the Court's ruling.

CARSON MCCULLERS'
REFLECTIONS IN A GOLDEN EYE (1988)

A BOOK MAY suffer "neglect" in ways beyond being ignored. A subtly insidious form occurs when, though well known, it is widely misinterpreted, and dismissed. That dismissal is inherited, and the real book remains unseen. Now even those who have not read it will dutifully mouth the entrenched judgment.

John Dos Passos, Gertrude Stein, Thomas Wolfe, Djuna Barnes, Eugene O'Neill—all have inherited restrictive reputations, verdict rendered, no appeal allowed.

Carson McCullers is not ignored in modern American literature. *The Heart Is a Lonely Hunter, The Member of the Wedding* (novel and play), and *The Ballad of the Sad Café* continue to be admired. But *Reflections in a Golden Eye* is considered something of an ugly aberration because of original misreading.

After high praise for *The Heart Is a Lonely Hunter,* McCullers became the object of assault with her second novel. According to biographer Virginia Spencer Carr, her very future became uncertain. The book was "pounced upon," castigated for its "obsessive preoccupation with abnormality," its characters deemed "too preposterous;" McCullers "had much to learn about reality." With patriotic fervor someone named Edward Weeks—forever a footnote—wrote in *The Atlantic Monthly:*

"... if this is a fair sample of army life, and if the country is soon to pour itself into the army, then God save the Union!"

To view *Reflections in a Golden Eye* as "realistic" guarantees a misreading. It is an exaggeration removed from conventional reality. By pulling away from "real life," exaggeration allows a fuller kind of exploration, events and characters magnified for closer scrutiny. Through her odd gallery of characters, McCullers exposes an extremity of human capability, from tiny to giant horrors. A short, tight horror story of surprising humor, and unmarred by the sentimentality that intrudes in McCullers' other books, it is as unreal as a story by Poe.

McCullers herself viewed this book as a "fairy tale." Since fairy tales abound in exaggerated horrors and are populated by "preposterous" characters, that is an apt description. She contended her book was meant to be "funny"—and it contains a current of black humor so strong it is difficult to believe that that aspect is still missed: In the barracks of the army post where the book is set, "one old Corporal wrote a letter every night to Shirley Temple making it a sort of diary of all that he had done during the day, and mailing it before breakfast the next morning." Extending that exposure to the mailing of the love-token "before breakfast the next morning" is obviously satirical, illuminating, by projection, Shirley Temple's own grotesqueness as a movie-child.

In its exaggeration and in its ritualization of the accidents that shape fate into retrospective inevitablity, the book evokes Greek tragedy. Its controlled prose creates an effect that might be compared to that of modern ballet, formalized movements interrupted by jagged surprise, sudden lyricism.

The book opens with an impeccable paragraph of sculpted prose:

> An army post in peacetime is a dull place. Things happen, but then they happen over and over again. The general plan of a fort in itself adds to the monotony—

the huge concrete barracks, the neat rows of officers' homes built one precisely like the other, the gym, the chapel, the golf course and the swimming pools—all is designed according to a certain rigid pattern. But perhaps the dullness of a post is caused most of all by insularity and by a surfeit of leisure and safety, for once a man enters the army he is expected only to follow the heels ahead of him. At the same time things do occasionally happen on an army post that are not likely to re-occur. There is a fort in the South where a few years ago a murder was committed. The participants of this tragedy were: two officers, a soldier, two women, a Filipino, and a horse.

The calm prose, creating a sense of banal ineluctibility, does not shift to introduce the fact of murder, which flows out of unremarkable events. It is introduced by the laziest of syntactical constructions—"there is." The unaroused prose, employed throughout with two general exceptions, contrasts with the narrative turbulence to augment the book's tension.

McCullers distorts for effect. The horse is not strictly a "participant" in the tragedy. Its inclusion adds suspenseful strangeness to the events to be chronicled.

Exaggeration demands risk-taking into possible excess. McCullers does not resist the challenge. We learn that Captain Penderton, one of the participants, once stuffed a kitten into a mailbox. As a child of seven "he had become so infatuated with the school-yard bully who had once beaten him that he stole from his aunt's dressing table an old-fashioned hair receiver as a love offering." The same Captain was raised not by one maiden aunt but by *five!* When years later as an adult, he steals a little silver spoon during a formal army dinner, the reader is ready to laugh aloud—exactly as McCullers intends. At that precise point, she allows Alison, another of the participants in the tragedy, to laugh *with us.* Sitting near him, she "laughed so hard that she choked herself and someone had to beat her on the back." McCullers is guiding the reader carefully into her exaggeration.

She dislikes her characters. That allows her to expose their every meanness and stupidity. In the view of Alison, her husband, Major Langsdon, is "as stupid and heartless as a man could be," Leonora, the wife of the Captain and the mistress of the Major, is "an animal," the Captain is "hopelessly corrupt." "Even she herself she loathed."

The author does nothing to separate herself from the evaluations. Twisting the screw, she signals her own disdain and adds evidence: Decrying his wife's proclivity "for classical stuff," the Major proclaims his own choice of music: " 'The Merry Widows' Waltz'—that's the sort of thing I love. Tuneful music!" For him, only two things finally matter—"to be a good animal and to serve my country." Disgusted by his newborn daughter, he thinks that "if he had to touch that baby he would shudder all over."

Lush, sensual Leonora has "a gay cliché for everyone." "Think of it!" she marvels at each tiny banality that baffles her. She stumbles over Scripture: "They giveth it and they taketh it away." Wickedly gratuitous, McCullers informs us: "The truth of the matter was that she was a little feebleminded."

Not surprisingly, McCullers comes closest to compassion with Anacleto, Alison's devoted houseboy. Still, he is not beyond her glare. When the Major, the Captain, and Leonora do not stumble over three bricks he has planted in their path, he is "so vexed that he gave his thumb a mean little bite." Although entirely uncomfortably, he sleeps in a position imitating that of Alison. McCullers allows him some lovely moments—and shatters them. Pretending to be a great, acclaimed dancer, he stumbles—with "a thud." He longs to own a linen shop, with Alison.

Fragile Alison prefers the possibility of "managing a prawn boat" with Anacleto—if she leaves the Major. She is capable of much greater excesses: In a rage of self-loathing, she mutilates her breasts. Her "broodings of decay" lead her to disinter the remains of her child—to be cremated.

The pivotal participant in the drama is Private Williams. Although he will soon be transformed into an object of sensuality, McCullers does not allow him to escape her tight scrutiny: When first introduced, he has "a round sunburned face," and he seems "a bit heavy and awkward in his bearing." Later, "the pure-cut lines . . . of his slim body glistened in the late sun." Still, he retains "dumb eyes, heavy sensual lips" that are often wet, and "childish page-boy bangs." Once he stabbed a Negro—"in an argument over a wheelbarrow of manure."

"My God, what a choice crew!" Alison remarks when she looks about the expensive institution she is being committed to. The exclamation might be McCullers'—in admiration of her own bizarre crew with which she goes about illuminating nothing less than tragedy "as a subtle scheme," the conspiracy of accidents that resolve fate.

The murder announced is set into motion when Private Williams carelessly spills coffee on the Captain's new pants. Assigned to do some landscaping for the Captain, Private Williams happens to see Leonora naked inside her house. Equally accidentally, in the secluded woods, the Captain sees Private Williams nude. Thus begins "the strange hate" that creates the book's violence. The Captain becomes aware that his state of agitation was "not caused by forces within himself and others, things that in some measure he could control—but by some menacing outward circumstances." He makes a "wondering resumé of the steps that had brought about this condition, beginning with the carelessly spilt coffee." The Captain does not know that Private Williams has begun to keep a quiet vigil—unperceived—by Leonora's bedside.

McCullers' unbudging scrutiny of her characters allows intimate epiphanies: "The Captain suddenly looked into his soul and saw himself. . . . 'You mean,' " he says to the complacent Major, "'that any fulfillment obtained at the expense of normalcy is wrong and should not be allowed to bring happiness? In short, it is better because it is morally honorable, for the square peg to keep scraping about the round hole rather than to discover and use the unorthodox square that would fit it?'" He relies on Seconal for sleep: "... the drug gave him a unique and voluptuous sensation; it was as though a great dark bird alighted on his chest, looked at him once with fierce, golden eyes, and stealthily enfolded him with dark wings."

After the murder of the black man, Private Williams "had felt a certain wondering, numb distress, but there was no fear in him, and not once since that time had the thought shaped definitely in his mind that he was a murderer. The mind is like a richly woven tapestry in which the colors are distilled from the experience of the senses, and the design drawn from the convolutions of the intellect. The mind of Private Williams was imbued with various colors of strange tones ... void of form."

McCullers alters her cool style somewhat in these discoveries—but more so in moody descriptions that evolve eerily throughout the book, auguring the dramatic events: "In the autumn darkness outside the window," Private Williams begins his spying, while "the sky glittered with icy stars." As the dangerous night watch extends, "the bare branches of the trees made a sharp filigree against the winter sky. In the early morning there was a frost on the dead grass." From her window, Alison discovers the Private's secret visits: "There was no wind and shadows lay still and dark on the lawns." When we learn that Private Williams is capable of murder and that the Captain has begun searching him out in fascination throughout the post, "the days were growing short, and at this time in the late afternoon a hint of darkness was already in the air."

Now only the enigmatic presence of the Private can hold the Captain's attention, he realizes. The weather, that afternoon, "was extraordinary. There were dour storm clouds in the sky, but down near the horizon the heavens were still clear and the sun shone with gentle radiance." When the Captain comes close to approaching Private Williams—and to do so with "a wild tirade of curses, words of love, supplication, and abuse ... the rain that had been threatening held off."

Then: "The rain stopped at midnight. . . . But there was no moon." The Captain sees Private Williams enter his house and believes that it is him, not Leonora, he is seeking.

Leaving all humor behind, insinuating the ominous descriptions of dying days, McCullers paces the horror of her ending perfectly. This novel—McCullers' best—assumes a glowing strangeness like that of the bird with golden eyes.

POSTSCRIPT: In my writing workshops, I often use this novel as a strong rebuttal to the nonsense that one must always have a sympathetic character to relate to.

MUSCLES AND MASCARA (1988)

IN THE MID-1950s a revolutionary event occurred with the publication of a few small-format magazines with names like *Physique Pictorial, Male Physique,* and *Tomorrow's Man.* Featuring muscular men wearing only posing straps (a mere peek of pubic hair guaranteed legal prosecution) those "pictorials" were aimed unapologetically at gay men, no pseudo-workout routines, no health tips, just titillation.

Simultaneously, circulation plunged among so-called bona fide bodybuilding magazines like *Muscle Power, Strength & Health,* and *Iron Man.* Since the '40s, those "muscle" magazines had featured lots of workout routines, lots of health tips. Virtually every editorial comment made it clear that those publications were aimed at heterosexual men, and that their goal was to encourage the hyper-masculine activities of weightlifting and bodybuilding. That did not keep those same magazines from carrying, in every issue, several modeled photographs of men in tiny posing straps, photographs aimed at gay men and offering the same titillation the new gay pictorials were providing without subterfuge.

Instead of lamenting the real reason for their distress, the decline in subscriptions, editors of "muscle" publications decried this catering to "perverts."

Bodybuilding had, in a sense, been outed. Not only had the subscribers to muscle magazines "come out," but so had the models in "physique" magazines, models often well known in gay circles. "Out," too, were some of the photographers who had contributed to muscle magazines—Bruce of Los Angeles, Lon of New York, Kris of Chicago.

What did not "come out" were the muscle magazines themselves. While no longer overtly disdaining gay readership, those publications still continue to assert that their subscribers, and the bodybuilders appearing in their pages—especially the "stars" of physique competitions—are super heterosexual.

There have always been those who have known otherwise. Many years ago, a sage queen, observing this writer and modest bodybuilding-practitioner loitering—shirtless chest oiled—on a Hollywood street late at night, cut to the core of the matter by declaring, "Hon, your muscles are as gay as my drag."

However denied by its professional practitioners, bodybuilding fits squarely in the realm of gay theater. On that stage, there are three main categories of players, the queen, the leatherman, and the muscleman. All rely for effect on visual assault—they are living *trompes l'oeil*: the queen with her sequined drag, the leatherman with his stud-sequined leather, the muscleman on stage with his oil-sequined body. (All apparently share an impressive knowledge of the decorative power of sequins.)

In extremity, artifice, and effect, all three presentations are forms of glamorous camouflage. They reveal roots in common, an aversion to appearing to be a "sissy." All convert the "wearer" into someone else. The drag queen becomes a "woman"; the leatherman displays himself as a menacing presence; the muscleman signals, with his pumped armor, that he will not be the proverbial object of "sand in the face" as depicted in the famous Charles Atlas comic-strip ad.

In that comic strip, a painfully thin, nervous man—a stereotype of a kind of gay man—is ridiculed by a beefy man who kicks sand in his face. The assaulted man learns his lesson, orders the Atlas course, as so many of us did, and is transformed into a bully himself. Muscles bulging, he can now face, *mano a mano*, his oppressor. Perhaps, after their ardent encounter on the beach, they went home together.

Now a few words are in order about the tawdry beauty of professional bodybuilding. It's a world that is at once sleazy and alluring, cheesy and elegant, hypocritical and honest. While extolling ultra-masculinity, it indulges a bitchiness that makes squabbling divas seem tame. Self-avowed heterosexual bodybuilders resort to bizarre meanness, "psyching out" rivals, remarking on "bitch tits," a condition caused by steroids. Widely derided, bodybuilding is in ill repute because it is spectacularly narcissistic.

There are grounds for considering it an art form. The self-sculpting of a body requires as much discipline as ballet and acting. Bodybuilding has a rich heritage. Atlas, Hercules, and Michelangelo's God and Adam are its progenitors in art and myth. So is Sisyphus, who must have developed a terrific physique from having to cope with that infernal rock. In paintings, martyred saints have killer abs and obliques, exhibited lovingly to the very edge of sexy loincloths. Christ on the cross has awesome definition—and knows how to pose sensationally.

There's poetry in bodybuilding. In magical synergy, muscles grow out of confusion that results when they are forced to perform "unnatural" motions with increasingly heavy weights. Alerted to such repeated assaults, they become stronger and larger in order to cope, achieving miraculous rhythm between breakdown and rebuilding. "Muscle memory" allows idle muscles once trained to sprout quickly. The barbell is the catalyst for recaptured "memory," not unlike tea and Madeleines in Proust's search for lost time.

Top bodybuilders know their bodies as intimately as a painter knows hues, a writer the nuances of metaphor. Scholars flaunt their intellect, writers their prose, artists their art. Why, then, disdain a sculpted body? But, too, why deny its gay implications?

The two questions link to provide one answer. The sculpted body is disdained because it is widely perceived by the general populace as being in the domain of gay males, and the entrenched denial of that fact by its top practitioners and the magazines that record their performance forces it into a limbo as a kind of sweaty, roustabout sport (like wrestling!), thus denying its aesthetic overtones and thwarting its correct placement within the realm of other exhibitionistic arts, like ballet, acting, modeling.

Indeed, from its humble beginnings in dingy high-school basements—droopy sheets employed as contest backdrops—bodybuilding has always had a heavy gay context. Some early bodybuilders became famous figures in the gay world. Bob D., the owner of a well-known gym on Hollywood Boulevard—outside of which he often recruited young men—specialized, with his recruits, in livening up a gay party. Nude photographs of Jack LaLanne in his prime were favorites among gay collectors. The "Jeannette MacDonald and Nelson Eddy" of early gay porn did everything but sing. A Mr. America sponsored by several wealthy men enjoyed a brief career in gay porn, until he was "born again" and renounced his earlier life.

Today, many bodybuilding contestants and titlists advertise in gay-solicitation columns, even on billboards, as "personal trainers," "escorts," and "models," often euphemisms for prostitution.

Although the vast majority of competitive bodybuilders proclaim themselves to be "straight"—Mr. Olympia competitor Bob Paris is an exception—and although muscle magazines perpetuate the charade that they are involved in a strictly heterosexual sport certain revealing intimacies are allowed to participants in the activity. Preferred exercises often seem to mime sexual acts. In the gym, while "spotting," one man straddles the head of a prone lifter—to lend nominal support in handling an otherwise prohibitive weight. During "donkey raises"—calf exercises—a helper may mount the buttocks of a bent-over lifter—to add resistance to the move. During the near-orgiastic frenzy of "pose-down"—when makeup is permitted—finalists on-stage (wearing "trunks" that are much like the posing straps of old) press quivering bodies against sweaty tensed bodies.

Nothing has brought bodybuilding more clearly into the realm of gay performance than the recent emergence of a new gay man, the effeminate bodybuilder.

When some of us began working out with weights back in the 60's, our trained bodies stood out among gay men. Today, hundreds of muscular men populate gay arenas. Many of these men exhibit new defining characteristics. As they walk, there is a bit of a swish now and again. It may be caught just in time, but often it is allowed, and refined expertly. A wrist may melt. Although it may be quickly rejected by clasped fingers, just as often it is left to wilt. A deepened voice cracks into a shriek of "You *go*, girl"— and it may deepen again, or sustain its high pitch. Faces glow with tans enhanced by bronzers. A touch of subtle mascara is allowed. This out-of-the-closet muscular figure has become as identifiably gay as drag queens and leather queens.

Gay-male porn performers have long influenced, and powerfully so, what physical types are to be sexually idealized, and, therefore, imitated—and the influence of pornography on gay culture extends far beyond those who watch it, even strongly determining the types of models that populate "straight" male-fashion advertising. Today, those "masculine" prototypes of the "new gay man" are paradoxically being shaped in major part by a giant drag queen named Chi-Chi La Rue, the pre-eminent director of gay pornography.

For better or worse, this queen of high drag—who would, sadly, be ostracized from the turfs she depicts, refused entry into the very bars, bathhouses, and orgy rooms that her movies celebrate—is able, through her star-making power as a director, to set the standards for "stud-dom" among the very men who would reject her sexually, especially within the dead-serious domain of leather she often records. Replete with puffed wig and mascara-drenched lashes, looking uncannily like Divine, she is often photographed laughing triumphantly.

With all its contradictions, denials, and incongruities, the world of sculpted bodies—extending from competitive stages to street theater to pornographic images—possesses a gaudy splendor, an aggressive allure that, whatever its intentions, ends up celebrating a distinctly gay sensibility; and it's entirely possible that the prime manifestation of the world of sculpted bodies will turn out to be a new grand creation already shaping, the proud and elegant muscle queen.

POSTSCRIPT: I believe this essay was the first to give prominent attention to the emergence of the now-ubiquitous muscle queens. I do rue that emergence somewhat, however, because there was a time, in the '70s, the '80s when I was virtually the only "bodybuilder" along gay cruising and hustling turfs.

PART III: 1990–2000

SIXTY YEARS LATER
A GAY CLASSIC ENTERS (ALMOST)
THE MAINSTREAM (1990)

ALL WRITERS CHERISH "rejection" stories that end up success stories in publishing. What writer, ignored or mugged by critics, doesn't remind himself that posterity is quite often more easily satisfied than the surly book reviewer? Look at *Wuthering Heights, Moby Dick,* and ... and ...

A fine success story is happening now, but because it occurs within an arbitrarily constricted circle, it brings both pleasure and regret and arouses questions about what is currently permitted to qualify as "serious literature," what is banished, and why.

In the early 1930s, a young man sat down to write a novel he must have known had little chance of being published. It was on "a very sensitive subject," a euphemism for homosexuality. Fortunately there was at the time a publisher specializing in "sensitive" books, and Richard Meeker's *Better Angel* was issued by the Greenberg Press in 1933. It soon disappeared.

In 1987, Sasha Alyson, publisher of no longer necessarily "sensitive" gay books, reissued the novel (it is available in paperback from Alyson Publications for $6.95). It received wide attention and formidable reviews in the gay press, and it sold well. Too bad the author was dead, was the general lament.

At A Different Light Bookstore in Los Angeles, an elegant old gentleman asked for *Better Angel.* Approving his choice of the "quite popular and well written" novel, the clerk assured the customer: "You'll like it." "I'm sure I shall," said the dignified gentleman. "I wrote it."

Richard Meeker—almost ninety years old—was actually Forman Brown, recipient of the Los Angeles Drama Critics Circle Literature Achievement Award for his work in the Turnabout Theater.

Cut to Cambridge, Mass. An order is placed a the Harvard Coop for 150 copies of *Better Angel*. Why? Sleuthing by correspondence, Brown was put in touch with Robert Kiely, respected professor of contemporary writing. Kiely wrote Brown that he was teaching a course at Harvard on the literature of the twentieth century. Fourteen books were required reading: Conrad's *Lord Jim*, Morrison's *Beloved*, Chopin's *The Awakening*, Woolf's *Mrs. Dalloway*, Joyce's *Ulysses*, Nabokov's *Pale Fire*, Lawrence's *Lady Chatterly's Lover*, Ford's *The Good Soldier*, Kingston's *The Woman Warrior*, Orwell's *Homage to Catalonia*, Arendt's *Eichmann in Jerusalem*, Toomer's *Cane*, Beckett's *Three Novels*.

And Meeker/Brown's *Better Angel*.

Kiely explained that he had learned of the book from a student's thesis on the gay American novel. He found *Better Angel* in the popular tradition of American success stories: part romance, part dogged determination to be oneself—not only a novel of "literary merit" but "a fine evocation of the time . . . an upbeat narrative of growing up gay." In his course, he was teaching "the 'monuments'" along with lesser-known works, to provide a more nearly complete picture of the twentieth century experience and art."

During the recent American Booksellers Association Convention, Brown received a standing ovation from several hundred in attendance at a gay-awards publishing banquet. The reissued book has gone into a second printing, with an epilogue by Brown. Sales continue to be "steady," and reaction in the gay press is glowing.

I approached this book expecting a lovable artifact, convinced that Kiely's inclusion of it in his course was the sort of thing every college teacher does slyly—adds one or two unknown writers to his required list to show his independence and demonstrate the breadth of his knowledgeability. (I often mention Aphra-Behn in my literature class at USC.)

I was wrong. Long before gay liberation, *Better Angel* resounds movingly with "the anarchic note of pride in difference." At the book's opening, Kurt is a sensitive boy often taunted by school bullies. He would rather play piano and read than toss a baseball. Close to his mother and a stranger to his father, he wants to be the princess in a play he writes. Set in the past, the novel thus allows today's reader to look anew at a "gay stereotype—a present sacrilege—to find in the forbidden, but quite healthy, figure the spirit of endurance and courage. Boldly presenting themselves to a hostile world, stereotypes most often grow into figures of strength.

And so does Kurt, as he moves from Michigan to New York to Europe, back to the United States, encountering Chloe—a girl he longs to love—and Derry and David, young men with whom he experiences romantic entanglements despite the harsh strictures of the time. A homosexual act in some states was punishable with life imprisonment, and 15-year sentences and commitment to psychiatric asylums were not rare for "accosting."

Still, Kurt is often inspired to write "a page of jottings, ecstatic or sad, but always pregnant with promise of future joy." He comes to lament: "We go around ashamed of a thing we've no reason to be ashamed of." Not blind to the world he's living in, he "must go on with the evasion, the hypocrisy, the compromises that he despised."

Reappearing today, when general indifference is growing even as deaths from AIDS mount among gay men, and gay bigotry is expressed freely, *Better Angel* reminds of a time when hope was possible—the "promise of future joy"—simply because the full reality of prejudice had not yet been entirely exposed, not yet bitterly tested.

Thoroughly modern in its voice—despite words such as *invert*, which are nonetheless true to its time—Brown's book is not only a very good novel about coming out, as it has been called; it is a very good novel without qualifier, a book that contains excellent writing, sophisticated humor, universal insights. "The whole problem of life is to get enough moments crowded into it so the places between won't be so deadly." That is a sentence any writer would be proud of. And how's this for description: ". . . patches of graying snow thatched the earth outside; and a gray sky, tarnished with gold from a sun gone down behind the grove of oaks opposite, gave to the light a pale, cold, honey-colored translucence."

Kurt's mother, who encourages his "difference"—"Everybody who amounts to anything is different, all those generals, great men"—marvelously dismisses the importance of her ex-lover: "It's all silly now, for he's still a good friend of your father's and getting bald and fat."

And when the adult Kurt faces a young boy he knows will become gay, "the sense of destiny . . . of all such boys everywhere" sweeps over him "their heritage of . . . concealing the truth . . . Would such a one be better off . . . never to recognize his inversion . . . to live lonely and apart . . . ? No. No . . . Whatever advancing years might bring, knowledge was necessary."

Sadly, the present success of *Better Angel* is constricted because it will be kept in a new "closet"—available only in gay bookstores and on a few "Alternative Lifestyle" shelves in others—separate but not quite equal. Thus some of today's best writing—and yesterday's, like Brown's—is kept in a literary ghetto" that would have banished Gide, Proust, Genet from world literature. No prestigious awards possible, no *Paris Review* interviews, no discussions in serious literary volumes. Banished. (Professor Kiely's course is a thrilling exception.)

What a success story this could be if Forman Brown's *Better Angel,* which cut across old barriers, would slice away new ones to be read simply as the fine novel that it is. Then Brown's 90th birthday in a few months would provide double reason for celebration.

Postscript: I met the author, a kind, attractive and elegant man of almost ninety. He had once directed a popular puppet theater. He was very excited—and it was a pleasure to note his excitement—by the deserved, if late, attention. He died soon after.

THE OUTLAW SENSIBILITY: LIBERATED GHETTOS, NOBLE STEREOTYPES, AND A FEW MORE PROMISCUOUS OBSERVATIONS (1991)

ARGUMENTS ABOUND ABOUT whether or not there is a unique "sensibility" manifested in the arts by certain minority groups and women. A feminine sensibility? A gay sensibility? A black sensibility? A Hispanic sensibility? I suggest that such sensibilities do exist, and that they are linked by one main factor: the awareness of separation—call it exile—from the authoritarian "mainstream." That awareness shapes what I call an "Outlaw Sensibility."

Let's look at a few famous outlaws in myth and literary history and see what we may find in common, as we range from the plains of Heaven, to the mountains of Spain, the moors of England. Were Lucifer and his band of angels the first questioning outlaws, defying autocracy and the decreed singing of assigned hymns? Prometheus? He challenged a pouting Zeus to return light to the world. Pandora! She gambled for hope. We might consider Adam and Eve.

On the battleground of literature, we quickly encounter Don Quixote, whose most dangerous combat is not against windmills nor giants but against his own author, Cervantes, who tortured and ridiculed him. Yet in the myth that has evolved, Don Quixote thumbs his nose at Cervantes and survives as a hero of impossible causes, "impossible dreams." Always the questioning outsider.

Leap forward in time, and Camus's Mersault in *The Stranger* accepts, even welcomes, his alienation; but the world conspires to entrap him in its infernal machinery of banal conventions. Let's call that the power of the "mainstream." Mersault *chooses* to remain at odds with the world, longing for his execution to be greeted with cries of denunciation. May we add *choice* as an element shaping the outlaw sensibility, *choice* that accepts known dangers in asserting a proud, questioning alienation?

A. E. Housman may provide a poetic motto for our exploration: "And how am I to face the odds/of man's bedevilment and God's/ I, a stranger and afraid,/ in a world I never made." The outlaw artist provides his own answer in defiance.

Defiance, pride, choice to remain estranged, an acceptance of risks, a constant questioning of limiting assumptions—our shaping definition might lead us into a frightening trap, the criminal as outlaw, if, that is, we did not locate some further essential factors in the outlaw sensibility we're investigating: nobility of intention, respect for the individual life, and, in the artist as outlaw, a dedication to unique creativity.

In choosing the term "outlaw," let's differentiate among other seeming choices. "Outcast" suggests acceptance of defeat. "Exile" suggests resigned expulsion ("living in exile"). Intrinsic in the word "outlaw" is the implication that the "laws"—the conventions—questioned are wrong, repressive.

We'll borrow from the terminology of war in exploring some tactics that the artist as outlaw employs and that define him: (1) infiltration; (2) sabotage; (3) camouflage. Alas, there is also collaboration to consider, as well as counterattack by the "mainstream."

Let's watch some literary outlaws in action. We'll pit Federico García Lorca, Emily Brontë, and Luis Buñuel against William Wyler—yes, William Wyler—and see what significant differentiations we may uncover in identifying an outlaw sensibility. Briefly to introduce our cast in this epic battle: In his life, Lorca was a defender of the free spirit, the gypsies; he was slaughtered by fascists. In his art, he was able to insinuate tabooed sensuality into his writing because he employed it to explore sexual repression. In his life, Buñuel was the son of a rich landowner; he was educated by Jesuits and he rebelled. In his art, he infiltrated Mexican commercial films with his subtle assault on form in *El*, which prepared for his powerful sabotage of structure and convention in *The Discrete Charm of the Bourgeoisie*. In her life, Emily Brontë was a recluse, a brave recluse. On one of her many walks through the cold, windy moors, she battled a wild dog and won. She threw herself on her brother, Bramwell, when he set himself on fire. In her art, specifically *Wuthering Heights*, she redefined love and hatred, heaven and hell. Lorca, Buñuel, Brontë: a formidable team of outlaws indeed! They now face William Wyler, quintessential Hollywood director.

Here is Lorca speaking through Leonardo addressing the Bride who is about to marry another in *Bodas de Sangre* (*Blood Wedding*): "To keep still when we're on fire is the worst punishment we can inflict on ourselves. What good did it do me to have pride?— and not see you?—and leave you lying awake, night after night? . . . It only poured fire over me! Because you may believe that time can heal and walls can hide—but it's not true. . . . When things reach deep inside you, nothing can pull them out!" The Bride answers: "I can't listen to your voice . . . it draws me under, and I know I'm drowning. . . . I know I'm rotting away with suffering. . . ."

Now here is Brontë speaking through Catherine addressing the housekeeper Nelly about Heathcliff in *Wuthering Heights*: "All sinners would be miserable in heaven. . . . I dreamt once that I was there . . . heaven did not seem to be my home; and I broke my heart with weeping to come back to earth; and the angels were so angry they flung me out into the middle of the heath on the top of Wuthering Heights; where I woke sobbing for joy." Here again is the recluse speaking through Heathcliff cursing the dead Catherine: "I pray one prayer—I repeat it till my tongue stiffens— Catherine Earnshaw, may you not rest as long as I am living."

What a startling similarity in tone—heaven, hell, fire, lovers cursing each other, pushing love into a further definition.

In 1939 William Wyler filmed his version of *Wuthering Heights*. Although his movie is gorgeous, certain telling transformations occur. Catherine becomes Cathy. Heathcliff's accusation of Catherine occurs while he and "Cathy" are bathed in a white, redemptive radiance in a glorious bedroom; heather sways beyond spring-polished windows. The portals of hell have become fluttering organdy curtains. At the end, the fallen angels are sighted along a snowy path, blissfully on their way to a vapid Heaven, where they do not belong.

In 1953, Buñuel released his version of Brontë's dark novel. The ending of *Cumbres Borascosos*, shot in grainy black and white, reveals Heathcliff keeping his promise to claw his way into Catherine's grave if distance should separate them at death. Buñuel follows him as he melds into the shadows of a grave in search of her skeleton.

Have we found that Emily Brontë, the spinster recluse, had the heart of a passionate gypsy, an outlaw? Have we found that García Lorca had the heart of a passionate recluse, an outlaw? A third outlaw, Buñuel, adding his own unflinching vision, linked both.

Passion, the risking of the extremes of melodrama, and an uncompromising staring at what is seen recur as elements in the artistic outlaw sensibility.

An outlaw may not achieve full insurrectionary power until he springs into myth. Let's broaden our scope and deal now with another great practitioner of outlaw insurrection, a masterpiece of modern art named Marilyn Monroe.

According to biographer Lawrence Guiles, her agent summoned her for a first assignment with these words: "I have a call for a light blonde, honey or platinum." In Arthur Miller's play *After the Fall*, Miller's alter ego says about her prototype—with staggering pomposity: "I see your suffering." According to Norman Mailer in his book *Marilyn*, many weeks after finishing *Some Like*

It Hot, Director Billy Wilder claimed, he "could not look at [his] wife without wanting to hit her because she is a woman." George Cukor—who was vaunted as a "woman's director" but often privately derided women—delighted in demeaning her. Angela Carter in *Sadean Women* saw Marilyn Monroe as "carrying the exciting stigmata of sexual violence," and she deduces, "that is why gentlemen prefer blondes."

To explore Marilyn Monroe as a masterpiece of the outlaw sensibility, we must deal with the artist, the creation, and the metaphor. The artist was an unwanted child named Norma Jeane from Hawthorne, California. Unhappy, abused, insecure, she kept moving from home to foster home, always an outsider, always fearing she might inherit the madness of her mother and her grandmother, abandoned desolate women.

Beyond that, the "truth" about her began to disappear when that only-somewhat pretty girl—even her last name, Baker or Morton, is in ambiguity—set out to create, with constant embellishments and contradictions, an extravagant fiction called "Marilyn Monroe." She did so, step by step, with marvelous lies and splendid variations—like the best art.

With the inevitability of fate in Greek tragedy, the created goddess would of course gravitate like a moth to the alluring destructive glow of the ruling American patriarchal dynasty of the Kennedys. A plaything for them, she was passed from John to Robert. Each discarded her when he had conquered every heterosexual-male's dream of that time. Can anyone doubt that with them Marilyn Monroe was always only Norma Jeane?

She died, a suicide, and Marilyn Monroe, the woman we now celebrate—the woman in the seductive photographs—sprang to life as redemptive legend. As such, the unwanted outsider was able to infiltrate the world she could not enter in life. Now the abandoned girl from Hawthorne is forever tied in history to the Kennedys. Her legend converts her into a subversive outlaw who triumphs over the powerful patriarchal dynasty, questioning and exposing the darkest caverns of Camelot.

Since it is often the outsider who graduates to outlaw, let's explore only two of the prominent sensibilities—there are more—that often produce him, the gay sensibility and the Hispanic sensibility, the two I am intimately and personally familiar with.

Homosexuals are the only minority *born* into the opposing camp; call it the "enemy camp." All other minorities are born into supportive environments—blacks into black families, Chicanos into Chicano families. Homosexuals originate out of a heterosexual union and must function in a heterosexual world. To reconcile secret desire with acceptable performance, the homosexual child learns expert camouflage, learns to mime, to seem to be what he is not. In later life that separation defines a prominent aspect of the gay sensibility. It includes a terrific sense of dramatic presentation that veers at times toward extremity. We might even call it gay theater.

On its stage, the drag of transvestites links with the drag of gay leathermen—both share an awesome knowledge of the decorative power of sequins. Muscles and mascara are reconciled; iron-pumped muscles, ubiquitous on today's gay horizon, are as exaggerated a form of decoration as high drag. Both bodybuilders and queens attempt with bruised arrogance to disguise wounds most often open by early derision.

We find variations of this duality in the literature of gay outlaws: William Burroughs' orgiastic anarchy is contained within a highly conceptualized form. Genet's super-hung studs become drag queens. Carson McCullers locates a very special beauty in grotesquery, and grotesquery in beauty. Gore Vidal's cool intellect allows a tone of "trashy dishing" that's right out of gay bars. Truman Capote wrote about criminals—and did so in a high-drag style, creating an effect not unlike that of the shimmery sequined darkness of Djuna Barnes' prose. Allen Ginsberg had a powerful low-drag voice.

Gay writers often produce a seductive prose that reflects elements of gay-bar cruising, a flirtatious prose full of subtle messages of constant courtship. Edmund White constantly winks at his readers. Tennessee Williams's tough Stanley Kowalski is as gay as is frail Blanche DuBois, who is more than just a bit of a fading queen, which, indeed, is what posturing-stud Stanley calls her—and *he* should talk.

On the Hispsanic sensibility, the most powerful influence emanates out of the Catholic Church. Whether the artist is himself Catholic or not, the church's historical and social dominance in Hispanic countries permeates the culture.

What Hispanic artist has not been blessed—or cursed, as the case may be—by simply entering a Mexican Catholic church? What artist would fail to be influenced by the assault of colors, the shift of lights on stained-glass windows, the gaudiest paintings in the world? What Hispanic artist isn't affected by early exposure to blood-drenched statues of saints writhing in exhibitionistic agony, bodies stripped only when they're suffering; statues real and artificial at the same time—like the best art; the grand melodrama of the journey to Calvary, performed by gorgeous agonized creatures; the operatic excess of Christ's Seven Last Words; the poetic ritualism of the Stations of the Cross; the glorious extravaganza of High Mass, which is the greatest drag show on earth; the aggressive mourning of Holy Week; the invited, not to say extorted, tears and breast-pounding guilt—all, all overseen by glamorous male and female angels.

Move to the peripheries of that religion, and you have more irresistible factors: the *curanderos*, sightings of the Madonna in sidewalk cracks, *beatas* whose impeccable timing would make Bette Davis weep with envy, the haunting wails of *la Llorona*. Don't you infer it all, in Orozco's perennially confrontational comic-strip-as-great art murals which dominate a surrendered orphanage in Guadalajara? In the rhythm of colors in Rivera's paintings? And in all of Gabriel García Márquez?

Catholicism deals centrally and powerfully with mystery, which it attempts to solve by "faith." Abandoning that leap required to accept "faith," the artist is left only with mystery. I think that much Hispanic art explores mystery itself, the ungraspable wonder of things—from Lorca to Isabel Allende, from Manuel Puig to Ana Castillo.

Machismo is an influence on the Hispanic sensibility, as is its tempering by the enduring—and tearful—courage of women. That melding of arrogant strength, endurability, and tears refines the sensibility. Yes, Hispanic men do cry a lot, often lamenting a vague sorrow, expressing a longing for an indefinable something lost "long ago." This sense of bewildered, deep loss recurs in the anguished ballads of mariachis and might be detected even in the sulky, wounded posturing of young Chicano gangsters. In male writers this produces a rough but sentimental prose—find that in the satirical exuberance in Luis Valdez. Hispanic women add superb, sad irony in their observations of all this. I think of Jessica Hagedorn (Filipina but closely associated to Hispanic culture) and Mary Helen Ponce.

High melodrama, rich symbolism, mythical resonance, a sentimental machismo, tearful strength—certainly we may locate these among elements shaping a Hispanic sensibility in the arts. By asserting its unique presence without compromised assimilation, by remaining itself unchanged, the outlaw sensibility gains insurrectionary power, challenging, and at best affecting the entrenched "mainstream."

Not long ago, strong taboos existed in literature. Sexual subjects were banished through overt censorship. Black people, Hispanics, homosexuals, other minorities existed only in the background of fictional landscapes—all as a result of a kind of "gentleman's agreement" among publishers. The only way to overcome these barriers was through infiltration by means of camouflage and masquerade.

Admirable subversives educated readers who did not know they were being educated, a taboo subject introduced without identification. Dorian Gray is homosexual, and Oscar Wilde's widely quoted wit is distinctly gay. The early Christopher Isherwood used pronouns deftly to disguise gender in sex scenes. In *The Remembrance of Things Past*, can we read the young Marcel's operatic anguish at the prospect of being deprived the reward of a mother's kiss without recognizing there a gay sensibility?

By ruling bestseller lists as the proponent of "magical realism"—though not its originator—Gabriel García Márquez becomes a major infiltrator and a most powerful saboteur. He has brought to the mayonnaisey blandness of writers sanctified by *The New York Times Book Review* an awareness of a most resplendent and distinctly unbland Hispanic sensibility, with its mixture of fables, religion, superstition, and history that would have remained otherwise invisible, and that now allows other writers to explore new subjects, new terrain. Pedro Almodóvar has practiced the art of infiltration through camouflage— and then followed with sabotage, and he has done so through dual sensibilities, Hispanic and gay.

There is hardly a member of *any* minority who has not had to deal with factors of imposed inferiority, self-hatred, aroused by the dominant society's insistence that it represents the desirable "norm." That creates the problems of "passing," the rejection of one's rich heritage and sensibility.

My father's background was Scottish. He was born in Mexico, but his family soon settled in El Paso, Texas. My beautiful Mexican mother was born in Chihuahua. She entered the United States illegally—and was almost deported. Eventually she received a passport. She did not become a citizen until the last ten years of her life. We spoke only Spanish at home.

I did not learn English until I entered school. My kindergarten teacher changed my name from Juan to John because when she taught us numbers and referred to "one," I thought she was calling me. I despised school because all Spanish-speaking children were separated twice a day, once when we were inspected for lice while Anglo children gasped and giggled. We were again separated for an hour in order to learn the astonishing difference between "sh" and "ch" while Anglo children played outside. (Even after we experienced the epiphany of "ch," budding outlaws would sabotage the Anglo teacher's testy example by converting it into a defiant refrain: "shuldren . . . Chihuahua, shuldren . . . Chihuahua.")

The temptation to pass became enormous. I would run home to secret poverty, having given a false address of a prettier house. After my family was finally able to afford a party-line telephone—and I remember indelibly how my mother applauded with delighted surprise when it rang the first time—an Anglo friend called me when I wasn't home. "I couldn't get the dumb Mexican maid to take a message," he told me. My beloved mother had answered. That violent awareness of the inescapability of bigotry ended any temptation to pass, despite extended invitations. "Oh, don't say you're Mexican," kind friends would offer absolution. "You must be *Spanish*." A similar "out" is often proffered to homosexuals, to become chic "bisexuals."

At one time passing was necessary for homosexuals to ensure survival. In the '50s and '60s, into the '70s, the accusation of having been involved in a homosexual act, even in private, might result in imprisonment of up to 15 years. And in some states, life in prison. Even today, for many, the closet may become necessary for survival. In the extreme of passing, collaboration may occur.

Edward Albee becomes irate when *Who's Afraid of Virginia Woolf?* is spoken of in gay terms. He insists that his play is about a *heterosexual* union, period—although part of that play's accomplishment is that it functions just as well as an exploration of a homosexual relationship. For having accomplished that perfect duality, Albee deserves praise as a most powerful infiltrator and saboteur. For denying his dual accomplishment, he becomes a collaborator.

The outlaw sensibility does not in any way restrict the artist from illuminating *all* aspects of human experience; indeed, it may enrich by a broadened perspective. It may be that there is more astute revelation of heterosexual relationships in Proust's *Remembrance of Things Past* than in all of Philip Roth's aggressively "heterosexual-male" explorations. Visconti, Fassbinder—those artists have at one time or another all practiced the art of infiltration through camouflage—and then followed with sabotage.

One of the saddest examples of the outlaw turned collaborator is John Dos Passos. His *U.S.A.* exposed more of the dark roots of the American psyche than a dozen history books of that time and later. Success lulled him, he retracted, collaborated, became . . . a Republican—and there are no Republican outlaws, not even gay Republicans. John Steinbeck, the man who gave us Ma Joad, lived to be smilingly photographed while aiming an assault weapon at the Vietnamese.

For some Latinos, Richard Rodriguez is a *bête noire.* Collaborator or masterful infiltrator? I suggest that he is an elegant saboteur. By adopting a formally "European-American" prose style that at times suggests the influence of Henry James, he has been able to infiltrate literary territories otherwise closed, and so to convey to a widened audience his unquestionably "Mexican" experience.

There is counterattack by the "mainstream" to consider. One of its main tactics to effect that countering is through the creation of "liberated ghettos."

When book chains assign labeled sections to "Chicano Literature," "Gay Literature," "Women's Studies," they segregate. So do "mainstream" publishers who aim minority books only at minorities and who promote such works, if at all, with restricted advertising.

Herdings of minority writers doggedly appear in *The New York Times Book Review, Time, Newsweek,* and—with pompous "correctness"—in *The Nation*; these purport to name the "best" Hispanic writers, the best Hispanic "women writers," the best "gay" writers—often proclaiming one as "*the* best," suggesting that the range of such literature is so narrow, its artistry so limited, that such an absurdity is possible.

To applaud such meager tokens of recognition as "success" is to accept and contribute to segregation. There is a vast difference between proudly proclaiming one's identity by ethnicity, gender, color, sexual orientation, and accepting the use of labels to separate one into a new, if somewhat relatively spacious, closet, where certain artists see and are seen, hear and are heard, only by each other. This is *literature*; this is *minority literature*. Still too often, minority writers are being allowed only into the peripheries of American literature.

The bias of imposed labeling becomes clear when you alter context. Have you heard John Updike discussed as among the best self-avowed heterosexual male WASP writers? Philip Roth as among the most important self-avowed heterosexual Jewish male writers? No, but restrictive tagging clings to the names of minority writers. (As far as being a self-avowed homosexual myself, as I am sometimes described: I don't remember ever having taken a vow of sexuality, although I believe at one time or another John Updike and Philip Roth may have.)

Political correctness increasingly threatens the individual voice. The demand is often made on the artist, especially the writer, to avoid aspects considered unflattering to one's own group, no matter that such aspects exist and require scrutiny. There emerges out of that attitude an insistence on a new conformity among former "outsiders." Homosexuals are today being coerced to call themselves "queers," in conformity with something called "queer theory" emerging out of some academic departments fleeing from deconstruction. I shall never call myself queer, in theory or otherwise. To use that word honors the hate-distorted faces that for centuries have shouted it, and still shout it, during gay-bashings, arrests, and murders. By extension, allowing the word "queer" into respectability permits a whole new vocabulary of vile terms, for women, African-Americans, Hispanics, Jews. Shall we now speak about nigger theory, kike theory, greaser theory, cunt theory, et al.?

I have always felt that a factor that extends bias against homosexuals is what we have chosen to call ourselves. Although I use it now, I am still not at ease with "gay." Christopher Isherwood once said that the pluralized "gays" made us sound like bliss-ninnies. I envy lesbians their grand designation, with literary and historical resonance. I wish we males would consider calling ourselves . . . Trojans. That would confound the football team at U.S.C., where I teach. It might even pull cute Tommy Trojan, already attired in a toga by International Male, out of the closet—and it would be a steadfast reminder of safe sex.

Language itself has been put into disarray by misguided correctness. Every year when I watch the spectacularly awful Academy Awards, I lament the passing of the grand word "actress" as woman after woman refers to herself as an "actor." (I imagine Sarah Bernhardt and Victoria Fabrigas stiffening their backs in resistance like affronted queens—not kings.) Doesn't that implicitly suggest that the male form is to be preferred? The Spanish, French, Italian languages award gender even to sexless objects. The sturdy rock is *"la roca,"* the flickering earring is *"el arete."* No sexism there. The male organ in Spanish—*la verga*—is honored with a grand feminine designation. Political correctness entrenches mythologies to prove its points.

The myth persists that gay liberation burst full-force on the last weekend in July 1969, in New York, when drag queens resisted arrest during a routine raid at a bar called the Stonewall. Overnight, the legend declares, gay liberation was born, although our darkest night was still to come with AIDS.

The truth is that the riot at Stonewall was only one event, one battle in the long war for sexual freedom. Used as the point of separation, the myth of Stonewall falsifies history. It demeans the courage of warriors who fought bravely on the front lines when it was even more dangerous to do so—and it shoves into relative unimportance their brave battles, equally confrontational acts of defiance and pride protesting police raids and roundups in the '50s and early '60s, in San Francisco and Los Angeles; but because of the censorious tenor of those earlier times, those cataclysmic events remained largely unrecorded, remembered only by the warriors who had fought in them.

The troublesome myth of Stonewall does damage to a whole body of literature. It draws a sharp demarcation, labeling everything before Stonewall an assertion of the repression of the times; everything after, "liberated." Yet Gore Vidal's *Myra Breckinridge*, William Burroughs's *Naked Lunch*, Isherwood's deceptively genteel *A Single Man*, other novels published before Stonewall—and let's not forget Radclyffe Hall's *The Well of Loneliness* in the '20s and Gertrude Stein's fabulous *Melanctha* soon after—each in its own way reveals a defiant consciousness that had nothing to do with Stonewall. Each possesses more insurrectionary power, more defiance, than the half dozen or so vaunted novels that now form the misguided canon of post-Stonewall "liberated gay lit," with its tortured gay men pining after impossible, often "straight," figures of desire; dishy Fire Island queens; rampaging sadists violating the objects of their lust.

Under the rigors of political correctness, it becomes sinful to "perpetuate stereotypes." Certainly stereotyping can be harmful, but at times some of those brushed away collectively as stereotypes may, on close individual examination, prove to be courageous revolutionaries.

On a balmy Los Angeles night of only mild Apocalypse in the City of Lost Angels, in the old, sinful Pershing Square of the late '50s, early '60s—rockin'-'n'-rollin' with undaunted hustlers of every ilk, whores of all sexes, mean cops, loony quivering preachers high on Thunderbird wine—a fabulous flaming queen called Miss Destiny swept into my life. Her breathless fabrications about a white wedding in significant part inspired me to write about the world of my first novel.

Miss Destiny's progenitors remain today, and although shunned and banished, they endure, grandly visible. Emphatically not a parody of women, the drag queen is a creation unto herself. Her flaming drag is a costume not a mimicry—brazen, unavoidable, superb at its best. One might even call it an elaborate uniform worn by a most distinctive army that constantly disorients the rigid concept of only two allowed "genders."

Within that same theater of visual confrontation, there exists another stereotype to be explored—the "macho" leatherman, profoundly linked to the queen by exaggeration of costume. Although I have long questioned and continue to question what I see as the ritualized self-hatred in the "leather world" of gay S & M, I admire the bold glamour of its uniform, its silver on black, an intricate crisscross of glittery designs. A mainstay on our horizon, the macho leatherman is as easily identifiable as "gay" as is the queen in highest beaded drag. There is much to explore in that elaborate stereotype, as there is in that of the iron-pumped bodybuilder, as proclaimed years ago by a young queen who assaulted my shirtless posturing on a street: "Hon, your muscles are as gay as my drag."

Another favorite stereotype of mine is that of the often-married Chicano woman who prefers to be called "Mexican-American," has a romantic penchant for telenovelas, and, often, for handsome—eventually abusive—men, especially with saints's names, like Salvador, Gabriel, Angel. Working mostly as a maid, she is unquestioningly Catholic, though she frequents *curanderos*. She has a "live-in boyfriend" who allows her to sustain rebellious children venturing into dangerous streets. I have just described Amalia Gómez, the protagonist in my tenth novel, *The Miraculous Day of Amalia Gómez*.

When I began her story, I had not yet entirely discovered my heroine. Then one day I went to a Thrifty's Drug Store and saw one of the most resplendent women I've ever seen: a gorgeous Mexican woman in her upper '30s, a bit heavier than she might believe herself to be but quite lush and sexy. She wore high-heeled shoes—and a tight red dress, to show off proud breasts, but she had added a ruffle there to avoid any hint of vulgarity. She had a luxuriance of black shiny hair, and into its natural waves she had inserted . . . a real red rose. She had created a fashion that defied all fashion except her own. Bedazzled, I followed her along the aisles. Aware of me, she added the subtlest sway to her walk. Just as I had been looking for her, I was then sure, she had been looking for me. But not quite. A dashing Chicano gentleman appeared from another aisle, and, obviously with her, asked me, "*Pós?*" "*Pós nada,*" I assuaged him.

Now to the woman I had seen, I would donate from the lives of the many women—those "stereotypes"—I had known when we lived in the government projects. Out of the memories of those brave women Amalia was born.

Look what Amalia Gómez revealed about herself when she challenged me to look very closely—and perhaps no other character of mine has acted on her own volition once created than my beloved Amalia Gómez, whom, at times, I still hear arguing with me. This is some of what she taught me: To survive with her religious beliefs intact, and still be "helped" by the necessary live-in male, she had to restructure all the tenets of the Church, so that it allowed divorce, so-called adultery. She resorted to lying at confession to retain otherwise banned sacraments. She must keep reality in abeyance, in order to trust risky romances. She manages to convert into strength all the negative aspects that make her a "stereotype"—and so she is finally able to *demand* a miracle, earned.

Perhaps no stereotype is more decried than the woman often derided as a "bimbo," a woman then defined only by her physicality, her overt sensuality. Attached to the definition is the deduction that she must be vapid, oblivious to serious events about her. So modern thinking often castigates her, pushes her away, leaves her unacknowledged. May we find telling antecedents for her in myth, religion, history? What of Helen of Troy? Delilah? The Whore of Babylon? We've already explored Marilyn Monroe, once considered the quintessential "bimbo."

All are transgressive women, sensual women blamed for enormous disasters—the Trojan War, the fall of the Temple, the birthing of "all the abominations of the earth." And what about Eve? She is the most heavily blamed woman, blamed for the very fall of man, for bringing to mankind pain and death and all sorrows.

But what may we find on close inspection? Admonished, absurdly, not to eat from dazzling fruit placed there to tempt, fruit said to contain the very seeds of knowledge, Eve becomes the first bravely to *choose knowing,* to assert her will against a most irrational warning, the first to question the arbitrary autocracy of God. She becomes . . . thrilling notion . . . the mother of free will, a most noble outlaw. The first outlaw!

May we not consider courageous the woman who today flaunts her sensuality—the way men are allowed to flaunt theirs—while she asserts, "This does not give you the license to rape. I am not asking for it"?

Banish all stereotypes and you banish figures of daring—outlaws who fought lonely battles before war was declared—questioning, redefining, challenging, courageous, these noble flaming queens, these roaring bulldykes. There are enduring lessons in courage to be found in stereotypes, those shock troops of the advance guard preparing for battles to come and proclaiming, "I am not what you want me to be."

May I suggest that, upon close inspection, the "stereotype" may gracefully become . . . an "archetype"?

Throughout history the voice of the outlaw has conveyed

from the frontlines urgent messages of impending struggles. Because that is finally where we may locate that figure, on the front lines—and, always, employing a voice much more powerful than that of the propagandist.

And so I would add this modest observation, made not as a gay writer, not as a Hispanic writer, not even as a possible outlaw writer—but simply as a *writer.* Those essential observations from the front lines—that is, the literature of our dangerous times—will be most powerful if they are delivered, not in the banal prose of the propagandist, but in the careful sentences of the artist, unlabeled.

POSTSCRIPT: When I gave a variation of this essay at Yale, the auditorium was divided into two "factions." On one side, there were macho "Chicano" men holding protectively on to—clutching—their girlfriends, who seemed bemused; on the other side were gay men, making sure their eyes never roamed over to the "heterosexual side," probably not wanting to be accused of cruising the insecure machos.

Years later, I gave a variation of this talk at Harvard. I was glad to note that there existed no demarcation in the audience, as there had been at Yale. I don't know what to infer.

Earlier than the time of this essay, I had begun to question the distorted importance given to the Stonewall riot, an importance that I, too, had awarded it—as indicated by earlier essays here. I had begun to see the negative aspects of that distorted importance.

Too, I had long surrendered to the use of the term "gay." But I will never use the word "queer" in approbation. How quickly that word was seized by academics, turning its ugly inference into yet another silly and arcane "discipline" dubbed "queer theory."

A TOUGH GUY FROM L.A. (1992)

THE DESIGNATION "Los Angeles writer" has become a negative qualifier, indicating a persistent irritant that refuses to go away and must therefore be noticed—just barely noticed: a euphemism for "minor." Thus Nathanael West remains relegated to the lesser leagues, although his short novels outshine many of the sanctified books of his time. No other city name is used to indicate a compromise in artistic creativity.

Charles Bukowski is the possessor of a strong, disturbing voice that has led his ardent admirers to consider his poetry among today's best and to compare his tough-guy prose to that of Ernest Hemingway. Yet he has long been dismissed as only a "Los Angeles writer." He has lived most of his 70 years in Los Angeles, writes mainly about Los Angeles, and does not apologize for either. Still published by a California press, he does not fit neatly within the boundaries of literary acceptability. Though celebrated abroad, in America his work is still begrudged respectful attention by the tomes that purport to establish literary importance.

Those restrictive barriers may have been at least cracked by two recent developments: ironically by his having been the subject of the Hollywood movie *Barfly* and by the appearance of Neeli Cherkovski's biography, *Hank,* a serious appraisal.

Beyond that significance, *Hank* provides a treasure trove for Bukowski fans. The fact that it was written with Bukowski's full cooperation by a former drinking pal accounts for both its strengths and its main weakness.

Cherkovski's access to his subject allows him an intimacy otherwise impossible as he guides us through the poet-author's miserable childhood, scarred by an acute assault of acne; his early drinking; his years as a serf in the post office; the poetry readings that became circuses; his often shabby affairs.

Cherkovski is generous with even the smallest details about his subject: Bukowski detests any poem that contains the words "moon," "star" and/or "infinity." He was given an "Outsider of the Year" plaque by a small-press editor. During a meeting about his movie, he was vastly annoyed by the bouncing of Dennis Hopper's gold neck-chains.

In Cherkovski's knowledgeable description of the little-magazine jungle out of which Bukowski emerged, the literary "underground" is revealed to be just like the overground—nasty, bickering, assaulting other writers, replacing old pontifications with new ones. Here's the editor of a tiny journal responding in lower-case bombast to Bukowski's poetry: "you have taken the art away from the college profs, the creeleys, the william carlos williams, the pounds & eliots . . . back to the financially unstable, ordinary people of the country. . . . YOU are the prime example that the poetry of tomorrow will be the poetry of the fighting, struggling, unprofessional poet."

I'm sure Bukowski's German publisher did not intend black humor, but it is certainly there, when, in the paraphrase of Cherkovski, he responds in exhilaration on first reading Bukowski: "Anyone who could write a line like 'I am going to rob a bank or beat hell out of a blind man any day now, and they'll never know why' needed to be heard in as many places as possible." At best, that is exalted silliness.

There are many poignant moments. As a teenager, feeling like "some kind of beast" because of his blemished skin, Bukowski stares only through a window at his own graduation prom. Cherkovski renders a lovely portrait of Bukowski's daughter, wisely allowing her to express in her own words her loyalty to her father, a loyalty enhanced when we see the rambunctious author at her wedding, subdued, a proud father in doting attendance.

Unfortunately, the same intimacy that provides the book's best moments also leads to its central shortcoming: Cherkovski admires Bukowski too much. That causes him to avoid delving into touchy areas that would more sharply illuminate this highly complex man—who as a youth thought no woman would ever look at him, who lost his virginity late in life, yet became— Cherkovski offers no telling transition—a man pursued by women, "a sex genius."

A woman Bukowski had lived with and loved, responding to his telephoned taunts about a new woman, grabs his typewriter and threatens to throw it onto the pavement. The man who railed against and was often in trouble with uniformed authorities calls the police and watches her taken away handcuffed. Because, Cherkovski declares, Bukowski found himself "not knowing what else to do."

Bukowski makes an outrageous remark about rape. "Just joking," Cherkovski assures. Perhaps fearful of judging the man he highly admires, Cherkovski does not question the attitude of a man who can confuse alcoholism with "manhood." Bukowski "fires" at the young Cherkovski, whose head is already swirling with booze: "Be a man. Have another beer."

Had Cherkovski pursued his subject into mined territories, Bukowski might have been able to clarify many such touchy areas, even if only with the elliptical logic that permitted him to denounce anti-Vietnam-war demonstrators yet champion the class out of which that war's casualties came.

Cherkovski provides evidence for the deduction that, for all his denunciation of postures, Bukowski has at times quite consciously choreographed his outsider's reputation. He makes tapes of casual conversations. A note to a foreign visitor seems written for effect: "Just step through the door. It's broken anyway. Welcome to the United States."

In the 1970s, poet-actor Gerard Malanga insisted that I accompany him on a visit to the author. I wondered why Malanga, a central figure in the Warhol circle of glittery superstars, was making what seemed a pilgrimage with the emphatic offering of a six-pack-to the decidedly unglamorous author. When we entered Bukowski's house—he summoned us in from somewhere within—I had the impression that I had wandered onto a set of carefully allowed squalor: dirty clothes displayed all over, crumpled papers like sculpture, cans and bottles gleaming on the floor. There was even a lonely barbell. Then Bukowski appeared. Hunched, slouching, making an entrance, he bent over something on the floor. Surely not rearranging the debris?

Soon, I was struck by how gentle and courteous this reputed "wild man" was. I left with the notion that Bukowski's rough image was as carefully cultivated as was the shimmery glamour of Warhol's darling people.

LETTER TO GORE VIDAL (1993)

MR. VIDAL:
When a friend of mine told me recently that you referred to Alfred Chester's 1963 "review" of my first novel, *City of Night*, in your recent collection of essays, I was sure that you had decried that personal assault. I was sure of that because I have admired your courage in surviving similar personal assaults veiled as criticism, ugly assaults like those by William Buckley and others, assaults I do not consider "funny," as I'm sure you do not, assaults on the level of Chester's on my novel.

And so I was taken aback that, instead, you chose Chester's vile review of my first novel as exemplary of "high" criticism. You call it "murderously funny, absolutely unfair, and totally true." Recognizing the contradiction in your own statement, you go on to refuse to "show . . . how it's done," while clearly implying that you know how.

"Totally true"? To the contrary Chester's review was itself totally fake. I would assume that you, having often been the object of such, would recognize that sort of fakery, the kind that a critic who has been personally assaulted by a book's subject, and its author, resorts to in order to disguise the fact that he has been disturbed, even wounded, by it. Instead of dealing with that, he attacks its quality.

Critics I respect highly have publicly objected to Chester's review: Soon after it appeared, Frank O'Hara wrote in *Kulchur*: "I cannot but be convinced that Rechy not only has his own voice, but also that it has an almost hypnotic effect on many other writers, which is able to bring out all sorts of bitchy and flatulent attitudes which are otherwise cleverly hidden in conditioned, or assumed, stylistics. He even manages to get Alfred Chester down to the 'Oh, Mary' level."

More recently, in response to a *Poets & Writers* interview with me, in which I referred to Chester's attack, Edward Field, a friend of Chester's and the editor of a recent collection of Chester's essays, apologized publicly to me (*Poets & Writers*, September/October 1992). He wrote: "It was with a good deal of sadness that I read in the John Rechy interview of the damage done to City of Night by the late Alfred Chester's bitchy review of it. . . . [I]t was himself [whom Chester] was savagely attacking in the review." Mr. Field went on to point out that the offensive title of the review—"Fruit Salad"—was not Chester's "but the *New York Review of Books*'s, which has long demonstrated homophobia in its essays and cartoons."

Last year in *The Advocate*, David Ehrenstein wrote an essay about the initial reception to *City of Night*: "To judge from reviews of the period, such unapologetic homoeroticism plainly made literary critics—particularly gay ones—distinctly uncomfortable. Poet Frank O'Hara was one of the brave few to hail Rechy in a completely straightforward manner. . . . Novelist Alfred Chester, by contrast, bitchily dismissed *City of Night*."

No, Mr. Vidal, Chester's type of murderous assault does not require "high" art. It is the easiest form of attack—and the easiest to detect. It merely requires a low nastiness (what Frank O'Hara labeled the 'Oh, Mary' level).

I'm curious about this, Mr. Vidal: Didn't the title *The New York Review of Books* donated to Chester's review—"Fruit Salad"—make you wince even slightly, especially when you saw it resurrected in their 1988 *Selections from the First Two Issues*? It did Barbara Epstein, belatedly. To her credit and in response to a letter from me protesting the exhumation of that spiteful "review" and its now even more offensive title, she wrote me: "You are right about the title 'Fruit Salad.' *Selections* is a collection of pieces intended to recall our first issues for new subscribers, and I see that when we reprinted the Alfred Chester piece, we should have removed the title. I'm sorry." Did the title, like the review, strike you as merely "murderously funny"? I would say that that screechy review and its outrageous headline are not exactly an example of the "comprehensive dignity" you ascribe to the journal you frequently write for.

If you had read any of my nine novels since *City of Night*, or at least the foreword by me that now accompanies all new editions of my first novel and refers to Chester's "review," you would find how unfair and untrue that man's bleatings were. You might, in your own words about first disliking Burroughs' *Naked Lunch* "begin to see things . . . missed first time around . . . what criticism is meant to do—show us what we missed or just plain didn't get." You might even find more evidence in Chester's "review" for your "Eckerman's" contention that "envy is the only credible emotion, isn't it?" Yes, very often, Mr. Vidal.

You are right when you say that Chester's review is—or, rather, attempted to be, since it did not succeed in being—"murderous." Despite advance praise for my novel from Christopher Isherwood, James Baldwin, Larry McMurtry, and others, Chester's review— being the first (eagerly printed weeks before publication date) and appearing in a journal that vaunts its literary authenticity— had an undeniably powerful effect on how my first novel was viewed critically; Chester's review was quoted by others, including Richard Gilman in the *New Republic* and the reviewer for the *Village Voice*, precisely because of its "murderous" tone. As you well know from your own experience, that is the sort of vitriol that journalists seize on eagerly.

The effect of Chester's malice lingers among some noisy "critics," those you yourself often decry and who, not incidentally, make the *New York Review of Books* their Bible, and even write for it. Indeed, I find myself, 30 years and nine books later, still often having to ward off the impact of Chester's assault on my reputation at its inception. Each time I battle *The New York Times Book Review* to give attention to a new novel by me, I detect the influence of what you call Chester's "murderously funny" denigration of me as a serious writer.

Still, I've gone on to write nine more novels; and my first novel survives, intact, highly respected, taught in major universities, never out of print, issued and reissued constantly in foreign translations.

Indeed, the Gallimard edition, just reissued with my new foreword, drew high praise from Hugo Marsan in *Le Monde* in July of this year and provided, from the crucial vantage of time, a view of it almost entirely opposite that of Chester's. Noting that "thirty years later . . . the novel has not aged a bit . . . one reads [it] eagerly," Mr. Marsan writes: "[W]e understand better its exceptional authenticity, its premonitory vision, its subtle literary innovations. The characters . . . have the tragic complexity of Vautrin, Charlus, or Morel, and the aggressive solitude of the marginal people of Jean Genet. . . . [I]ts poetry is not ostentatious nor imposed. . . . [T]he protagonists are individuals of flesh and blood."

I have, Mr. Vidal, produced a body of work that is as authentic and as worthy as that of any other writer of my generation, a body of work that I am proud of.

JOHN RECHY

POSTSCRIPT: Mr. Vidal proved most gracious. He answered me that he had been swayed by "the black powers" of the "monster" Chester. He expressed his admiration for *City of Night* and told me about the high regard one of Italy's most prominent critics had for my novel. Mr. Vidal and I exchanged letters, too briefly. Later, he provided a glowing quotation about my work. We've never met—although he lives in Los Angeles periodically. I'm sorry that we haven't met, because I would welcome the opportunity to express my admiration for one of the best American writers. What I would hesitate to tell him is that I think he likes to hide a kind heart.

On May 28, 1996, I wrote Barbara Epstein protesting the reprinting of Chester's review in their collected *Selections from the New York Review of Books*. I ended that letter by stating, "After thirty-three years of this, how about equal time, Ms. Epstein? . . . Allow me space [for rebuttal] in your journal . . . At the very least, how about reprinting this letter? For permitting overtly personal and destructive spite into the pages of your journal and for stubbornly perpetuating it for decades, Ms. Epstein, you *owe* me that much."

Instead of publishing that letter, Ms. Epstein extended to me six hundred words to rebut Alfred Chester's vitriolic review. The letter that follows, dated June 17, 1996, is the letter that was published in the letters column of the *New York Review of Books*, October 31, 1996, under the heading "Complaint."

LETTER TO *THE NEW YORK REVIEW OF BOOKS* (1996)

T0 THE EDITORS,
The New York Review of Books:

In May 1963, there appeared in your journal a piece of malice posing as a review of my first novel, *City of Night*. The "review" was written by Alfred Chester. You titled it "Fruit Salad." I was young, baffled by the personal assault, and I did not protest. I'm no longer young, I understand the attack, and I protest the abuse and its recent extension.

Chester questioned my very existence, a twist of meanness seized by others of his ilk in *The New Republic*, *The Village Voice*, and in tabloids. Consequently, impostors emerged, their behavior attributed to me in gossip columns. (I had chosen to retain my privacy.) The impact of Chester's "review" was possible because it appeared in your journal.

City of Night became an international bestseller, has never been out of print, is taught in literature courses.

Chester's "review" would have become at most a ridiculed footnote if you had not dug it up in 1988 in your collection of reviews, *Selections*. Again you exposed Chester's leering at my photograph, his giddy tone ("Oooo, Mary"), his attempted disparagement even of my name. The doubting of my existence was more offensive when I had gone on to write many more books. The original headline updated your imprimatur on the word "fruit."

You answered my objection: ". . . we should have removed the title. I'm sorry."

In May this year you offered a copy of *Selections*, with a new cover, inviting subscribers to learn what your reviewers wrote about Burroughs' and Baldwin's books considered "modern classics." Since *City of Night* is also referred to as a "modern classic," I assumed Chester's "review" was omitted. It was intact. A letter from you answering mine maintained that the edition was— "apparently"—not a new printing. Still, Chester's performance was extended.

Responding to an interview with me in *Poets & Writers*, Edward Field, Chester's once-editor, wrote to the magazine: "It was with a good deal of sadness that I read . . . of the damage done to *City of Night* by the late Alfred Chester's bitchy review. . . . It was a considerable understatement to call Chester 'notoriously disturbed.' . . . He was mad . . . cruel and destructive, as his review demonstrates. . . . In explaining and apologizing for [Chester's] disservice to Rechy, an author I greatly admire, I should point out that the title of the offending review . . . was not Alfred Chester's but the *New York Review of Books's*. . . ."

In his *United States: Essays 1954–1994*, Gore Vidal, discussing *Selections*, labels Chester's "review" "absolutely unfair," yet "murderously funny . . . a trick that only a high critic knows how to pull off"—a trick Mr. Vidal goes on to claim he, too, can perform. I reminded Mr. Vidal that he has been the object of "murderously funny" criticism. I asked him whether not even the title of the "review" had made him wince. He wrote back: "I very much admire *City of Night*. . . . Also . . . I admire a kind of performance in criticism which is often plainly gratuitously destructive but at the same time a sort of art. . . . Chester, a moral monster, one gathers, was, for a time, a master of this sort of thing. . . . I had forgotten about him entirely until I reread his 'totally unfair' piece and I'm afraid I succumbed yet again to his black arts. . . . I don't even recall the offensive title." Mr. Vidal's approval of Chester's malice—not art—remains in his volume.

Each time you exhume Chester's spite on a novel that has proven him wrong, you condone his dishonorable motives, motives Chester makes clear in his "review":

Categorizing the hustler in my novel as "the kind of person we now speak of as 'someone incapable of love'" Chester continues: "And, as with all these people, if you are hot for them enough, or bedeviled and tormented by them enough, and if you look and examine very hard, you will find that it is not at all true that they cannot love. They can; they do; alas, they love too much, which is the problem, for they are always loving someone else." But never Chester.

Postscript: I bristle at the exhortation that writers must never "talk back" to reviewers, etc. I do so when a review is clearly unjust, a personal assault, or when there is clear evidence—a writer can always tell—that a malicious reviewer hasn't read the book he's assaulting. The latter happens more often than not. I usually get a personal answer, even an apology, even a telephone call. I succeeded in getting Amazon to delete one or two of the more scurrilous letters that they allow "readers" to post on their Web site and that stick to a book like messy glue.

Once, I was told by one of my publishers that my letters of protest had put me on a "blacklist" at the *New York Times Book Review.* Too grotesque to believe. I'll continue to protest; and I tell writers in my workshops, at USC and privately, to protest, always, the abuse that too often appears in the disguise of "criticism."

I consider the printing of my letter to *The New York Review of Books* one of my most fulfilling protests, especially because of this: When I was receiving PEN West USA's lifetime achievement award in 1998, the director wrote Ms. Epstein informing her that the author whose identity had been questioned in her book review was being given PEN's top award. Ms. Epstein not only published that letter, but she headlined it: "Congratulations!" I cherish that exclamation mark, so rare in that publication; and I have become inordinately fond of Ms. Epstein.

SETS AND REPS:
BOB PARIS' *GORILLA SUIT* (1997)

T HE WORLD OF professional bodybuilding is rife with contradictions. Sleazy and glamorous, honest and hypocritical, it
extols ultra-masculinity while indulging a bitchiness that
makes squabbling divas seem tame. It may be an art form or
a sport but, accepted as neither, it is in ill repute because it
is spectacularly narcissistic and, however denied, homoerotic
at its core. Scandals lurk behind the façade of wholesomeness
demanded by its czar, Joe Weider, self-avowed "Master
Blaster." His credo on magazine mastheads commands:
". . . speak the truth, practice fidelity and honor your father
and mother." Only a witness from its heights could depict
this world that fits grandly in Southern California, capital of
narcissism, where, at land's end, the exposed body is
unabashedly celebrated.

Bob Paris has unquestioned credentials to be that witness. A
former Mr. America and Mr. Universe, he placed ninth in the
king of contests, Mr. Olympia. As the first major bodybuilder to
proclaim being gay, he possesses the requisite outsider's eye.

He details his unhappy early years. He smokes, becomes
drunk, inhales marijuana. His father banishes him. His beloved
grandmother poignantly sews his first posing trunks; he models them for her. He drops out of school. Bodybuilding becomes

his religion. Narcissists need love, too, and Paris falls in love with a man he courageously "marries."

Paris is at his lyrical best when conveying the excitement of lifting weights. "I fought the pull of gravity . . . and disappeared inside the fight." Even those of us who have only dabbled in bodybuilding share that thrill. While longing for sensational bodies, we hid muscle magazines under copies of *Life* to avoid the glare of owl-eyed clerks. We flexed before mirrors and almost wept. We sent for Charles Atlas' course, gasping at what became of the man whose face had been sprayed with sand. We ordered a set of York Barbells and struggled to unpack them. Little muscles sprouted. No shirt was tight enough. Someone asked, "You work out?" We held our breath for what—please, God—would follow: "You look like you do."

Dedicated, we learned the short history of competitive bodybuilding's main stages, marveling at its humble beginnings. In school basements, a few brave men in trunks straggled before droopy sheets, the only backdrop available. One man emerged with a grandiloquent title and a tacky trophy. Sean Connery was photographed looking disconsolate after not winning in an early dingy contest. In the '50s, Steve Reeves as Hercules made us proud by ushering in a somewhat more elegant era, that of bodybuilder as movie star, if only in cheesy Italian epics. Not every bodybuilder of the time lucked out. Many were enticed to Italy, offered nonexistent movies. Articles in muscle magazines pleaded for donations to bring back the stranded, starry-eyed musclemen. Broke ourselves, we lamented that fate allowed terrific bodies but supplied little regard for them.

Paris ignores much of the shabby richness that makes professional bodybuilding unique. His book is too often a labor of self-love. He forgets that interest in this venture relies not primarily on him, but on the exotic world he knew as a gay narcissist among narcissists. He downplays prime factors in competitive bodybuilding, narcissism and homosexuality: "Myths . . . to degrade anyone who took care of his body" and who was there-fore "automatically considered suspicious and narcissistic, and abracadabra, homo."

He emphasizes: "Few gay athletes are at the top of this sport. I can only think of one, besides me . . . however, the myth that all bodybuilders were gay caused great psychic unrest among the straight men who ran the sport . . . [as] a wholesome heterosex-ual pastime." He accounts for professional bodybuilding's gay fol-lowing: "It revolves around men's bodies taken to the arguably hyper-masculine limits . . . [T]hat appeals to some people." But not to him. "I don't find elite competitive bodybuilders sexy."

In fact, there have been at least five other top gay body-builders, all closeted. One became a prostitute and porn per-former—and, later, a minister, until God told him to make a comeback in physique competition. Three other titlists became gay porn models. Lesser contestants advertise in gay solicitation columns as "private trainers," "escorts" and "models," often euphemisms for prostitutes.

However subliminal homosexuality may be in exhibition body-building, Paris' claim of its paucity astounds. During the near orgiastic frenzy of "pose-down," finalists onstage match sweaty bodies, tensed biceps against tensed biceps, tensed thighs against tensed thighs. Training involves intense intimacy. While "spotting," one man straddles a prone lifter to lend nominal support in handling an otherwise prohibitive weight. To add resistance to donkey raises (calf exercises), a helper mounts the buttocks of a lifter, who is bent over.

Paris evades the subject of bitchiness. Yet contest competitors resort to bizarre meanness, "psyching out" rivals, offering spuri-ous advice, remarking on "bitch tits." A condition caused by steroids. Titlists who become commentators evaluate contests: "Holding water . . . needs work on his stomach . . . has no calves."

Paris contributes his own cattiness. One bodybuilder has "zits" and a "little pee-pee." He chides a competitor for allowing his posing to become "burlesque." About a gay photographer, Paris thinks, "My God . . . He's flirting with me" and indignantly throws the "lizard's" business card into a trash can. He rages against those who are by choice bulkier than he. They are "monsters . . . lugs . . . overbuilt caricatures . . . clanging through gruesome contortions." On the other hand, his own goal was "to build . . . the most perfect human sculpture" possible.

Not much evidence is required to establish bodybuilding's hard-earned narcissism, barely discussed but amply exemplified. Bodybuilders court reflections in myriad gym mirrors, staring, awed, as quivering muscles flirt back. Dissatisfied in contests, they walk offstage, smash lesser trophies, vaunt their own qualifications. Often exploited like starlets, contenders struggle—even triumph briefly—and vanish. Younger bodies populate magazines.

Paris misses a telling metaphoric connection between muscles and elaborate gay decoration. In terms of extremity, artifice and theatrical visual assault, Paris' "gorilla suit" is not unlike sequined drag and the glittery regalia of gay leathermen. Paris does recognize that muscles convert the "wearer" into someone else and insulate psychic wounds: "[As a boy] I hated myself . . . my limbs were in all the wrong places . . . And I was a fag." Later he deduces: "As long as I didn't let the little boy believe too strongly that the suit was really him, he was okay." Not all self-created narcissists have arrived at such wise discernment. Marilyn Monroe, Rudolph Valentino, Rita Hayworth, James Dean, those fabulous narcissists disastrously confused themselves with their creations.

Paris is much too restrained in his depiction of the phenomenon named Joe Weider, providing only a mildly scolding view of a man many may consider the Barnum and Bailey of professional bodybuilding. By the early '70s, Joe and brother Ben had formed an awesome empire of barbells, food supplements and glitzy physique shows. On the masthead of most of his glossy magazines, Joe placed a bust of his profile—it still appears today—atop a formidable chest he claimed was his. He promised "barn-door lats" and "coconut delts." He sold elixirs to guarantee them. He attached his name to familiar exercises and exalted them into "Weider Principles" and, more modestly, his "legacy to the world." A monarch, he exercised his power to exile subjects deemed disloyal, often because they had posed for a rival publisher or entered an unsanctioned contest.

Readers of Weider's magazines predicted contest winners by gauging who received the Blaster's blessing. A huge Austrian named Arnold Schwarzenegger appeared in every issue, endorsed every Weider product and principle and won Mr. Olympia seven times, the final time in less than top shape after having retired to make movies.

The age of drugs had arrived. A stupendous body emerged, not possible without steroids, every massive muscle clamped on, every vein etched like a tributary. Risks included death—and Paris movingly documents the death of a famous bodybuilder minutes after his posing onstage.

Paris blames freaky musclemen for the fact that competition bodybuilding is not widely respected, not "written about in the sports pages." But try to imagine the typical sports fan rooting for a man who stands onstage demanding adulation for his shaved body, dyed tan, oiled to a glassy sheen, wearing only a strip of cloth, and you get a picture of impossibility.

Top bodybuilders know their bodies as intimately as a painter know hues; a writer, the nuances of metaphor. Scholars flaunt their intellect; writers their prose; artists their art; dancers their leaps. Why disdain a sculpted body? Here is Paris' terrific assessment: "[Bodybuilding] is misunderstood, under-appreciated . . . considered to be the realm of freaks, but it is also beautiful and can be graceful and thrilling and lifted high above the dull thud of conformity."

At the end of his book Paris, 35, contemplates a comeback. He may again have to take steroid and will face homophobia.

Homophobia, he contents, robbed him of the Mr. Olympia title in 1985. He presents ample evidence for suspicion of ostracism. After he came out, he almost disappeared form the forefront of bodybuilding.

Paris is an inspired bodybuilder. He is still too involved with the profession ot be entirely daring, still courting the Master Blaster for a product endorsement contract. When he has no more at stake—or does not care about the risks—perhaps he will provide what this book does not: a truly bold depiction of his fascinating world in all its tawdry splendor.

POSTSCRIPT: I continue to regret that Mr. Paris did not write the book he might have written, a true exposé of an exotic world of perfect bodies and sexual repressions, a world like no other, vaunting health and steeped in depravity.

SERGEI EISENSTEIN: A LIFE IN CONFLICT (1999)

BIOGRAPHER RONALD BERGAN sets out to alter the view of Eisenstein as a "cold, intellectual artist," a "calculating" theorist "whose films lack humanity." He intends, further, to throw "light on his homosexuality."

Why Bergan felt that locating notable "humanity" in the director's films would elevate his art is baffling. Many great artists have been "cold," artfully calculating—Kubrick, Nabokov, Resnais, one of whose characters in "Providence" says, "Style is feeling."

Bergan largely fails in his lofty goal—fortunately, because the result is an engrossing portrait of the complex artist and a lucid examination of his work. Relying largely on Eisenstein's writings, Bergan illuminates borrowed entries with astute observations about the director's theories. He paints vivid scenes of the times, from Russia in turmoil to Hollywood by poolside.

First he strains to detect humanity within Eisenstein's adoration of Hollywood stars—Chaplin, Garland—and in the anguished faces he depicted. Yet what dazzles in Eisenstein's films is their almost-architectural composition, and faces are a part of the intended configuration, consistent with the director's theory of "visage," typecasting.

Bergan reveals a cold Eisenstein in his life, citing aloof treatment of his platonic wife, unmentioned in his memoirs. "A small, ridiculous woman died today," was his epigraph for his mother."

Bergan provides scant illumination into Eisenstein's homosexual life. He conjectures that the director must have visited homosexual clubs in Berlin, dwells on images of upraised cannons, describes homoerotic drawings, and notes shirtless men in his films.

He might have found equally substantial manifestations in the director's adoration of Judy Garland and in his gay wit. About Director Joseph Von Sternberg: "He has a predilection for well-built males. . . . even stayed at the Hercules Hotel." Eisenstein could be hypocritical about his homosexuality. "I've not felt any such desire." Still those were times when private consensual homosexual acts were punished with imprisonment.

Avoiding dizzying interpretations that Eisenstein's Freudian-influenced views invite, Bergan explores without jargon Eisenstein's theories of dialectic montage, conscious arrangement of shots so that the clash between two images creates a third impression resulting in an emotional or intellectual response. Among the masterful results of Eisenstein's "visual ideas" is his "reproduction" of gunshots by dots glistening on water. The famous, stunning sequence in "Potemkin"—the slaughter on the Odessa Steps—"against which the whole of cinema can be defined," notes Bergan—was rendered so powerfully that although there was no such slaughter, purported survivors attested to its authenticity.

Bergan employs telling black humor. Claiming enormous admiration for "Potemkin," Samuel Goldwyn wondered whether the director might make a film for him—"the same kind, but rather cheaper, for Ronald Colman." After finding Eisenstein's script of Dreiser's *An American Tragedy*, "the most moving script

I have ever read," David O. Selznick wrote to producers: "Is it too late to persuade the enthusiasts of the picture from making it?"

Eisenstein cherished his power. He claimed that if he cast a fat man as Ivan the Terrible, Ivan would be remembered as fat. Yet he was challenged repeatedly by a much more powerful man, Stalin. Once, he was summoned to meet with the Russian dictator— whose favorite movie was *The Great Waltz*—to discuss adjustments in the epic *Ivan the Terrible* to conform to revised views of Ivan as heroic. The dictator's spokesman objected to "Comrade Eisenstein's fascination with shadows . . . and Ivan's beard," offensive especially because "Ivan lifted his head too often." Wryly, Eisenstein promised: "Ivan's beard will be shorter." That was not the extent of his cooperation with Stalinism.

Events in Mexico had destroyed his intended masterpiece, *Que Viva Mexico*. Funds withdrawn, footage seized and scattered from Russia to Hollywood, pieces spliced into B-films, a vulnerable Eisenstein returned to turbulent Russia. Unlike other artists—some imprisoned, some executed for their views—he apologized, reversed his theories. "My subject is patriotism," he declaimed, and was awarded the Stalin Prize. Still, there is evidence that Eisenstein only camouflaged his denunciation of Stalin in latter films.

In his memoirs, Eisenstein retold a Persian legend about a man who felt a calling to fulfill a great task. At a bazaar, tanners demanded he lie in filth so they could walk over him. "And the hero-to-be, saving his strength for the future, humbly lay at their feet in the filth." Later, he "attained the full mastery of his unprecedented strength and performed all the feats of unheard-of difficulty that lay before him." Expressing admiration for the humiliated man's "unheard-of self-control and sacrifice of everything, including his self-esteem" as he prepared for great achievements, Eisenstein wrote, "I have had on several occasions to stoop to . . . self-abasement."

Finally, Bergan finds the humanity he strove to locate, found in that moving lament, and subsequent artistic triumph, of a great artist trapped within violent political crosscurrents.

POSTSCRIPT: Twice I turned down reviewing the book, feeling I wasn't knowledgable enough about the man or the subject to do them justice. But the book review editor, for reasons unknown, kept insisting I write it, sending the book back. So I researched both the life of Eisenstein as others had seen it and I read extensively about his theories, especially about montage. I was able to write a review I'm proud of. The insistent assignment, however, caused me to wonder: How many books are carelessly assigned?

PLACES LEFT UNFINISHED AT THE TIME OF CREATION (1999)

I T IS NOT difficult to find evidence for the claim that Mexican-Americans often suffer from a sense of alienation, a confusion of identity. That sense of abandonment lies at the heart of mariachi ballads that bemoan something lost, not recognized. In popular telenovelas of today, the main characters are virtually always anglicized. The only ones who look Mexican—that is, Indian—are servants, especially *criadas*, poor women retainers who, to the point of martyrdom, are loyal to their rich and arrogant *patronas*. Ricky Martin, his hair growing lighter, sings a few words in Spanish, but he has been converted into every teenage girl and boy's dream of a cute American kid. Even his last name is a disguise. In Spanish it would be pronounced Marteen. There is confusion about what to call oneself—Mexican-American? Hispanic? Latino? The most prevalent designation, Chicano, was, for decades, a term of disrespect among Mexicans.

Not too long ago in Texas, children, if they were fair, were warned by well-meaning friends not to call themselves Mexican, but Spanish. Down-sloping "Indian eyelashes" must be curled into a tilt. Those attitudes of European superiority have a strong historical parallel. The war against France produced a dictator, Porfirio Díaz, a mestizo, who nevertheless became renowned for his European pretensions.

In his impressive memoir, Santos (the name means saints) attempts to locate the origin of that lingering loss among the descendants of the conquered Indians, and he does so with grand success, reimagining lives, roaming through myths, history, and borrowed dreams.

He embarks on several journeys of discovery: to find the truth of his grandfather's drowning in the San Antonio River; to trace Hernán Cortés's symbolic conquest of Mexico; and to retrieve the banished stories of his own family.

A sense of awe permeates his impressive book and lifts it above its easy categorization as the memoir of a "Tejano," an appropriately elegant word for a Mexican-American born or raised in Texas. (Santos does not use the word "Chicano.")

Was the drowning of his grandfather at age 49 the result of a heart attack? Murder? Santos's search leads him to an old retired fireman who may have pulled the body from the river. The addled man responds to questions with a rendition of "The Eyes of Texas Are upon You." That, and the reticence of his family to recall the event, lead Santos to search for a deeper meaning, within the heavy fog that persisted that fatal day, the *niebla*, which means fog in Spanish but also suggests psychological and psychic confusion.

Santos moodily describes an ominous fog that infiltrates the mythology of the Nahuac and Aztec cultures, a fog that occurs "as if all the heavens have been stilled." In San Antonio, "the body and its senses begin to retreat from the outside world." Was his grandfather's death a suicide in response to a command buried within the ancient melancholia of conquered ancestors, a melancholia "handed down, wordlessly, through numberless generations, inscribed onto the helical codex of the DNA"?

As Cortés—"the grandfather no Mexican wants to admit to"—swept into Mexico, he devastated ancient temples and traditions, squashing a complex culture knowledgeable in mathematics, medicine, architecture. He also carved deep wounds into the psyche of the Indians, spawning children often born of rape, mestizos, "the mixed ones," outsiders from the two worlds that produced them. That conquest still "runs through most Mexican-American families like an active faultline." It creates an epic of defensive forgetting among a people who, like Santos, easily weep.

"We have made selective forgetting a sacramental obligation. Leave it all in the past, all that you were, and all that you could be. There is pain enough in the present." He wonders: "Could you tell a story about centuries of forgetting?"

In answer, he restores the lives and memories of his family in San Antonio. With loving humor, he presents a gallery of snapshots within portraits.

He brings to life *las viejitas*—"doñas who held court in shady painted backyard arbors and parlors across the neighborhoods. . . . To the uninitiated, [they] might look fragile, with their bundled bluish hair, false teeth, and halting arthritic steps . . . grandmothers, great-aunts, sisters-in-law. . . . But under the all-knowing gazes . . . we never felt oppressed or downtrotten." That is so because within all Hispanic culture, these ubiquitous women are symbols of indomitable spirit and endurance.

Among the *ancianos,* Uncle Lico suffers a terrible ignominy. He is buried not with the grandiose melodrama of Catholic tradition but with the stingy recitations of "born-agains" who claim his last days, and his defenseless dead body.

Santos is respectful of the lore some might label superstitions, and his accounts are aptly tinted with magical realism. A double rainbow augurs smooth passage past purgatory. A dream of "luminous pears, glowing bright green against the midnight sky," will end turbulent sleep. The Inframundo of the Aztecs is a limbo "where all that has been forgotten still lives."

Susto, a sudden fright with religious overtones, can traumatize forever, as when the corpse of an Anglo woman is being carried by two sisters for preparation, and a stumble causes it to fly from their grasp. A veil falls, revealing the face of death to Aunt Madrina, who sees the woman's soul "spiral upward like smoke." That *susto* causes her epilepsy.

Santos's sense of awe allows him to leave mysteries unresolved, to yield, instead, strong metaphoric meanings, mysterious epiphanies. As a child, he is fascinated with *"los Voladores,"* men in Indian garb who perform a kind of dance, spiraling downward in widening circles while roped to a tall pole atop of which another man stands singing. The adult Santos believes that the dance—men seeming to fly away, liberated from punishing gravity—holds a secret intended only for him. When he asks the stationary performer what he thinks of as he surveys the field others will fly through, the man answers, "I think about nothing."

In Texas, an aunt stares in horror at a captive wolf in a cage. In its desperation to escape, the wolf has shredded its own flesh. In her country, wolves roamed freely, "a part of God's wild creation that always seemed beyond human control." Their howls were "like a conversation in an old language . . . everyone but the wolves had forgotten." When she recovers from a blackout at the terrifying spectacle of the martyred wolf, she knows: "We have been taken to purgatory. Soon the chastisements would begin."

Santos's early background is suggested in references to "fields," to "pickers. Bigotry provides a subtle but strong strain throughout. There are intimations of "refugee camps," of immigration agents sweeping through neighborhoods in search of wetbacks, "greasers." Bicycle tires are slashed, the word "Meskin" scratched on a desk. Santos is made ashamed of the gaudy old Cadillac his uncle drives. There are warnings of Texas ranchers shooting Mexicans.

In school, he is taught a history populated only by Anglo settlers, not the Indians or the Spanish who built the city, "a secret history." He deduces: "The struggle against the conquest was still alive."

The book's flaws attest to its power. A trip to visit the chapel of the Virgin of Guadalupe, the blessed brown lady revered perhaps even more than Jesus, is propped beautifully, arousing expectations. But there is, finally, no sense of unique revelation before that staggering presence, who is awesome beyond religious belief. That great apparition assumed Indian coloring—though not Indian features—to become the Mother of Mexico.

In a disturbing passage and with perfect honesty, Santos documents his shooting of a doe, for meat. He fires three times. The doe will not fall. He refuses to feel guilt. Yet the reader anticipates a revelation beyond the event as the stricken doe continues to move accusingly toward its killer—not unlike the people Santos describes, wounded by a conqueror but still enduring.

Nor is Santos beyond a stumble in his graceful delivery. "It felt like" recurs awkwardly. A misplaced phrase may jar his refined imagery. "Like others of her generation, the present—"

Those are minor lapses in writing that seamlessly combines a formal literary tone with that of a *cuento,* a folk tale. Some sentences seem sculpted. Here is Grandmother speaking: ". . . her sentences moved in one steady arc, like a bow across a violin, and her words were delicately pronounced, so that you could hear every tinkle of an old chandelier, every gust of a Coahuila wind falling to a hush, and the grain of a rustling squash blossom."

Later, when he journeys as a documentary producer, Santos is able to link the world of his ancestors with that of other people's history of ancient grief, other worlds God forgot. In a famine camp in Sudan, starving bodies beg a television crew for food. He realizes that all he can offer to do is to tell their story.

What a wonderful story he has told here, in a memoir that is a brave and beautiful attempt to redeem a people out of a limbo of forgetting.

POSTSCRIPT: I welcome writing about a subject that allows me to discuss my Hispanic/Latino/Chicano roots, as I have in many articles, including earlier ones. Although one or another of my books (especially *The Miraculous Day of Amalia Gómez* and even *City of Night*) appears on the curriculum of university "Chicano Lit." courses," I'm still a dubious figure among a few Chicano academics who seem to believe that you can't be Chicano and gay.

BROTHER PAUL, SISTER JAN, BROTHER HINN, GOD, AND THE FOLKS (1999)

L ORD HAVE MERCY, here they come! What we folks been a-waitin' for in front of our television screens. The dang-lucky folks are in the audience, live!

On a giant sound stage that looks like a Las Vegas suite redesigned by a berserk born-again to look like a posh rectory, with fake mosaic windows, puffy sofas, thronelike gilded chairs, and a huge picture of a happy Jesus in splendid robes approvingly surveying it all, Brother Paul, Sister Jan, and Brother Benny Hinn are revving up for the highlight of tonight's *This Is Your Day* show from the Costa Mesa Head-quarters of the Trinity Broadcasting Station, beamed to more than 768 TV stations, worldwide.

Looking like a would-be gigolo turned mortician, Brother Paul Crouch stands in a dark suit that manages, on him, to look gray, stands there smilin' at the thought of Jesus expected soon. Next to him, wife Sister Jan is jiggling her tambourine and screeching, "Praise Jeez-usss!" at every tremor from Brother Benny Hinn, who is front stage center and preachin'; and Sister Jan weeps in joy and sorrow—and, oh, Lord, mercy does she weep. She cries rivers of tears, canals of tears, lagoons, tributaries, oceans of tears, but there are never enough tears to melt the thick black mascara that sticks to her lashes like clumps of tar. Nor does her jiggling and giggling—she giggles bubbles between tears—perturb a single hair of her gigantic blond wig that sits on her head like a yellow wedding cake melting in the sun; unperturbed even as she flounces about, a 70-year-old country teenager, in ruffly skirts and girly blouses that reveal her impressive God-given upper endowments, shoved into greater prominence by her cruelly pinched waist.

Brother Hinn's doin' his fancy preacher-strut—hop, hop forward, hop back once, hop forward once, hop back twice, reachin' for Ezekiel's angels and speakin' in tongues, punctuating his chat with angels to exhort the congregants before him and beyond the screen:

> *Send a love donation to Jesus, get a personal reply! Show him how much ya love him! The larger the pledge, the more generous the donation, the bigger the miracle! Give your savings, and show God there's no limit to your love! Pledge, give, give, give, pledge, love God and Jesus, pledge!*

"Give!" begs Sister Jan, weeping and giggling. "Please give with your generous heart to spread the message of Jesus!"

"Show how much you love him!" pleads Brother Paul.

Brother Hinn halts midway between a hop-hop back preacher-strut! "Stop!" he orders.

Is Jesus here and Benny's asking him to wait until he's through with his strut? No. Brother Hinn has just had a vision of a man with a critical heart condition—the man may drop dead now, that serious—and he's moving away from his home TV.

"Don't turn your back on Jesus!" Brother Hinn shouts—and waits. "Good! Now touch the screen, touch my hands!" He reaches out with his hands, which, in closeup, reveal bristly dark hairs. "If you make that pledge that the Lord knows you've been with-holding, God will heal your heart tonight!"

The man does the former, and Brother Benny trumpets the latter. "He is healed!"

Offstage but revealed by the camera, a squadron of drab volunteers for Jesus answer telephone calls from good righteous folk offering donations in response to the long-distance miracle. Grant me mine! Inspired, Sister Jan does a skirt-flapping jig, while Brother Paul clenches his hands and thrusts his eyes heavenward basking in awe of the Lord and Brother Hinn's miracles.

"Come and be saved in the blood of the Lamb!" Brother Benny invites the congregation.

Motley squads of women in dated prints, men in aged suits, oily-faced young women and young men with bad complexions—the old and gnarled, the young and gnarled, the stammering young and the stammering old, dozens of them, the bruised, the pleading, the desperate, the destitute—all rise, march forth, advance, crawl, roll on wheelchairs, are carried to the stage, hurt bodies, pained souls, dozens of them, dozens and dozens, advance in a tide of God's wounded army toward Brother Hinn, who is basking in the radiance of a heavenly stage light. Arms outstretched, he welcomes the bereaved.

"I have headaches that never end!"

"Be gone, accursed misery, festering evil!" Benny Hinn plants a hand on the woman's forehead, shoving her back for "catchers" to intercept as she falls "slain in the spirit." She quivers in the arms of the catchers before she staggers up. "I yam cured! Head don't hurt, pulsin's gone, praise the Lord! I yam cured!"

"Let's hear it for the Lord!" Benny exhorts, selflessly.

"Can't see, gotta grope 'round, keep stumblin'."

With a jolt and an assertive push from Benny's hand, the man falls back onto the arms of the catchers, who thrust him forth, and he hops about in circles. "I can see, I can walk!"

"Let's hear it for the Lord!" screams Benny, generously.

More supplicants come, more, more, still more—begging, suffering witnesses to the mysterious ways of God and the healing powers of Brother Hinn, who understands their hurts, don't you know, feels their miseries, longs to heal them all, God bless, Lord love. Brother Hinn knows because he's one of us, hear us, Jesus.

"I cast you out, Satan!"

A pretty, out-of-place young girl trembles, falls into eager arms, is shoved forward and shouts, "I am saved from sins of the flesh!"

"The devil done possessed *me*." A stout woman, meaning serious business, thrusts the saved girl away.

"I cast you out of this good soul, demon!" Brother Benny declares war.

The heavy woman does not budge, does not fall back into the arms of the catchers. Her face grows fierce, fiery red. She growls. "Debil still done got me! Won't let go! Grrrr, grrr!"

Benny hammers his fist on her forehead, harder, again, harder, the catchers grab her, hold her back, down. The woman wrests free, screeches, growls, moans, twists. "Debil don't let go! Grrrr, grrrr!"

(Well, Lord, if da Debil don't let go, push him outta the damn picture, Benny Hinn!)

The camera sweeps away, and when it returns to Brother Benny the woman is gone—trotted off with da Debil—and Brother Benny is ministering to more cooperative sinners.

Lord, Lordee, what come here? A jar! What do the jar contain? A tumor! A tumor ripped out by the Lord from the very flesh of a lonely old woman who was sitting in her living room praying with Benny on TV and she touched the screen and out pop the tumor, which she sent special delivery in a jar, along with a pledge of all her savings that she had long begrudged the Lord.

"Let's hear it for the Lord!"

"Praise Jesus!"

Soon the show will end. An old star from Grand Ole Opry is singing happy gospel. Paul and Jan swing and sway. Brother Hinn takes a bow for Jesus, humbly.

What next, after all this? What to do with the empty hours before more relief from pain is proffered, more donations made that attest to a responsive, caring God? Sad, lonely, abused folks before their TV screens—what, now, for them?

They shift to the Shopping Channel and wait for tomorrow and the possibility of less pain.

POSTSCRIPT: Recently, the whole thing blew up in scandal. A helper at the ministry accused Brother Paul of having a homosexual affair with him, and of being paid hundreds of thousands of dollars (in donations from the pitiful souls who give their savings?) to keep quiet. There are now bruitings of investigations into the fund-raising activities of the ministry, something, I am proud to say, I had, in fictionalized form, foreseen in my novel The Life and Adventures of Lyle Clemens, in which "Brother Bud and Sister Sis" are main players.

PART IV: 2000—2004

LAY OF THE LAND: CHRISTOPHER ISHERWOOD'S *LOST YEARS* (2000)

W HEN CHRISTOPHER ISHERWOOD died in 1986, his literary reputation seemed solid. He had written several fine books
that revealed him to be a masterful stylist, including *Prater
Violet* and *The Berlin Stories*. His novel *A Single Man* is, in this
reviewer's opinion, that rarity in literature, a "perfect" work,
every word exact in its wise, sad, and funny documentation of
one day in the life of an older man who wakes, remembers, and
may perhaps, at the end, die.

His respected literary standing allowed him to survive con-
troversies: There was his fleeing London on the eve of World War
II; his avoiding conscription as a conscientious objector after
he became an American; his association with Vedanta, on and
off intending to become a monk; his affairs with very young
men—and intimations of anti-Semitism. The publication of
this so-called memoir may challenge his reputation more critically than anything else in his life.

In 1971, during an arid creative period, Isherwood began
this "reconstructed diary." "It might keep me amused, like knit-
ting. . . ." He attempted to record, from memory, events of years
left out in his formal diary, the years 1945–1955. He abandoned
the reconstruction in 1977, stopping with an entry dated 1951.
The protagonist of the reconstruction is referred to as

"Christopher." In copious footnotes, the older writer comments as "I" from the vantage of about 20 years past.

When the *Diaries* appeared posthumously, former friends and champions were jarred by the vituperative treatment of them by a man who had courted and praised their friendship, often lavishly in public. About a close writer-friend and ally he wrote in the *Diaries*: "[H]e exudes . . . a cynical misery and a grudge against society which is really based on his own lack of talent. . . ." About another: "[M]ost people dislike [him] because he is ugly and unchic and not quite talented enough."

Many who knew Isherwood and liked him (including this reviewer) saw someone else revealed, a mean-spirited man, although in forced retrospect one was able to detect avoided hints of that new person. *Lost Years* compounds the nastiness of the *Diaries*, and Isherwood emerges as even more of a stranger, an abusive, vindictive stranger.

Some of the most apt descriptions of this book may be borrowed from Isherwood's remarks about others: "[His] name-dropping soon got to be a bore and his tale-telling was so indiscreet that you became afraid to open your mouth. . . ." About another "friend": ". . . his approach was demure until he had detected your weak points and was ready to play on them." Isherwood's name-dropping becomes as rote as a mantra—"dinner with the Knopfs . . . Supper with Peter Viertel." No matter how "demure" an encounter might have seemed to others, everyone who crossed his path was exposed to later-recorded malice that exploited vulnerabilities he detected, like a spy.

How is *Lost Years* different from other candid accounts that put an author's life in a negative light? Flaubert's letters to Louise Colet reveal him violating her trust with false expectations of a permanent union. Dealing primarily with the author's theories on the novel, the letters illuminate his work, become literature. There are many other such works—Rousseau's *The Confessions*, Virginia Woolf's *A Writer's Diary*, Boswell's *London Journal*.

Even a generous definition of the word would disqualify *Lost Years* as literature. A torrent of slights and gossip, relentless renderings of messy affairs—so similar that only names change—it contains little about the author's art, his novels, his philosophical views. It is not even reliable as a historical document of repressive times: Major historical events surrender to chat: "The next month passed without any remarkable incidents. . . . It sounds crazy to say this, when, in fact, Mussolini and his mistress were killed. . . . Hitler's death was announced. . . . Berlin fell . . . and the Nazis surrendered. . . . [T]he day-to-day diary records that, on the 28th, [Christopher] took a taxi to the beach. . . ." In retrospective notes that might have allowed him ironic perspective about changing attitudes toward homosexuality, he chooses instead to extend the gossip.

Curiously driven to find fraudulence in others, he becomes insensitive to genuine confusions. "What really repelled Christopher [was] his dishonest, tricky bisexual posture. . . . [H]e became maudlin over his marriage, and his responsibilities as a father. Stephen Spender is deeply false in the same way, but not nearly as disgusting. . . . They are both utterly untrustworthy." (Apparently Isherwood forgot that in his *Diaries* he claimed at least one bisexual seizure: "I made violent love to that Russian girl.")

One of his sexual partners is described as "an essentially ridiculous character, even a bit of a fake." What Isherwood dismissed as "fakery" was the clash between the man's desire to have children and his homosexuality. Years later, even more conflicted by that confusion—married and with children—that same man attempted suicide, an attempt that put him in a wheel chair for the rest of his life. (The latter information is not noted in a strange name-dropping "Glossary"—not Isherwood's—odd mini-biographies of all the people, especially famous ones, whom Isherwood met even cursorily; Hedy Lamarr is included although she was merely present at a recital he attended.)

There are some fine sentences tinged with wit: "Collier found it thrillingly Proustian to look out of his office window and watch the discreet flirtations of the messenger boys." A notable section documents Isherwood's return after the war to siege-devastated London, the "dead city" he abandoned. Other good passages—a visit to a Veterans Hospital—provide welcome respite from the slush. But the awkward, gossipy voice takes over: "Guy asked Christopher if he was in love with Jack, so Christopher had to assure Guy that he was—though he doubted it. . . ."

One of the most disconcerting aspects of this book lies in the author's treatment of his own sexuality. Claiming 400 sexual encounters (not an exceptional number, really, in those times), he informs us that in his middle years he gained such accolades as "the best lay in the Pacific Coast." He guides us through the tiniest details of his sexual predilections, including scatological sex. Even with an unattractive partner, "Christopher managed to get an erection." One of the 400 sweeps him aloft onto an awaiting bed.

There are endless accounts of flirtations and crushes, of which he—"a born flirt"—is always the object. "Jack flirted with Christopher," "a very good-looking young actor . . . flirted with Christopher," "Truman [Capote] . . . flirted with Christopher," "Gore [Vidal] was flirting with Christopher." "Almost instantly Andrew Lyndon started to get a crush on Christopher," "Christopher was well aware that Jack would get a crush on him," "Sam had a slight crush on Christopher." Even poor "Rachel . . . had a terrific crush on Christopher." From his present vantage, he does not even pause to comment on the fact that even during repressive times an open homosexual life was possible, despite dangers.

He goes after writers: Camus's *The Stranger* is "faky," Sartre's *No Exit* is "phoney," Huxley's *Ape and Essence* is "cheap and nasty."

In locating the "postures" of others, he ignores his own. He informs that he "almost never made a direct pass until he was certain of success." "[H]opeless passes [were] something that senile queens did." In truth, he was aggressive, especially when drunk. Rejected, he became spiteful.

The most despicable aspect of this book is Isherwood's flaunting of his repugnant anti-Semitism. He recounts an affair with a "Jewboy . . . about eighteen." Later, he refers to "an almost classically Jewish Jew, bald, bearded, sly eyed, somewhat rabbinical in his manner, full of hostile mocking flattery, aggressive humility, shrewdness, rudeness, taste, vulgarity, wit and fun."

And this: "The first evening in bed together, Barry said, 'How extraordinary this is! Here am I, a Russian Jew, making love with Christopher Isherwood!' His remark jarred on Christopher; it seemed indecent, masochistic, sexually off-putting. But, as Christopher got to know Barry better, he found a different significance in it. When Barry thus called attention to his Jewishness, he wasn't really demeaning himself. He wasn't at all a humble person. Indeed, he had that Jewish tactlessness, argumentativeness and aggressiveness which always aroused Christopher's anti-Semitic feelings. Only, in Barry's case, Christopher's anti-Semitism quickly became erotic. It made him hot to mate Barry's aggressiveness with his own, in wrestling duels which were both sexual and racial, Briton against Jew. Barry's aggressiveness became beautiful and lovable when it was expressed physically by his strong lithe body grappling naked with Christopher's. As they struggled, Christopher loved him *because* he was a pushy arrogant Jewboy."

Even in the area of homosexuality, Isherwood exhibits a reactionary attitude toward sexual roles, references to male partners as "unalterably female," a "wife," "efficient as a nanny," "a good woman," a "truly feminine soul . . . properly domestic."

How reliable is this memoir? It depends on self-serving, years-ago recollections about a period when Isherwood might find himself "lying on the floor, dozy with drink"—not the clearest time for retention of memories. There are editorial vagaries to be considered, including confusion about the nature of profuse footnotes. Ellipses appear in ambiguous brackets. Occasionally the "I in the footnotes lapses into the "Christopher" of the memoir.

It would be good to think that Isherwood did not intend these journals to be published, that he did not want to be remembered the way they portray him; that they were private exercises to keep him writing. It would be good to think that he abandoned this Memoir because he recoiled from its damaging betrayal of friends, that he was repelled by its rancid attitudes. Perhaps he intended both the *Diaries* and *Lost Years* to find a place in his archives, not in leering public.

The rationale for their publication is emphasized in the foreword by editor Katherine Bucknell: Though "never completed," these entries were "also never destroyed."

The final irony of this shoddy performance is that, for all its broadsides at others, the figure most assaulted is Isherwood himself.

POSTSCRIPT: Why those related to Isherwood allowed this embarrassment to be published is a mystery. It makes Isherwood look silly, childish—and he could be both. His claim that he never made hopeless passes yanked me back to the time, before *City of Night* was published—only a few sections had appeared in literary quarterlies—when he invited me to dinner and a visit to his home. Flattered by the attention of this famous writer, I accepted gladly. Because I didn't have a car at the time, he picked me up. We had a wonderful dinner and terrific conversation back at his home in the Canyon, near the ocean. Before the fireplace, I felt very much a writer, talking literature. I accepted his invitation to spend the night in his guest room, since it was then about 3 A.M. Instead he led me into his own bedroom—"It is a big bed," he said. It was, but he wouldn't stay on his side. So I insisted on sleeping in the guest room he had offered. I had barely gotten into bed there, when there he was. He became very angry at being turned down. I was at that time conflicted and disoriented about whether I was being viewed as a writer or a hustler, and I found it difficult to shift from being seen as one, and, then, the other. He refused to drive me back. So I had to walk down the canyon, down, down, to the Pacific Coast Highway, to hitchhike my way back to downtown Los Angeles, miles away. God was with me, and I was picked up by a gentleman who gave me a ride and made me $20.00 richer. . . . Now I wouldn't be telling this story if Isherwood hadn't written, in his published diaries, malicious tales about all his guests, who had previously considered themselves trusted friends, friends he courted. Both the diaries and *Lost Years* exhume a nasty voice from the grave.

And this: He once gave me sagacious advice about using "real people" in fiction, something he had done in virtually every one of his novels. "You can say anything about their ethics, their morals—even call them evil—as long as you describe them as attractive," he advised. I did just that in a novel *(Numbers)* in which he thought he saw himself. I describe him as quite attractive. (The artist Paul Cadmus said it was too flattering a portrait.) Even so, Isherwood was mightily miffed.

This remains: He was a superb prose stylist, and his *A Single Man* is a flawless jewel.

RANDY DANDY: LIBERACE, AMERICAN BOY (2001)

OFTEN CONSIDERED THE most popular entertainer of the twentieth century—his extravagant performances set still-unchallenged attendance records—Liberace (dubbed Mr. Showman in tribute to his theatricality) sued a London columnist in 1956 for implying he was gay. He won. At the same time, virtually everyone in gossipy gay bars knew that he was not only gay but very active in his homosexuality; and in his popular television and concert shows, he flaunted queeny ways, cultivated a purry lisp, donned glittery costumes. Still, up until before his death, he refused to admit publicly that he was gay.

A pervading atmosphere of homophobia in his time kept him in the closet, and today he is excoriated by an assertive faction of gay activists for staying there, considering him a reprehensible reactionary, and—in severest politically correct judgment—a "stereotype."

In his intelligent biography of this complex man, Darden Asbury Pyron makes an unusual confession: "Insofar as the criticisms identified the entertainer as a womanish, lower-class, consumer sissy who corrupted art ... I was not eager to justify, much less identify with such a figure." His agent warned against undertaking the biography: "What does a dead, closeted queen performer ... have to say to contemporary gay men?" As Pyron persevered, his view altered: ". . . I came to respect him, in some ways even to admire him. And . . . he never bored me." That duality of point of view allows him to explore contrasting aspects of the star. Like the performer, he never bores.

Wladziu Valentino Liberace, born in West Allis, Wisconsin, 1919, made a spectacular entrance at birth: The survivor of male twins, he appeared with a mysterious membrane veiling his head, a caul that, among Italian-Polish Catholics of his ancestry, was believed to portend an exceptional life, perhaps genius. It certainly augured later dramatic entrances: He once swooped onstage strapped to wires, rhinestone-spattered cape flying.

Classically trained, a child prodigy, Liberace idolized Ignace Paderewsky. At age 23, he soloed with the Chicago Symphony Orchestra and won praise. He shifted to more lucrative venues, supper clubs, and television; he produced successful record albums. With eminently less success, he starred in two movies. Hugely popular at his height as a concert entertainer, he broke attendance records at Madison Square Garden, the Hollywood Bowl and Radio City Music Hall. He dismissed disdainful critics by claiming: "I cried all the way to the bank."

Blessed or cursed with good-boy looks, he fawned over his "Mom," often bringing her onstage, smiling her a toothy good night when she wasn't in the audience. Middle-aged and older women adored him. He became every American apple-pie Mom's ideal son, the son who would never leave her, never find another woman as wonderful as she, and if he was gay—and didn't he deny it?—he would never embarrass her by coming out. (Pyron, who sweetly dedicates his book to his own mother, suspects incestuous yearnings among Liberace's female fans; but those doting Moms were much too plain, too unglamorous, too unsexy for anything as exotic and un-American as incest.)

In private, Liberace could be notoriously assertive in his homosexuality. During a formal dinner, an attractive male (this modest reviewer), seated next to him by compliant hosts (anticipating a return favor, perhaps a gold-leafed "antique"), was startled by a hand wandering under the table long before dessert. The performer was crafty. If tears were needed to achieve a seduction, he would cry, lamenting his starry isolation. (A performance this reviewer had occasion to be exposed to when it was strategically staged in the star's Hollywood mansion while pampered beribboned black and white poodles skittered nervously about on black and white marble floors.) If more tangible blandishments were required, he would extend them—jewels, a cottage in Palm Springs. He was famously generous, lavishing gifts on friends and assistants. He would provide salaried positions in his entourage to former intimate companions. Still, his gifts could be grotesquely selfish. He paid for plastic surgery to be performed on longtime companion Scott Thorson, in order to make the young man look like him. (More likely, Thorson became, then, a version of what Liberace would have liked to look like when he was young—masculine, handsome.) The performer's generosity had strict limits. Those who violated his expectations were banished—like Thorson, who, after exile, sued the star for palimony and won a meager out-of-court settlement.

Relying prominently on previous biographies, media accounts, and Thorson's memoir, *Beyond the Candelabra,* Pyron surprisingly includes few unpublished reports by those still living who knew Liberace. That creates gaps, at times mistakes. Left a tantalizing blank here is what became of Thorson after his banishment and well-recorded involvement with drugs and mobsters. (In recent televised biographies of Liberace, Thorson, in apt paradox, has begun to look and act like the middle-aged Liberace.)

Pyron recounts a version of the wandering-hand interlude at a formal dinner and places it ten years earlier than its actual occurrence, thus rendering askew his contextual conclusions about the performer's developing "randiness" (Pyron's quaint word). Citing this reviewer as a source, he attributes to Liberace's Palm Springs excesses a spooky "dress-only-in-white party" that occurred in Hollywood and was not given, nor even attended, by the performer.

What makes Pyron's book impressive is his astute interpretation of the forces that shaped Liberace. He draws a sharp picture of the Midwest during the Depression. He analyzes the pressures to succeed among Liberace's immigrant ancestors, and the consequent entrenched conservative values that the performer absorbed. He details the sexually restrictive influence of Catholicism on Liberace, who as a boy considered becoming a priest. He quotes Eve Kosofsky Sedgwick's provocative *Epistemology of the Closet* on the allure of the priesthood for young gay males: "the possibility of adults who don't marry, of men in dresses, of passionate theatre . . . images of the unclothed or unclothable male body, often in extremis and/or ecstasy . . . to be gazed at and adored." (Although he did not become a priest, Liberace discovered substitutes for that vocation. His costumes found antecedents in the bejeweled ostentation of high priestly garb, draggy cassocks, swishy robes, winking pendants. Votive candles evolved into his trademark candelabra. His acolytes were muscular attendants.)

Because Pyron located virtually no record of Liberace's sexual activities during early decades, he assumes that the performer must have frequented what is pervasively referred to as "the homosexual underground." However flawed that conjecture may or may not be, it gives Pyron a chance to roam with lively zeal through the landscape of outlaw encounters—movie balconies, sweaty bathhouses, and—famously—the standing-room section of the Metropolitan Opera (where gay men related to each other, as the divas they worshiped displayed their own throaty talents onstage).

Pyron falls into the prevalent trap of dividing gay history into only two steadfast periods, "pre-Stonewall" and "post-Stonewall," the former judged as repressive, the latter extolled as liberated. Overemphasis on that single event (a gay riot in

New York in 1969) distorts the history of gay courage and diminishes other acts of equivalent defiance, several occurring years earlier, but not as widely documented or eulogized, in Los Angeles and San Francisco during much more dangerous times. Nor did repressive elements disappear after the New York riot. They lessened. As before, there were advances and regressions. Within arbitrarily branded territory, however, Liberace is easily relegated to "pre-Stonewall" purgatory as a cowardly stereotype, judgment affirmed.

True, the performer obsessively denied his homosexuality in public. At the libel trial in London, he swore under oath that he was not gay. He often pretended to be on the brink of marriage (not unlike many other gay stars of the time and of today, several of the most famous of whom are aggressively married). He boosted his denials by pointing out that he was a Catholic, and that the Church judged homosexuality a sin.

To accurately evaluate Liberace's behavior requires placing him within the social climate of the country as he grew into it. Homophobia was accepted even among so-called liberal intellectuals. *New York Times* Critic Howard Taubman waged a war of innuendo on Liberace, and soon extended his assaults to an imagined "homosexual mafia" that included William Inge, Edward Albee, and Tennessee Williams. *Confidential* magazine destroyed Singer Johnny Ray with only a suggestion of attempted homosexual activity. Movie studios bartered with that magazine: Withhold a scandal about a moneymaking heterosexual star in exchange for revelations about expendable gay actors.

There were graver dangers. Police followed cruising gay men home, waited, and then broke in and arrested them having sex. Such consensual homosexual acts, between adults, in private, were punishable with five or more years in prison, lifelong registration as a "sexual offender," and, at times, with simultaneous aversion shock therapy. (Vice arrests in private are legal even today; a 1986 Supreme Court decision let stand the arrest of two consenting Georgia adults arrested at home; imprisonment is still possible.)

In context of those dangers, Liberace may be seen as a radical *trompe l'oeil* by the very nature of his "flamboyant" presentation. Like other banished "stereotypes"—those easily spotted, often noble early transgressors (including drag queens) who, reexamined, may reveal a powerful source of pioneer courage—Liberace may be viewed as a saboteur, an infiltrator unsettling homophobic consciousness. To judge him for his refusal to come out during very perilous times is to ignore the fact that even today there are, for some, dangers in doing so. Barbara Walters—all daggery smiles and arm-locking hugs—flirted with wrecking the career of a young male star recently when she tried to corner him into answering whether he is gay.

The weakest passages in Pylon's book involve attempts to pin down Liberace's sexual activities. What positions did he assume? What types of men did he choose? Did his tastes shift? If he had a liaison with Rock Hudson, who did what? Pyron thereby succumbs to another prevalent trap, the attempt to categorize homosexual desire, to assign staunch sexual roles—an impossible task.

At the end, Liberace's life shifted from gothic to tragic. The man who sued to prove he was not homosexual contracted AIDS and retreated in now-doubled despair to his Palm Springs mansion. "I don't want to be remembered as an old queen who died of AIDS," he said.

He died a sad figure in what must have been brutal physical and psychological pain. More horror was to come. Angling for a share of fame at the star's expense, a small-town coroner recalled the performer's body on its way to burial, in order to perform a further autopsy that would assert death by AIDS. The performer was cruelly outed as a corpse.

Pyron's recounting of Liberace's life provides a strong answer to his agent's question about the relevancy of the performer's life:

Liberace, Pyron deduces, lived as "an American Boy"; but, as a member of the conservative political and religious wing of Americans, "he confirmed their values even as he transgressed them." That courageous form of transgression makes Liberace relevant today, certainly it provides an admonitory example to factions of politically conservative homosexuals.

Still, Liberace's many fans will choose to remember the remarkable performer for a reason uncompromised by other aspects of his life and death, the sole reason for his endurability: "He put on one hell of a show!"

POSTSCRIPT: Liberace exemplified the song "Looking for love in all the wrong places." After the groping dinner described here, Liberace left and called our hosts to ask me to please visit him because he was very lonely, on the verge of tears. Naive as that may sound, I responded, thinking the famous man felt rejected, truly despondent. In his mansion—again I confess horrible naïveté, but I truly felt sorry for him—I was genuinely disappointed to discover that his invitation was for reasons other than to talk—he was ushering me into his bedroom (his bed was a throne), and I ended the visit, again disoriented by the change in expectations; we ended up on good terms though. . . . Later he sent my mother—a major fan, who loved, she told me, the way he ended his programs by saying, "Goodnight, ladies"—a miniature piano and an autographed photograph." I liked Liberace; he was a kind man.

HOLY DRAG! (2001)

Impressions of an entirely lapsed Catholic on attending a performance of High Mass presided over by the cardinal in Rome on a recent visit:

AFTER THE MASS: there they came, the opulent squadron of prelates making their processional way toward the sacristy, past entranced parishioners in the pews, the cardinal at the helm, followed by high prelates—the young good-looking ones cherishing their coveted place close to the cardinal, and he clearly cherishing theirs. Their gorgeous red gowns, topped by blousy hip-length cassocks, barely kissed the floor, making seductive sounds—swish, swish, sigh, sigh. The procession of priests drifted on like red ships with white sails. They accepted with a nod the hands stretched out to them by the congregants, and the cardinal gliding by waved airy blessings at them, the way movie stars blow kisses at the fans in the bleachers during the Academy Awards, and all amid the wafting of perfumy incense emanating from swinging censers—swing, swing, swing, sigh, sigh, swish, swish. Oh, and the glitter of rings and necklaces and pendants and belts—sparkle, sparkle, swish, swing, sigh—and on they swept, the cardinal and his prelates in their stunning gowns and spangles and flirtatious beeds—and the cardinal, catching sight of a muscular man in a tight shirt, paused to stare appreciatively—

and then, swish, swoosh!—out of sight, into the sacristy to change into less glamorous but still stylish attire, a subdued black outfit, with only a touch of contrasting white, a long dressy cassock, a shock of bold red. Irresistible temptation: a peek into the sacristy while the prelates changed! Why, it was like the dressing room of Las Vegas showgirls, red gowns swooped and scooped up by eager little acolytes—sweep, sweep, scoop, swish, sigh, sparkle, swoop!—and there it was, a crush of red velvet and coy sequins, removed gowns and smart accessories that young acolytes cherished and held close to themselves, garments worn by the cardinal and his favorites. Sweep, scoop, swish, sigh, scoop, sparkle, sparkle, wink!

Then it all turns ugly. These men are the hypocrites who uphold the strictures of the political party they represent—the Church—strictures that have condemned and damned and tortured and persecuted and prosecuted and ostracized countless human beings throughout history: during the Inquisition, burning and torturing innocent people for blasphemy, sexual transgressions; strictures that today account for a climate of condoned hatred toward all who deviate from their sanctimonious admonitions and prohibitions and accusations about sex, homosexuality, divorce, birth control, and (until recently but the entrenched hatred lingers) the "complicity" of Jews. These are the men, these prelates, who today uphold some of the most corrupt notions about society, resulting in gay-bashings, unchecked births creating poverty and hunger, the lessening of women. These are so-called abstinent men! (Abstinent? Really? Surely the hypocrisy extends beyond their mouthings of abstinence, into their guarded cloisters.) Yet they presume authority over all sexual matters! . . .Why abstinent? In early centuries, popes and cardinals and priests married and had children—and kept mistresses and misters—and amassed staggering wealth. Marriage produced heirs, though, and that contained an explosive threat to the Church's vast wealth. What if the heir of a prelate laid claim to the Church's wealth? The demand for celibacy solved that detail.

PostScript: Even greater hypocrisy is revealed daily now, with accounts of rampant child molestation, about the men who uphold strictures for others, men who continue to stigmatize homosexuals in an attempt to exorcise their own desires. During the 2004 presidential campaign, a number of priests apparently took time out from molesting children in order to decry as sinful a vote for candidates who supported a woman's right to abortion.

THE HORROR, THE HORROR: THOUGHTS ON THE AFTERMATH OF SEPTEMBER 11 (2001)

"THE HORROR, THE horror." So says Colonel Kurtz in Joseph Conrad's *The Heart of Darkness* about the spectrum of atrocities that war creates. Those words express the reaction of all civilized people to the murder of more than 4,000 men and women, and the wounding of as many others, in the homicidal attacks by Osama Bin Laden terrorists on the World Trade Towers in New York and on the Pentagon on September 11, 2001.

So vast is the multiplying horror—more anticipated terrorist strikes, intimations of germ warfare and nuclear attacks, the protracted bombing of Afghanistan—that new events occur each day like stark projected images quickly supplanted by others, resulting at times in surreal juxtapositions, many assuming clarity only in retrospect.

"I think it's the end of the age of irony," *Vanity Fair* editor Graydon Carter proclaimed. Whatever that vague statement meant exactly, irony was not dead; it abounded on the surrealistic landscape carved by the terrifying events of that branded day.

While those still alive dealt with the bloody aftermath of the assault on the Towers, ex-governor Bush of Texas (appointed as their own president by a partisan Supreme Court) and Dick Cheney fled into hiding, the ex-governor emerging to echo

Franklin Roosevelt's "We have nothing to fear but fear itself." While the imminent threat of anthrax to mostly minority postal employees was ignored, a similar threat on congressional representatives sent them scurrying away—after they sang "God Bless America." With glittery lapel pins depicting the American flag, Wall Street investors panicked, sinking the economy further.

In a speech announced as being about terrorist threats to the nation, ex-governor Bush instructed the country to give a boost to his brother, Florida governor Jeb: "Go about your business, fly, go to Disneyland in Florida." Ostensibly to speak once again about the anthrax crisis and the looming bombing of Afghanistan, the ex-governor pushed at businessmen his "stimulus package" that amounts to war-profiteering, allowing large corporations huge gains derived from the current quagmire.

In turning the undeclared war against Afghanistan into a "crusade against evil," he became a strutty Western sheriff in a B-movie. He wanted Bin Laden "dead or alive." He continued to pepper his speeches with Bushisms: "We will fail," he said, meaning—perhaps, "We will prevail." He warned that this is not "an instant gratification war," and reminded: "I'm a lovin' kinda guy." In an attempt at folksy camaraderie at the site of Ground Zero with cameras attending, he leaned so heavily on an old veteran fireman that the man threatened to topple over.

Swamped with millions of dollars in contributions for the victims of the September 11 bombings, the Red Cross floundered about how and to whom to distribute the donated amount, while the survivors and the families of the victims—now that the tributes and ceremonies for the dead were over—were left to face not only the sorrow of their loss but a future snarled in red tape. Criticized, the charitable organization offered to return donations to angered donors, then retracted.

Flags proliferated in an ocean of patriotism. But patriotism was not under assault, was it? Why not a new flag expressing unique sorrow over this disaster, and a sense of hope for the future, like the yellow ribbons that anticipated the return of veterans? The relevant question, How dare they do this? was reduced to: How dare they do this to us? Artifacts from the Cold War resurged: "America: luv it or leave it."

Amid the wash of patriotism, the question recurred: Why do they hate us so much? Nothing condones the murderous assault of September 11; yet it is not a slight on the tragedy to state that much of the hatred of America is self-induced. Despite the increasing calamity of our own homeless people and the poverty and hunger of millions, there is a worldwide perception of opulence in America. Consider only these minor current manifestations: An ad for baubles from Tiffany that appears almost daily in the Los Angeles Times, located beside a page-two condensation of world events, offered a diamond necklace for just under a million dollars; juxtaposed with the ad were news photographs of tattered Afghans fleeing the bombings. An Associated Press item was headlined: "How to Accessorize the Perfectly Pampered Pet."

It became dangerous to say that America has a checkered historical past, that it often flaunts its arrogance as the mightiest power. That power has often been misused in support of despots—Batista, Pinochet, the Shah of Iran, many others. America, too, has blood on its hands, bloodshed in Vietnam, Cambodia, the Middle East. Treason! Anyone who dared suggest that not all was righteous on the darkening horizon was denounced—Susan Sontag, Bill Mahers, dotty old Andy Rooney, and even that stalwart figure of integrity Walter Cronkite, who decried the imperious, and impervious, American belief that "the power of our arms will dictate a quick victory."

The splash of patriotism led to wretched excess: At a Calvin Klein fashion show, male models in jockey shorts later held hands and sang "God Bless America." In Laguna Niguel a cluster of nubile girls gathered at a street corner with signs proclaiming: "Honk if you love America." At each honk, one pretty little girl jumped and did a patriotic split, causing a male driver to make a dangerous U-turn to reassert his patriotism. In Louisiana, three teenagers who terrorized a group of elderly bingo players with squirt guns that the elders confused for terrorist guns were sentenced by a patriotic judge to write an essay titled "Why I'm proud to be an American."

Even self-announced liberals deserted logic and draped themselves in patriotism. After issuing a cominiqué from one of her mansions stating, "I get very upset when I see big business and corporations getting [favored] over working people," Barbra Streisand hurried to toss her support to the ex-governor of Texas. If Barbra speaks, can Warren be far, far behind? Mr. Beatty ("the technology is to blame," he keeps declaring in answer to any question) followed in dogged flaggy support. Eminem has not been heard from; but fickle Elton John prepared to recycle his all-purpose "Candle in the Wind" (first awarded to Marilyn Monroe, then snatched away to be given to Princess Di—nothing for Mother Teresa) to honor the victims of the assaults. The Emmys finally went on. ("Let history record that," said the president of the Academy). In dutifully mournful clothes, the Emmy attendees shed rivers of tears at each patriotic reference. Even those performers who were secretly watching the World Series wept along.

Impervious to trivialities, Cuban exiles in Florida opened the Elian Museum, displaying to the world his precious toys, togs 'n' things.

In a closing message by the Assembly of Bishops, their holinesses from around the world condemned terrorism. Their statement, released by the Vatican, went on to decry "the fact that 80% of the world's population lives on 20% of the income." Was the report sent aloft from one of his highness the pope's palaces, or from one of the lesser palaces occupied by the blessed cardinals and bishops?

Vultures hovered and scratched with their talons. Creepy things crawled out from under rocks: Pat Robertson and Jerry Falwell justified the treacherous attacks by terrorists as God's deserved wrath against feminists and homosexuals. Falwell's son asked devoted followers to soothe the subsequent criticism of his father by sending in a donation of fifty or even a hundred dollars. TV evangelists and millionaires Paul and Jan Crouch hosted quivering preachers who echoed Falwell's denunciation. In empathy, Sister Jan perpetually wept giant tears under the huge blond wig that threatens to swallow her head and the mascara-laden eyelashes that might blind her first. The son of Sister Jan and Brother Paul (Brother Son?) said God had timed the raid on the Towers and the Pentagon to correspond with the release of a dingy apocalyptic movie he produced. In Afghanistan, as Taliban forces caved in to the so-called Northern Alliance of often-warring tribes, opium-poppy growers celebrated the restoration of their only sure means of gaining big wealth, the production of heroin.

On the Internet, cheap "survival kits"—gloves, masks—were hawked for high prices; for a hundred bucks you could buy an anthrax detector, batteries included. An advertisement in the *Los Angeles Times* exhorted people to face the world bravely—with a new face created by the advertiser, a plastic surgeon.

Meanwhile ...

A million-dollar investigation by independent media about the irregularities of voting in Florida during the turbulent presidential election resulted in findings that asserted ... nothing. What remains clear is that if all ballots (including those with indications that they were intended for Gore) had been counted, Gore would be president. What remains more emphatic is that Gore was elected by a large margin of the popular vote. What remains equally unassailable is that Cheney, from his hiding place (only God and Allah know where he and Bin Laden are) is the real president. (President Clinton—the last elected president— please come back!)

Polls declared that the approval rating of ex-governor Bush had soared. Not surprising, since support grows for any president during war, especially among the majority of people who remain initially uninformed and so confuse support of the government with patriotism. It happened during the Vietnam war until the reality of the debacle infiltrated the general consciousness and drove Lyndon Johnson out of office. That shifting of consciousness is increasingly reflected in newspapers by the majority of letters to the editors that question current dangerous trends, abroad and at home.

Whose side is God on?

Ex-governor Bush of Texas asserted that the Deity is on our side, members of the Taliban asserted that Allah is on theirs. More chilling "religious" words were uttered: "Our young men love death the way Americans love life," Bin Laden was quoted. A checklist left behind by one of the four hijackers noted: ". . . remember that this is a battle in the sake of God, which is worth the whole world and all that is in it." A little boy in San Francisco shouted on television: "Kill a thousand of them for one of ours!"

Amid revelations of ignored years-ago warnings of impending terrorism and germ warfare, squabbling FBI and CIA officials admitted they lacked expertise to deal with further threats, despite millions of dollars spent on a new crime lab and special units for hazardous materials and instruments of mass destruction. Was the FBI overworked in its pursuit of pornographers? Finally a break occurred in the million-dollar hunt for the perpetrator of anthrax terrorism when the FBI announced: The criminal is "a man, a loner who possibly has a connection to a lab." Now let's go get 'im!

The fifth victim of anthrax, a 94-year old woman, Ottilie W. Lundgren, provided—and even her sweetly benign name contributed to—a metaphor for the whole, grotesque cruelty and indifference of the perpetrator of the mailings, increasingly believed to be a home-grown right-wing maniac.

What about the four Tommies? Director of Health and Human Services Tommy Thompson claimed the first case of anthrax came from a contaminated river. Tommy J. Ridge, head of the Office of Homeland Security, was stunned into silence by direct questions during his first briefing after the disasters; he stuttered, visibly perspiring, through stage fright. Tommy J. Pickard, the number two man at the FBI, announced an untimely retirement, abandoning the investigation into the anthrax mailings. General Tommy Franks, commander of U.S. troops, granted few briefings and said nothing about casualties of the bombings, nor about the extent of destruction, but he did emphasize: "We are winning." (In current military jargon, dead civilians are called "collateral damage.")

Though not a Tommy, Defense Secretary Donald Rumsfield (Donny?) contributed to the unique, evasive performance of ex-governor Bush's cast of characters. Asked whether certain Taliban forces were dead or running out of Afghanistan, he provided this answer: "Life isn't perfect."

Without the necessary requirement of a declared war, ex-governor Bush granted military tribunals the right to try and to sentence—and to carry out punishment on, even to execute—those deemed to be war criminals. Consistent with such a robbery of due process, thousands of foreigners have been rounded up (like the Japanese during World War II); they remain incommunicado, even from their families—400 agents, 1,200 suspects; and on the airways there is talk of government-condoned torture of the detainees. The FBI admits it has no evidence that any of the confined are connected to the terrorist act. Now it is creating software that, planted secretly via the Internet, will record every stroke of a computer.

At the Museum of Television & Radio in Beverly Hills, Walter Cronkite addressed those violations of human rights and intimations of censorship, blaming the federal government and the military: "Americans aren't getting enough information about the U.S. military effort in Afghanistan." He denounced "a violation of everything that we believe in, our rights as citizens of a democracy."

There were still more violations. Old people and the poor became silent victims of the burgeoning events as campaign promises of relief for expensive drugs and of insurance for the vulnerably uninsured were shoved aside.

"Yes, I call CEOs 'honey.' but to me, that's wry Texas humor," laughed the woman appointed by ex-governor Bush to persuade the Muslim world that the U.S. is not the enemy. The Madison Avenue executive went on to describe her style at client meetings: "I'm likely to say the most outrageous thing in the room—to liven things up." ("Muslims, honeys, we're not for y'all, just against y'all. Just kiddin', honeys, jumblin' up words like my boss, to get your attention an' liven things up.")

To assert its alerted consciousness to critical matters, the Supreme Court considered definitions of . . . pornography. Antonin Scalia, looking more and more like a judge of the Inquisition, made a startling admission: "I don't know what simulated sex is." Even within his busy schedule in keeping track of terrorists—unsuccessfully—Attorney General John Ashcroft (as fanatic a Christian fundamentalist as are some Afghans about their own Muslim fundamentalism) found time to file a suit against Oregon's right-to-die ordinance.

Amid the chaos, there remain memories of acts of courage. The passengers on the hijacked Boeing 757 on flight 93, alerted by cell phones that they were on a forced mission of destruction, took over the airplane, choosing to crash it in a field that would kill no one but them and the terrorists. (The deserved celebration of those men and women does not undermine the unknown acts of those on the other disastrous flights, who were not aware, until the exact moments of horror, that they were being used to assault the Towers and the Pentagon.) There were equally courageous individual acts—most of them unrecorded—of people who helped others, often the handicapped, out of the fiery inferno of the Towers; and there were the men and women of organizations aiding survivors of the victims in America as well as victims of the bombings in Afghanistan.

There were moments that stirred joy: photographs of Afghan women removing their veils, symbols of their brutalization; a picture of an Afghan soldier placing a flower in the mouth of his rifle while Taliban forces fled.

As the flags that proliferated after the bombings in America grow old—strips of red, white, and blue often fall along freeways, whipped up by speeding cars—there are new, daily realities to cope with: The reality depicted by photographs of long lines of displaced Americans applying for a few jobs; accounts of families waiting for promised relief in seeking new shelter while they attempt to renew their altered lives; photographs of other families, Afghan families, huddled in rags, fleeing the bombings against a drought-seared gutted background of desolation.

The bombs continue to drop—along with packages of food containing messages informing Afghan civilians that the bombs may fall on them but they are not aimed at them. Delivered by airplanes in the dark morning hours, some food packages crash into mud-brick dwellings, injuring people. Some packets land in mined areas.

While Bin Laden hides after unleashing new violence on a ravished country as a result of the murders in America, more than 6 million Afghan civilians—as innocent as the thousands who died in the terrorist attacks on September 11, as innocent as the Afghan civilians who have died in the bombings—face starvation during the freezing winter in a country of entrenched poverty. News photos of ragged children haunt almost daily now, some—who have never known a time of peace—scavenge through garbage; others roam deserted streets. Those children inevitably reveal pained, ancient eyes, eyes that don't seem to know whom to accuse.

The horror, the horror.

BEATIN' AROUND THE BUSH (2002)

I N HIS RECENT war talk about "the axis of evil," ex-governor of Texas George Bush promised he would not "wait on" events to unfold in the war on terrorism. Is ex-governor Bush intending to become a waiter?—a true servant of the people, "waiting on" tables at his next fund-raiser? Or is it possible he meant he would not "wait for" events? Difficult to tell when someone is trying to sound like plain ole folks but also happens to be just a tad syntactically challenged.

What this nonelected official is clearly not "waitin' on" is shredding the Social Security surplus, allowing the environment to be poisoned, the land plundered—all in order to give Big Business Big Breaks (forget about Enron), at the same time continuing to pack his cabinet and the circuit courts with appointments that can only be compared to allowing foxes to assure the safety of the chicken coop.

The Democrats? They're still playing dead, the way they did (along with the major media, led by the *New York Times*, the first major newspaper to take up the Republican chant that Gore must concede "for the good of the country"), when the presidency was being stolen, right before all eyes, right on television. True, Democrats seem to have awakened at least briefly to pass the campaign reform bill in the House.

Now what about Sheriff Bush's media-vaunted "success" in the conduct of the war on terrorists? The sheriff's goals—y'all remember—were to "git bin Laden, dead or alive." Success? Where is the monstrous terrorist? Hiding in a cave, like Cheney? (Is it possible they're together?) Success? The only man charged with planning the September 11 attack on the Towers was released on bail by a court in England pending hearings on extradition, released because there was no solid evidence against him. (God help us if, despite that lack of solid evidence, he *was* involved in the atrocity and is now again dangerously on the loose.)

Success? The threat of terrorism increases daily; and those in charge of the country's safety can't locate even the local anthrax terrorist. Success? New Yorkers displaced by the Twin Towers bombings still struggle to stay afloat, still choke on red tape—and dust-polluted air—while trying to get needed treatment for injuries, despite promises of huge amounts of aid—and now, they must hear only echoes of patriotic songs and tributes. Success? Afghanistan, already pillaged by famine and poverty, is left to cope with even greater devastation, and the bombings continue.

Success? What success? Is it possible that the same relentless machinery of manipulation that shoved the ex-governor into office is now churning out propaganda about his "success"— asserting it by repetition (the way the manipulators kept repeating that the ex-governor had been elected) and making the assumption of complete success synonymous with being patriotic, thus sending his approval ratings soaring so he can get away with his destructive policies on the home front?

Yes, and what about the cast of odd characters that surround the sheriff? They seem to want to top him in . . . uh . . . unique behavior.

1. Prissy Attorney General Ashcroft spends $8,000 of taxpayer money to cover the proud breasts of the classic statue of a woman (the Spirit of Justice) that he was forced to stand

before—under—during his briefings in the Justice Department. What profound childhood trauma did those mighty breasts arouse in the attorney general?

2. In clarifying the current administration's decision to treat Afghan prisoners humanely but not as prisoners of war under the Geneva Convention, President of Military Justice Eugene R. Fidell (the name!), citing the very real need to gather information about possible future terrorist attacks, said: "You cannot torture, coerce or starve [the prisoners]. You can tell them they can have two slices of layer cake if they talk." Ah, cummon, Eugene, let 'em eat the whole cake, and I'll jist bet ya they'll spill th' beans!

3. At hearings about the limits or nonlimits of pornography and of digitally produced young cyber-figures simulating sex on the Web, intellectual giant Antonin Scalia, instrumental in pushing the illegitimate contender into the White House, thundered: "What great works of Western art should be taken away from us if we were unable to show minors copulating?"

Justice John Paul Stevens reminded ole Tony that Shakespeare's *Romeo and Juliet* involves an affair between two teenagers—Juliet is not yet fourteen, Romeo hardly older.

While snorting that he had not seen "that version" (oh, uh, Tony, did you ever-uh—have occasion to read the play?) Tony made a startling confession (somewhat wistfully?): "I don't know what is meant by simulated sex."

As the song says: "Send in the clowns. Don't bother, they're here."

Devastating clowns, these, eh?

POSTSCRIPT: I suspect that the reign of George Bush may augur the death of satire. Not even Swift could match the surrealism of this man's moronic declamations and devastating power.

SINS OF THE FATHERS (2002)

THEY CAME TO Rome in their black cassocks and red caps, like decorated penguins, the princes of the Catholic Church, 13 cardinals, responding to a summons by the pope, to deal with the revelation that more than two hundred American clergymen stood accused of sexual abuse of mostly young men, a few women. Like good Germans, their excellencies surely did not know what was occurring within their parishes, did they? They did know, had known for years, and had quietly transferred offending clerics to fertile new grounds, at times silencing victims with million-dollar settlements. (Now where do all those millions come from?)

The sins of the arrogant Catholic Church! From the time of the Inquisition, when hooded prelates sentenced to torture and painful death those they deemed a menace to their authority, on through the present, the church has contributed its power to some of the most evil acts on humanity. Centuries-long accusation of Jews as the murderers of Christ entrenched the detestation that culminated in the Holocaust, the murder of millions of Jews and thousands of other "undesirables," gypsies and homosexuals. Its attitudes concerning sexuality have rendered women inferior, chattels for child-bearing; have attempted to exile into imposed shame divorced couples; have created a climate of hatred that bashers use to legitimize violence against homosexuals; are responsible for a huge population of children, mostly minority children, children whose destitute families cannot care for adequately, children almost guaranteed turbulent lives, children born because birth control is forbidden. (Surreal paradox! Men who swear to be abstinent dictate the sexual conduct of those who aren't.)

Even before the parade of cardinals arrived in Rome, pretending like movie stars to dodge the press, cassocks hissing at the cobblestones, the pope had asserted adherence to the concept of celibacy among priests; there were bruitings that the subject might come up. Almost nodding off, the dotty pope extolled the "value of celibacy as a complete gift of self to the Lord . . . [a] life of chastity . . . willingly embraced and faithfully lived." He went on to remind the princes of the church of their vow of poverty, and did so from his opulent Roman palace (while one of his cardinals basked in his own summer villa on Lake Como, along with his neighbors, the Versace family and Catherine Deneuve; and Cardinal Mahoney, of Los Angeles, surely longed to hurry back to his parish, and to his private airplane).

The concept of celibacy has been upheld for nine hundred years. Before that, high prelates had wives, mistresses (and misters). And children. As the wealth of the church burgeoned and its power spread across continents, the threat of children claiming rights of inheritance loomed. Out of such was born the lofty concept of "celibacy as a complete gift of self to the lord and his church"—a masquerade for greed; and the church did become abundantly rich, became one of the largest, wealthiest corporations in the world, with a powerful CEO, a tough board of directors. It is, however, one of the few corporations that does not offer to reward its investors financially.

Would allowing matrimony solve the problem of sexual predators within the clergy? Cloudy nonsense. Present allegations of abuse involve two women impregnated by priests and coaxed to abort. Pedophilia occurs far, far more often among heterosexuals, many married, than among homosexuals. Like the armed services, police corps, and other institutions that appeal to male exclusivity—and share a tight code of silence that shelters transgressors within their ranks—the priesthood naturally attracts its share of repressed homosexuals.

The accused priests are also victims of the Catholic Church. Before they became victimizers, they, too, were abused by the repressiveness of the church. A type of child raised in an atmosphere that bans all sexual activity other than as a means of procreation will feel trapped in a quagmire of guilt over sexual yearnings. The priesthood may seem the only salvation, offering surcease from "evil" longings, longings branded "unnatural . . . sinful." (Yet what is more "unnatural"—against nature—than to reject sexuality?) So the guilt-ridden priests seek escape from their "evil"—in an atmosphere of erotic masochism epitomized by a beautiful, naked male figure nailed to a cross, and emphasized further by icons like that of St. Sebastian, stripped chiseled body pierced by multiple arrows and twisting in passionate agony.

Freed from the pressures of the Church's crazy judgments, those men might have found natural outlets for desire, of whatever sexual orientation. In what is a cycle of molestation within the priesthood, they, too, were likely molested by older priests, even threatened into silence themselves, as later they would threaten their victims, often with intimations of hellish damnation.

As the scandal ramifies with daily disclosures—a six-year-old boy raped in the confessional—and with revelations of decades-long cover-ups and lies by the hierarchy of the church, there may develop a wave of baseless accusations of innocent priests, accusations like those that flared during the McMartin trials in Los Angeles, heated allegations about "naked movie star" games, secret tunnels. There are many good men in the priesthood, though far fewer in its power-driven hierarchy.

Now it is the Catholic Church that is under indictment for sexual abuse. But all rich, apathetic, greedy religions that purport hypocritically to serve the needful are guilty of violations that indict them all by the very nature of the existence of such abuses. Among those are the abuse of migrant children who grow up deformed from stoop labor; the abuse of the impoverished old; the abuse of runaways, often fleeing from molestation among their own families, sentenced to living under street tunnels; the abuse of the homeless, bundles of stirring rags everywhere.

No religion is blameless in the territory of injustice, and such injustices are perpetrated all too often in the name of God, Allah, G-d, Jehovah, et al.

CRUISE NOT GAY!
THE JUDGE HAS SPOKEN (2002)

THE NEWS THAT the besieged world has been awaiting is finally here, although it's taken some time for the impact of the revelation to sink in because of its cataclysmic enormity: Not only is actor Tom Cruise not gay, he "is not, and never has been, homosexual and has never had a homosexual affair." So agreed a Superior Court judge in accepting a stipulation to that effect. In exchange, Cruise dropped a $100 million defamation suit against the publisher of *Bold* magazine for claiming to be in possession of a picture of Cruise having sex with another man. Cruise's lawyer trumpeted the victory: "[Cruise is] not gay, and the judge so ruled."

The judge so ruled! Never before has a court of law been called upon so overtly to establish the sexual orientation of a party. Although ludicrous, the matter carries nasty implications.

Cruise's rise to fame began when he danced in his shorts in a movie called *Risky Business*. Although then he was a somewhat pudgy ordinary young man—not yet extravagantly remade— that scene allowed viewers to peek in on the naughty boy-next-door, arousing what is for some a gay fantasy. (Ironically, the truly sexual presence in the movie was sensational Rebecca de Mornay, and if that remark is interpreted as an indication that this writer is heterosexual, he will claim defamation and ask a judge to rule that he is gay.)

Cruise's court action is not the first involving such libelous overtones. In 1956, Liberace sued a London columnist for implying he was gay. Under oath, the performer swore he was not. Legend claims that with the money he collected—$22,000—he gave the gayest party in Hollywood history.

Nor is Cruise the only actor pursued by intimations of homosexuality, incorrect or not. In the past, several movie star careers were compromised, some wrecked, by such implications. Rudolf Valentino was derided after he was labeled a "powder-puff." Singer Johnny Ray was destroyed by an article in the infamous *Confidential* magazine that implied he had attempted a drunken pass on a man.

Other movie stars were able to overcome the rumors, even disregard them; some used them to enhance their sexual reputations—Errol Flynn basked in the aura of polysexuality. Tab Hunter survived a report of an arrest at a gay drag party. Rumors did not impede Laurence Olivier from becoming a British lord. Cary Grant flourished as a romantic leading man while living openly with Randolph Scott; *Photoplay* magazine featured the couple "at home." Grant even seemed to acknowledge his sexual orientation in one of his films. ("I've gone gay!" he blurts in *Bringing Up Baby* while donning a woman's nightgown.) Rock Hudson was widely known to cruise gay bars, and that did not affect his heterosexual image. In his autobiography, Marlon Brando informed that he had had a few homosexual affairs when he was young and that he was "not ashamed" of the fact.

Tyrone Power, Gary Cooper, even stalwart John Wayne and quintessential heterosexual idol Clark Gable were objects of similar rumors, and all survived them. Throughout the years, virtually every new young male star has been labeled gay, often only wistfully. Even performers who have made reported homophobic statements have come under suspicion, and they apparently remain uncompromised, including ex-Calvin Klein underwear model Mark Wahlberg, rap singer Eminen, and Eddy Murphy (even after being apprehended with a Santa Monica Boulevard transvestite).

Many of today's performers who find themselves objects of such rumors feel unthreatened and so are able to deal with the matter without panic. Recently Barbara Walters, all knifey smiles and arm-locking hugs, tried to coax Ricky Martin into declaring whether or not he is gay. Martin answered with cool composure that the matter of his sexuality is private. Though few seriously believe that they are other than close friends, Ben Affleck and Matt Damon disarm the innuendoes by joking about them, even allowing themselves to be photographed on the same bed. Being called upon to deny being gay, each has stated, is an insult to gay people.

True.

What sets Cruise apart from all this is the stridency of his reactions, the bombardment of statements vaunting his exclusive heterosexuality, the numerous defamation suits, threatened and actual. Perhaps dictated by those who influence his career, Cruise's magnified responses insult gay people (including gay fans he apparently welcomes at the box office) by conveying that it is so devastating even to be thought to be gay that one must go to court to be declared otherwise—and seek $100 million for the gross insult. Although Cruise, through one of his spokespeople, has denied harboring ill attitudes toward homosexuals, his actions resound in contradiction. Perhaps the worst aspect of those actions is the negative impact the offensive implications must have on young gay men struggling to come out.

Paradoxically, Cruise's conduct fuels the accusations. In a paraphrase of Shakespeare, "The laddy doth protest too much." It is not the scurrilous stories about him that find their way into the mainstream media. It is his response to them. Otherwise the gossip would be relegated only to tabloids barely glimpsed by most people while they wait in grocery-store checkout lines, gossip quickly disregarded along with tales of folks dining regularly with green aliens. Before Cruise's court action, who had heard of *Bold* magazine?

Now that a court of law has asserted his heterosexuality, Cruise would gain stature if he ignored any more gossip about him with silent dignity, secure in his court-decreed heterosexuality and knowing that such accusations are staples in all public careers and that most people view them as such.

It might surprise Cruise to learn that very few people, including the vast majority of gay people, care whether he is gay or not, and that many within that gay majority have long hoped that he is not.

POSTSCRIPT: The man becomes pitiful in all his ferocious denials. I very much hope that he isn't gay.

BLONDE (2002)

WHEN DOES THE freedom of fiction become license?
That question occurs on reading Joyce Carol Oates's novelization of Marilyn Monroe's life, a question particularly relevant since, in a dumbfounding statement ("On the Composition of 'Blonde'") sent out with the book, the author claims permissive authority over her subject: ". . . the sole voice of BLONDE is Norma Jeane's, as if she's speaking to us, at last, out of her body and out of time. . . . I felt her fingers encircling my wrist. . . . I came to feel that Norma Jeane had no one but me to tell her story from the inside. How it felt, how it feels, to have been her . . . to be her. . . ."

Joyce Carol Oates as Norma Jeane?

Oates's musings would not be out of place in a coven of Hollywood channelers, nor in the mind of a Methody actress auditioning for a role she won't get. Coming from a reputable author, they require scrutiny.

Oates has taken on a formidable subject, Norma Jeane, who became Marilyn Monroe.

Indeed, the legend of Marilyn Monroe may eventually overtake that of Helen of Troy. Her image reigns over all others on the outside wall of the Chinese Theater. Her visage enthralls on street murals. Psychics proclaim visitations from their gorgeous

Madonna. Accounts of twentieth-century highlights acknowledge her commanding presence, right along with Einstein's. A single name evokes her. Marilyn!

While, according to Homer's *Iliad,* Helen's face launched a thousand ships, Marilyn has launched a thousand books. She is a Rorschach test for authors. In nonfiction accounts, Truman Capote discovered a playmate; Norman Mailer, a dead mistress; Gloria Steinem, an embarrassment for many women before tragedy transformed her. (This writer mythologized a possible daughter of hers and Robert Kennedy's.)

Did she suspect she would inspire such staggering attention? Biographical evidence indicates otherwise. She had been discarded by two most powerful men, John and Robert Kennedy. (But history will link them to her forever.) She feared she had inherited her mother's insanity, once committing herself to a psychiatric ward, unable to get herself out. Believing her beauty gone (though final photographs reveal greater beauty), addicted to prescription drugs, her career in disarray, she died despondent at age thirty-six in 1962.

Her real last name is in ambiguity—Baker or Mortensen?— her father unknown. She revised important details of her life (contending her mother was dead although she was in an institution). When she was discovered dead in her bedroom in the only house she ever owned, mystery swirled around her, especially since she was still clutching a telephone. Calling whom? Was she murdered? Did she commit suicide? Did she surrender to an accidental overdose? She died virtually insolvent, but, in harsh paradox, her estate, controlled by a woman she never knew—the second wife of Lee Strasberg, a man Marilyn purportedly intended to remove as heir—is worth millions; even in death, her features are owned, jealously guarded, expensively rented.

She is now lovingly celebrated—and grossly used. The fact that she was a real woman—with a life of her own, with feelings of her own—is increasingly forgotten, undermined, or ignored.

The result is the almost-daily exploitation, the reckless looting, of her life and death. In his biography *Goddess: The Secret Lives of Marilyn Monroe,* Anthony Summers included a brutal photograph of her after autopsy. At Christie's, everything she touched went to the highest bidder. The famous dress she wore when she sang, "Happy Birthday, Mr. President" was sold for $1,267,500. An advertisement for unofficial stamps commemorating that auction exhorted: "Own a piece of Marilyn!" And now along comes Oates claiming to "be" Norma Jeane. In order to deal, first, with her novel as a novel, one must try to keep in abeyance her eery claim of ghostly intervention. Oates's characterization of Norma Jeane's mother as a wounded monster is plausible. Believing herself threatened by fire rimming the city, Gladys flees in a ragged car with Norma Jeane, and then shifts, toward the fire. "I want to see Hell up close. A preview," she says.

Oates effectively converts the burial of MGM mogul Irving Thalberg into a funeral of contrasts: Behind barricades, a throng waits: ". . . for film stars and other celebrities to arrive in a succession of chauffeur-driven limousines, enter the temple, and depart again after a length of ninety minutes, during which time the murmurous crowd . . . appeared disoriented, as if they'd suffered a great loss without knowing what it was."

A good scene depicts surfers saving Marilyn from a possibly suicidal drowning, then quietly recognizing her. Oates's fascination with the bizarre creates Boscheian surrealism throughout. Fans are: ". . . creatures of the under-earth. Hunchbacked gnomes & beggar maids & homeless females with mad eyes & straw hair. Those among us mysteriously wounded by life. . . ."

Matters go quickly awry. In turning Los Angeles into a hellish city as a backdrop for her dour narrative, Oates shoves grotesqueness into hysterical parody. She conjures an annihilation of children, ". . . nowhere in greater numbers than in southern California . . . their little corpses, often charred beyond recognition, were hastily swept off Los Angeles streets by sanitation workers, collected in dump trucks to be buried in unmarked mass graves. Not a word to the press or radio! No one must know." Except Oates?

Soon, "Death" bicycles through "the warm radioactive air of southern California where Death had been born." Death born in southern California!

Chapter titles like "The Lost One," "The Vision," and references to the "Fair Princess," the "Dark Prince" augur imposed allegory. Foggy loftiness sweeps into the language in italics: *"For what is time but others' expectations of us?"* That vasty tone is further elevated by the recurrence of the archaic conjunction "for," several on virtually every page, at times even in dialogue, and hundreds of biblical "ands." (*"For there is no meaning to life apart from the movie story. And there is no movie story apart from the darkened movie theater."*)

Allegory drains life from Oates's characters; and although at its best the agitated prose assumes urgency, her familiar literary stunts (exclamatory running sentences, racing ampersands, gasping blank spaces) serve only to interrupt an intrinsically powerful story.

Oates emphasizes: *"Improvising, you don't know where you're headed. But sometimes it's good."* Often, it isn't. As the novel stretches, the impression grows that it is an unusually rushed improvisation, an improvised first draft, by this admirably prolific author.

How else to account for pages of loose writing resulting frequently in unintended humor? ". . . Elsie kept Norma Jeane out of school for part of the morning to help her with the leaky Kelvinator washing machine and the wringer that was forever getting stuck and toting baskets of clothes outside. . . ."

How else to account for effects that have no discernible adventurous stylistic or narrative reason and that cause bafflement? Essential information (the death of Norma Jeane's grandmother and Gladys's contamination from film-cutting chemicals) is referred to, then explored, chapters later, as if introduced for the first time.

How else to account for murky observations straining for profundity? "Film is the repository of that which, failing to be remembered, is immortal." How to account for forgetful narrative reversals where required? A doll scorched by fire turns up again. How to account for an invasion of "suddenlys" and "somehows" instead of clear narrative reasons? ". . . for suddenly I realized . . ." "Yet somehow it happened." How to account for endless repetition and double-talk? "The Fair Princess . . . is so beautiful because she is so beautiful and because she is the Fair Princess. . . ." How to account for made-up undecipherable epigraphs on acting, like this memorable one? "The power of the actor is his embodiment of the fear of ghosts."

How to account for this? Halfway into the novel a character—not a Canadian—ends sentences by asking, "eh?" Soon everyone is asking, "eh?" Ava Gardner enters briefly and asks, "eh?" Peter Lawford asks, "eh?" Then "the president" asks, "eh?" Finally Marilyn asks, "eh?"

An "Author's Note" informs: "*Blonde* is a radically distilled 'life' in the form of fiction . . . synecdoche is the principle of appropriation." That disclaimer reads like a blurred excuse.

Of course, Oates is in firm territory within the literary tradition of fictionalizing real figures. Recent practitioners include Susan Sontag, E. L. Doctorow, Gore Vidal; all used historical persons, none cited visitations. Many writers have fictionalized Marilyn without employing her name (Paddy Chayefsky, Doris Grumbach). Michael Korda used Marilyn's name in *The Immortals,* a dismissible novel of almost sublime vulgarity, told from the point of view of a reporter.

Oates's synecdochic "appropriation" differs from all others in its presumed seizure of Norma Jeane's voice, an intermittent first-person voice that pretends to reveal Marilyn's most intimate thoughts—in self-recrimination. (". . . her own harsh judgment of herself," Oates unabashedly insists.) Thus, she takes lines from an actual interview in which Marilyn praised her own sexuality ("sex is a part of nature, and I go along with nature"), and, without differentiating, interjects her own lines, in order to twist Marilyn's celebration into the author's verdict: *"sad, sick cow piece of meat cunt that's dead inside."*

Writers are free to roam uncensored whatever territory they choose. But Oates should be called into account for taking a few salient and familiar events ("a selected symbolic few") from an actual life (one proximate in living memory), and from the lives of others still living (including Marlon Brando, Arthur Miller, and Marilyn's first husband), and then attaching lurid contrivances as a way of fitting them into evidence for her preconceived judgment upon that life, even going so far as to assert that her subsequent distortion has been spookily spoken—"at last"—by the subject of that distortion.

Rejecting a trashy script about Jean Harlow, Marilyn Monroe reportedly said, "I hope they don't do that to me." Reacting to proofs of photographs by Bert Sterne, she drew X's with red ink over those she disapproved of. They survive, shamelessly blown up, published. The slashes seem inked with blood.

"When confronted with the choice of enhancing Norma Jeane, or degrading her, as others have, I opted always for enhancing," Oates' statement about her novel maintains. Yet evidence abounds that to fulfill the allegorical requirements for "blonde" martyrdom, the author needed more abuse and heaped on her own. Is it conceivable, otherwise, that Norma Jeane's "fingers encircling [Oates's] wrist" would guide the author's hand to write passages included in this novel? Ignoring Oates's silly arrogation of Norma Jeane's identity, one may wonder how Marilyn, protective of her image, would react to portions of this book. She would encounter the following among many more linked to her name:

A scene in which her first husband ("the Embalmer's Boy"), redolent of embalming fluid, makes her up with cosmetics used on corpses—and takes erotic "before" and "after" pictures of her.

References to her soiling herself, her "hot scalding" urine, harsh periods, demeaning sexual positions.

Remarks ascribed to a nameless chorus but which Oates invents: "Look at you! Cow. Udders and cunt in everybody's face." "Can't get enough of Polish sausage." "You no more could predict what might emerge from that luscious Marilyn mouth than you could guess, or estimate . . ." etc.

A scene of her being sodomized with a "Thing . . . hard rubber," next to an aviary of "dead stuffed birds."

An account of her returning to "the Playwright" in graphic squalid disarray from an earlier sexual encounter, with "the semen of another man leaking from her cunt & the stink of the other's cigarette smoke (Camel's) in her matted hair. . . ."

A list of "Her lovers!"—including "Z, D, S, and T . . . Lugosi . . . Karloff . . . Roy Rogers and Trigger . . . Lassie. . . ."

An incident during which "a Valentine" turns out to be toilet paper with the word "WHORE" written in excrement.

A passage during which she fellates an indifferent "president," after which she's raped anonymously, urinates in the hall, is slapped by a secret serviceman, bleeds, and has a "wad of toilet paper" pressed to her wound.

A crassly cruel joke exchanged between "the president" and "one of his buddies" (in the presidential box!—as she "coos" "Happy Birthday" to him from the stage), derisively comparing her singing with her sexuality.

Yet Oates's character pleads with a photographer—as Marilyn pled with her last interviewer: "Don't make me into a joke . . . I beg you."

If, indeed, Oates opted for "enhancing" Norma Jeane when another choice would "degrade" her, and since those passages and others more audacious (the worst is reserved for her death) are Oates's fabrications, what alternatives occurred to her that would be even more degrading?

In constant expressions of disdain for her own male characters, Oates repeatedly describes their penises: "angry as a fist," "engorged with urine, sizzling and steaming into the toilet," a "tumescent sword," an "unruly pet," "frantic, bobbing," "limp and spent . . . like an aged slug." Even the ringing of a telephone becomes: "That jarring sound, that sound of mockery . . . that sound of male reproach."

In the single understatement explaining her novel, Oates acknowledges the "harshness of certain male portraits," but she hastens to inform that "these are from the perspective of Norma Jeane." (So! Norma Jeane made her do it!)

In a further bizarre distortion, Oates transforms two heterosexual men (minor Hollywood actors remembered only because of their famous fathers) into a pair of the most malicious gay men in memory. Marilyn's brief affair with Charles Chaplin, Jr.—known for affairs with women—ended when he found her with his brother. In Oates's reversal, Marilyn finds Chaplin, Jr. in bed with Edward G. Robinson, Jr., himself not known to be gay. To extend their villainy beyond the grave, she has Chaplin, Jr. die before Marilyn. (He outlived her by six years.) He leaves behind a note that finally reveals a vicious years-long charade the two devised involving Marilyn's lost father. The note is carried to her by "Death" mounted on a bicycle.

Is there a touch of rancid bitterness and resentment in morose accounts of Marilyn's life that attempt to undermine the fact that she accomplished what she set out to do, at least early in her life—to become a quintessential figure of desire? That is no mean attainment for a woman or a man. Is there a trace of envy in compromising Marilyn's exultation of her beauty? Is it possible to view her famous photographs and doubt that she delighted, justifiably, in her glorious body and face, and in the projection of her sensational sensuality?

However tragic Marilyn Monroe became, however abused by men (and she did become tragic, and she was abused by men, and by the women who ridiculed her), in turning her into a symbolic martyr, Oates demeans Marilyn's genuine sensuality, strips her dignity, reduces her strengths: surviving ruinous scandals, remaining financially independent during marriages to dominating men, and not relying on alimony afterwards; challenging the House Un-American Activities Committee; founding her own production company; proving herself a splendid actress and a highly intelligent woman.

Despite Oates's many disclaimers, the emergent portrayal is one of scorn for Marilyn Monroe. Without denying Oates's right to convey it, one may, with equal authority, assert one's indignation.

But no one, finally, can diminish Norma Jeane's grand triumph, the creation of the most astonishing figure in Hollywood history, the masterpiece called Marilyn Monroe.

POSTSCRIPT: I praised Ms. Oates too highly in this piece. I am still trying, unsuccessfully, to decipher: "The power of the actor is the embodiment of his fear of ghosts."

LAWRENCE BRINGS IT ALL BACK HOME (2003)

IN STRIKING DOWN the Texas law that made consensual sex in private between members of the same sex a criminal act, Justice Anthony M. Kennedy, speaking for the majority of the Supreme Court, wrote that the Texas law "demeans the lives of homosexual persons . . . entitled to respect for their private lives." By emphasizing the word "respect," Justice Kennedy was not only upholding the right of privacy, he was asserting human dignity. For many gay people, it is difficult to feel grateful. That the matter came up at all is disgraceful to every concept of human decency. For veterans of not-so-long-ago battles for equal rights, the decision will stir memories of outrages survived.

In the late 1950s, the McCarthy hearings aimed at identifying Commmist sympathizers had spread their poison to ferreting out homosexuals in the government. That created an exodus to California, a state always known for its liberal attitudes. Perhaps it was that new wave of homosexuals into the state that intensified entrenched prejudices—and what occurred in California was reflected in varying degrees throughout the country.

A series of sweeps on Hollywood Boulevard by police netted hundreds of homosexuals, who were stopped, harassed, even taken into police stations for further interrogation. A scurrilous Hollywood newspaper trumpeted the news: "100's of Deviants

Detained, Warned." The arrests were for "loitering." Any two men sitting in a parked car on streets near the Boulevard risked being ordered out by the police, separated, and grilled with questions about each other. Such questioning was meant to determine whether or not they had just picked each other up, a signal of lewd intent. That tactic was so widespread that gay men together, on sensing the presence of the police, whether in bars or on the street, would hurriedly exchange names and brief backgrounds to suggest a friendship, as opposed to a quick connection.

Throughout the '50s and '60s, and even into the '70s, being in a gay bar was dangerous. At any moment a bar might be flooded with light from a squad car. A bullhorn ordered all "queers" to march out in a single line, ostensibly to be checked for ID. Gay men would be insulted, mauled, and in some instances beaten. As many men as could be fitted into a squad car or wagon were taken to headquarters for questioning. Anyone who protested would be threatened with being held on "open suspicion" for forty-eight hours, released, rearrested, and held again.

Since it was illegal for members of the same sex to dance together (heterosexual women were exempted), a "private" club in Topanga Canyon adopted a system of lights to signal a hostile presence. Bulbs would blink and partners would shift, with gay men dancing with lesbians. The illegality of gay men touching each other even while dancing produced the Madison, a dance during which lines of gay men faced each other, not touching, just going through the motions of a dance.

In 1968, the murder of silent film star Ramon Novarro by two young drifters resulted in the trial not only of the killers but of the star's life. Newspapers all over the country routinely quoted the defense lawyers' reference to the silent-film star as "an old queer." The fact that his murder was brought to trial and the killers convicted was exceptional, occurring mainly because of Novarro's one-time fame. Other incidents of violence against gay people, even murder, were left uninvestigated, even unreported, since it was known that in courtrooms, if the perpetrator of violence against a gay man claimed he had responded in anger at having been the object of a homosexual pass, he would be assured a not guilty verdict.

Plainclothes cops would sit in cars outside gay gathering places in order to trail men leaving together. Without warrants, they pushed their way into private homes, just as, years later, the Texas police would invade a private home and arrest two men in the *Lawrence* case. Men caught in such situations often went to prison; a sentence of up to five years was not rare.

Entrapment was rampant. Vice cops dressed in the tight white pants popular at one time might, while hanging out in a gay bar or on the street, court or accept an invitation for sex at someone's home, and then arrest the gay man for solicitation. In 1965, a man attempting his first gay encounter was arrested in 29 Palms, California, after a plainclothes cop struck up a conversation that led to a mutual agreement to go to a motel. The gay man was sentenced to six months in jail, where he remained incommunicado, the judge claiming he was "insane" and needed to be "scrutinized." After he managed to get out, he became a recluse, petrified for life by the incident.

Countless lives were destroyed by such arrests: men lost their jobs, were ostracized by their families, were threatened with electric shock treatment, ordered to stay away from any place catering to "perverts"—in effect sentenced to a life of loneliness, away from their own kind. All men convicted of a gay sex offense had to register for life as "sex offenders." As such, they were frequently summoned out of their homes at night to participate in lineups for unrelated offenses, heterosexual rape, or child molestation.

Fledgling political groups, such as the Mattachine Society, met in secret, their blinds drawn. Their newsletters—mimeographed sheets—were confiscated by the Post Office even though they had no erotic content. Such a fate awaited the first gay activist magazine, *One*, which was entirely nonerotic.

In 1973, hundreds of gay men in Griffith Park were rounded up, not on hidden trails where sexual encounters occurred, but simply as they walked along on open roads or gathered publicly around their cars, a traditional gay practice on a warm Sunday afternoon. Suddenly a helicopter, a fleet of squad cars, and more than a dozen police on horses launched an invasion, proceeding to herd dozens of gay men into a wired compound at the foot of the roads. The routed men were kept in the compound for several hours, names and addresses were checked out, and 39 were taken to police headquarters for booking. Those who were released from the compound had to trudge up the miles of road to their cars. Those taken to the station had to abandon their cars along the darkening roads. *The Advocate* (at that time a small newspaper) described the maneuver as "a full scale military operation, with command post, detention buses, jeeps, a helicopter, marked and unmarked cops, uniformed and vice police . . . and a contingent of mounted cops," concluding that it was "a new harassment strategy." The *Los Angeles Times* reported only that "39 men . . . were cited . . . for possible prosecution under city ordinances, prohibiting sections designated as hazardous. . . . They could face penalties of up to one year in jail and a $500 fine."

On an early evening in 1977—four years after the repeal of California's anti-sodomy laws—while driving home from UCLA, I saw muggers fleeing from a man they had assaulted on the street as he walked home with his groceries along a nongay area. I stopped to be sure that the man was okay: he was bruised and shaken. With him in my car, I attempted to flag down a squad car in the area. Hands readied on their revolvers, the cops got out. The muggers would still be in the area, I told them. Glancing at the wounded man, who was clearly gay, they drove off. I took the bruised man to the police station to report the crime. The desk sergeant studied him knowingly. "What did you try to do with those guys?" he asked.

After I wrote an account of that night for the *Los Angeles Times*, and an investigation was ordered because the matter was now public and no gay context had been indicated, I became the object of retaliation, culminating in an attack by baton-swinging cops in Barnsdall Park, a cruising area I often frequented. As I got out of my car, two cops rushed at me with batons raised. I was able to get back into my car and speed toward them. As I drove past, they swung their batons in an action intended for me. I heard the sickening strikes on my car, leaving deep dents. For months afterward, I received threatening anonymous calls.

In 1983, a vice cop and his plainclothes partner, having made an entrapment arrest for lewd conduct in Griffith Park, lingered along the main road with a handcuffed gay man as a trophy until other gay men had gathered. Summoning a park ranger, the arresting cop asked loudly: "Think anyone would mind if I set fire to this part of the park to burn these faggots?" Intending to bring that statement into the court hearing as indicative of the cop's vengeful intent to entrap, the city attorney prosecuting the case said he did not believe that an officer would say that, nor would any judge or jury accept it. The statement was not introduced, and the entrapped gay man was convicted.

There was resistance throughout those years in Los Angeles, however. As early as 1958, as the cops pursued a routine, hour-long harassing tactic of checking IDs at a crowded after-hours gathering place for gay men, Cooper's Donuts on Main Street, the men inside pushed en masse past the cops, and a violent rumble ensued. After the notorious raid on the Black Cat Bar in 1967, riotous disruptions against the police spread to L.A., where two hundred gay men marched against a line of heavily armed cops. In early 1969, the nearly fatal beating of a gay man in downtown L.A. created skirmishes and demonstrations sporadically for days.

But the same prejudices that allowed myriad outrages against gay people caused these acts to be ignored by the mainstream press. Unacknowledged, their insurrectionary power was curbed.

Although the history of gay oppression is long, its recorded history is brief. For many gay men, history begins with the moment of their last sexual conquest. Many younger homosexuals have no knowledge about what occurred not so long ago—and still occurs away from relatively safe havens, those deceptive gay ghettos. It could all have returned ferociously as long as repressive laws like the one in Texas existed.

On the memorable day of June 25, 2003, in decent, moving words, Justice Kennedy and the four justices who joined him in effect denounced those past horrors as inconsistent with the respect and dignity owed to all human beings. Without in any way belittling the decency of those justices in their opinion—and the courage and commitment of those who fought to bring it about, especially the Lambda Legal Defense Fund and its attorneys—many gay people might view the decision as a vastly imperfect apology for the lives devastated by cruel laws that made possible the myriad humiliations of gay people, the verbal and physical assaults, the screams of "faggot!"—the muggings, the suicides, the murders, trumped-up arrests, incarceration—still occurring even during this time of victory.

The flagrant dissent by Justice Scalia and two of his colleagues—in an effort to uphold the Texas law—will help to keep fertile the atmosphere of hatred that recently allowed three men to mangle Trevor Broudy in West Hollywood and two others to butcher Matthew Shepard in Wyoming. A great battle was won on June 25, but the war continues.

POSTSCRIPT: The chasm between generations of gay men was again revealed after this finding: Those who remembered the ugliest of times became newly angered at the past while many of those who weren't around to remember, didn't want to know about it.

FROM *SUNSET BOULEVARD* TO *MULHOLLAND DRIVE* (2003)

I S IT POSSIBLE to define a "real" Los Angeles, or has the city been so forcefully imagined in literature, art, and especially in films that only a mythological city now exists? The mere mention of Los Angeles in the title of a film arouses presuppositions. *To Live and Die in L.A.*, the title of a William Friedkin film, resonates, just as does the phrase "Only in L.A.," with implications of edginess. To Live and Die in Fort Worth? To Live and Die in Rhode Island? To Live and Die in New York?—not even that creates as definitive an impression.

No other modern city draws more fascinated attention than Los Angeles as depicted primarily by film. In Rome, London, Paris, mention the city, and intrigued questions pour out, along with repeated expressions of longing to come here, where there is still the offer, at least the offer, of dreams fulfilled; that is, of getting into the movies.

Los Angeles is a city of daily apocalypse—fate swirls on the freeways. The city constantly prepares for natural disasters (and, now, very unnatural disasters), disasters that include Sant'Ana winds, fires, earthquakes, floods, sliding cliffs—no tiny catastrophes; they're immense, dramatic, extreme, even melodramatic. Los Angeles is not only metaphorically edgy but literally on the edge. Nightly, the sun falls off the Malibu cliffs and sinks into the ocean bringing night.

Against such a dramatic backdrop—this last frontier that at any moment may tremble toward apocalypse, this last-chance frontier—against all that, almost-biblical concepts of good and evil, morality, ethics, explorations of complex identity—these themes play well. After all, this is the City of Angels, a city of promiscuous spirituality—every religion and cult group settles here—and of physicality, a city of bodies and souls. It might be the place of exile for rebellious angels who refused to sing the praises of the celestial dictator.

As a result of so much inherited mythology and associations, Los Angeles has become a readied set for films. A set is prepared for performance; and Los Angeles inspires grand performances. Furthering that sense of performance is a strain of self-reflectiveness running through these films; of film looking at film looking at a Los Angeles recorded by Hollywood.

There are ample locations for unique performance: Forest Lawn, with its glamorous statues shrugging off death in Tony Richardson's film version of Evelyn Waugh's *The Loved One* extends its commentary on silly death. When Ma is about to "get it" in the back in *White Heat*, the dark Sant'Ana wind, rustling leaves ominously, adds heat to the treachery. The racist betrayal by a rich white man of his mulatto lover in *Devil in a Blue Dress* is rendered profound by its being played out in the distance, silently, against the backdrop of a deserted Griffith Park Observatory at night. The same setting elevates the rebellion in *Rebel without a Cause*, just as it augments the universal implications of Robert Wise's *The Day the Earth Stood Still*.

Like other great cities, Rome, Pompeii, and as a city of daily apocalypse, Los Angeles has been destroyed in movies over and over, but unlike those ancient cities demolished by the same disaster depicted repeatedly, Los Angeles has been destroyed by a spectrum of grim calamities. It has been wiped out by a volcano erupting on Wilshire Boulevard. It has been stung to death by giant spiders, ants, and killer bees. It has been set aflame by asteroids, and gnawed at by moll people. It has been ravaged even by a giant baby seeking gallons of milk and intent on finding his mother—even in the sewers of Los Angeles—in order to eat her up; the latter occurs in that underrated masterpiece *It's Alive! Part One*.

John Schlesinger's rendering of Nathanael West's *The Day of the Locust* includes not one but three apocalypses possible together only in Los Angeles. A literal movie set for a costume epic collapses, killing and wounding dozens of extras. An earthquake—augured earlier by the image of a cracked wall decorated, like a camouflaged scar, with a rose—strikes. A riot erupts simultaneous at a Hollywood premiere when a grotesque painted child, Adore, is mauled. (An aside: the hideously cute painted child Adore may be the close cousin of Baby Jane in Robert Aldrich's *Whatever Happened to Baby Jane?*—and that aged child star, played deliriously, all eyes, by Bette Davis, might be what Shirley Temple would have become if Richard Nixon hadn't appointed her ambassador to some country or other.)

L.A. Story attempts to define the city only through ridicule, distorting all that's imposing about Los Angeles.

The screenplay was written by Steve Martin, who often takes swipes at the city when he's in New York—nothing, though, that equals Woody Allen's fatuities or Ms. Bette Midler's recent announcement of why she fled Los Angeles. "There are," she said, according to that unassailable bastion of truth Liz Smith, "too many sick people here." Guess where she went?

L.A. Story opens with a montage of clichés: a shimmering pool, beautiful women lounging about, a helicopter floating overhead with what looks like a large penis in a bun but is really a giant hotdog, mustard oozing; rainbows of sprinklers on identical lawns; a man in bizarre shorts lugging a Christmas tree to the garbage under a shower of sun; an old couple abandoning their walkers to creep into a convertible while donning sun-glasses; earthquakes ignored in favor of nonsensical conversations at the Ivy; batty Venice West denizens, including an aging Lolita, neurotically obsessed with "colonics"; drivers firing at each other in congested freeway lanes. (About the city's congestion: have you noticed that in films, everyone finds a parking space right in front of his destination?)

A clownish weathercaster, played to the manner born by Mr. Martin, informs: "I was deeply unhappy but did not know it because I was happy all the time." Sara, a London journalist, arrives to write about Los Angeles; the clownish weatherman offers to show her "cultural Los Angeles"—in fifteen minutes.

In seeming rebuttal to her ex-husband's claim that Los Angeles is for the brain-dead, the English reporter delivers this cloudy reprieve: "They turn the desert into their dreams, and no one is looking to the outside for verification that what they're doing is all right." What no one is doing, either, is asking what the hell she means. She confesses that she's met some intelligent people here, like—The camera shifts to the clownish weathercaster skating through an art gallery that contains glass cases which allegedly contain: Verdi's baton, Mozart's quill, and Beethoven's balls.

Throughout, rich visuals counter the sophomoric silliness. Lofty palm trees, lush sunscapes, sweeping seascapes, streams of red and white lights on the freeways at night—these brush away the insults.

On the freeway the clownish weatherman encounters an electric sign that flashes messages to him: I'M A SIGNPOST HUG ME. It also flashes Martin a liberating riddle, a riddle of he sphinx for the braindead: HOW DADDY IS? Now will Martin sing to it a rendition of DooWahDo? The riddle is solved, and from all this the daffy weatherman draws this profound lesson: ". . . deep in the heart of Los Angeles love is possible." It isn't truly clear whether he's referring to the prospect of an affair with the braindead electric sign.

If only because of the preponderance of self-love in this proudly narcissistic capital of the world, Los Angeles might well be viewed as the City of Love, a city to which the constant influx of immigrants bring new variations of romance, of courtship.

Los Angeles is also a city that suggests passion, terrific possibilities for illicit love. Films set in Los Angeles borrow the city's sensuality, its physicality. Even murder becomes glamorous in Billy Wilder's *Double Indemnity* the moment the camera glides up Los Feliz and enters a Glendale mini-mansion and locates Barbara Stanwyck wearing only a towel and high heal pumps, and a sexy sneary smile that kills Fred MacMurray long before she shoots him, a unique love story. "I love you, baby." "I love you, baby!" Growl, growl, shoot, shoot, come, come, die, die." It may also have redefined terms for fidelity.

In other sweaty "noirs"—whether in black and white or Technicolor—the setting of Los Angeles contributes a sense of fate conspiring, just as the city's undercurrents conspire to grind. "The machinery had started to move and no one could stop it," says MacMurray about his fatal passion with Stanwyck. A similar sense of inevitability augments the drive toward injustice in Robert Wise's *I Want to Live!*

Among the voyeuristic films that stare in fascination at themselves and reflect a city enthralled by its many reflections, Billy Wilder and Charles Brackett's *Sunset Boulevard* sets the pattern, a narcissistic, consciously self-conscious film about narcissism in a narcissistic city. Its metaphoric title appears on concrete. The film wasn't shot on Sunset Boulevard. It was shot on Wilshire Boulevard.

Not only is Gloria Swanson's performance as Norma Desmond appropriately stylized; but so is the structure of the film. When at the opening Norma Desmond summons the man she believes to be an undertaker claiming the body of her pet-monkey, she also alerts the audience: "You there, why have you kept me waiting?"

Viewed in retrospect by a dead man, the film links past and present into a journey toward inevitability, fate asserted; it links the past and the present without flashbacks through a series of reflections: Early photographs of Norma Desmond abound. Led to believe we're watching a clip from one of young Norma's famous movies, we're actually viewing a clip a Gloria Swanson film. That actual film was directed by Erich Von Stroheim, whom Swanson, the mistress of Joseph Kennedy, fired and who here plays her butler. Silent film stars pantomime themselves.

When Norma Desmond returns to Paramount, Wilder's wicked sense of irony about Hollywood is displayed: Cecil B. DeMille informs Norma Desmond that Hollywood has changed, at the same time that he's directing an actual biblical clunker, *Samson and Delilah*, while Norma Desmond is offering him her not-dissimilar treatment of "Salome."

At the end, the film's structure winds into a circle of reflections. A Paramount newsreel camera, filmed by the movie's cameras, arrives to capture the filmic action. Norma Desmond snaps out of a trance when she hears that the cameras are rolling again, but they're newsreel cameras. Simultaneously she converts a small mirror into her key-light, the prized glowing territory of light given to only a few great stars. Her mansion turns into a set within the set of this Hollywood movie.

As she descends to face the deceiving cameras, her indictment of the audience in the opening sequence extends: "This is all there is, just us, and the camera, and those wonderful people out there in the dark"—the people who kept her waiting, abandoned her, the audience now watching her decline in fascination.

The film fades into a shimmering backdrop. Is that the pool into which Narcissus drowned in search of his own reflection? Or has Norma Desmond been saved by disappearing into her own stardust, her particular salvation?

Even ostensibly "realistic" films emphasize performance in incorporating the set of Los Angeles. Several borrow from *Sunset*

Boulevard, some subtly, some overtly; I have often observed that there is a vast difference between "homage" and "pillage."

In *Star Maps*, directed by Miguel Arteta, a shabby Mexican young man selling star maps is picked up on Sunset Boulevard by a beautiful rich actress who offers him stardom, albeit limited. Perceived by many reviewers as a realistic film, *Star Maps* is largely fable and sexual fantasy. Sunset Boulevard has never been a hustling avenue for map vendors; the director employs the street clearly because of its associations; it was in a Sunset Boulevard pharmacy that, legend insists, Lana Turner was discovered.

Other elements in Arteta's film abandon verisimilitude. A pimp and his boys make loads of money but the boys continue living on the street. A fight that is a highlight of the film occurs on an actual movie set and is allowed to proceed uninterrupted by any of the various burly grips. Paradoxically, the most "realistic aspect of the film is the dream-hallucination of an dying old Mexican woman being escorted into heaven by Mexican movie star Cantinflas.

Luis Valdez's *Zoot Suit* is a film whose story bears a strong historical antecedent. In the early 1940s in Los Angeles a climate of anti-Mexican racism resulted in the railroading of a group of zoot-suiters tried on spurious murder charges. Subsequently, squads of marauding sailors, marines, and soldiers raided East Los Angeles in a violent vendetta against "pachucos."

Valdez's film mythologizes the harsh event. The action is performed—and at times literally choreographed—on an actual set, at times a theater. The actual stylistics of pachucos easily become theatrical representation: the stride—a stalk—slow, rhythmic; the language, a cadenced incantation; the clothes, a complexity of hat, often plumed, pegged pants, wide shoulders, dangling key chains.

As Wilder did in *Sunset Boulevard*, Valdez acknowledges the audience, capturing it as it enters the theater. El Pachuco, the quintessential zoot-suiter, freeze-frames the action in order to comment. During an emotional high in the drama, he warns an agitated protagonist: "Don't take the play so serious, mano."

The film employs the standard props of socially conscious Hollywood movies: the happily grumpy mother, the protesting but supportive father, the suspicious attorney who turns out to have integrity, the left-wing woman blinded by her social commitment. Other ironic reminders of performance are black actors playing prison guards, Mexicans playing cops—in the '40s.

Although the Pachuco reminds, "Life ain't like that," Valdez flirts with a happy ending, extending three possibilities about what became of the railroaded man, once released: he committed other crimes and died in prison, he was killed in the war, he became a happy family man, despite the racial whirlwind that had sucked him in and was still churning during his release.

Like *Sunset Boulevard*, like *Zoot Suit*, Robert Altman's *The Player* opens by announcing itself as a performance on the set of Los Angeles. "Action!" a grip calls. There follow several minutes of an uninterrupted tracking shot as two men discuss famous long no-cuts. There are reminders of film as film everywhere: The camera glimpses glamorous Hurrell photos of great stars; there are sequences of movies within the movie—in one of which Julia Roberts as a woman doomed to execution in the gas chamber is saved by Bruce Willis, an ending the screenwriter of the movie-within-movie has dreaded from the first day of his pitch.

IN THE NAME OF ALL WRITERS, I AM GOING TO MURDER YOU, warns an anonymous letter to a big film executive who had promised to "get back to him" in five weeks that have stretched into five months. We learn from the hunted executive that out of fifty thousand yearly collective pitches, only twelve will become films. The wronged writer was not one of the twelve, because: ". . . his script lacked the necessary elements for a successful movie: laughter, violence, hope, heart, nudity, happy ending, mainly happy ending." With zestful irony, Altman provides a deliberately forced happy ending, as the film we just watched turns into the film now to be made.

Los Angeles is often depicted as a city to which many seek happiness, and often end up redefining it. Is the goal no longer to find love, but . . . stardom?—as in *Star Maps*. Or is it just hope redefined?—as in the third proposed ending of *Zoot Suit*. If indeed Norma Desmond drowns in the glitter of her legendary stardom, then she has found her version of salvation. It is found in "dolls" by the ladies of *Valley of the Dolls*. (Incidentally Jacqueline Susann made that up, the word "dolls" for pills; nobody else ever used it.) The *Pretty Woman* finds redemption on Rodeo Drive, the clownish weatherman a lasting affair with a freeway sign.

Roman Polanski's and Robert Towne's Technicolor "noir" film immediately pays homage to its classic antecedents (especially John Huston's *The Maltese Falcon*): A not entirely noble detective occupies a not quite elegant office within which slatted venetian blinds allow slabs of light and an overhead fan whirrs lazily. In walks a mysterious woman who makes a proposal for the detective to hunt a missing girl, somehow connected to one of the city's most powerful figures. (It also casts Huston in the film.)

That is only the beginning, because *Chinatown* intends to deal with large themes that play out perfectly within its setting: a desert city bordering the ocean and on the brink of destruction because of the threat to one elemental need, water—"where," one character reminds, "life began." On this vast plain, evil of biblical proportions looms, murderous corruption links with incest.

Water, gallons of water, are being discarded into the ocean during a severe drought that may destroy the city. L.A. IS DYING OF THIRST, SAVE OUR CITY, a poster informs. In an eerie silent scene, viewed from a distance, a lone Mexican boy mounted on a horse meets a tall imposing man we learn later is the man stealing water—an unheroic Prometheus. Placed on the sun-baked Los Angeles River barely veined by water, this scene of conspiracy assumes a quality of desolation and moral aridity. An angled overhead view of a girl being sought conveys her sense of unique captivity by its being framed by beautiful flowers.

When asked, "What more do you want?" the powerful Mulwray conniving to rob the city of water so he can buy the resultant cheap property, answers, "The future, the future," a motto of unchecked power that extends into his rationalization for incest and murder: "Given the "right place, right time—we're capable of anything." Setting the ending of the film in Los Angeles's Chinatown—early on identified as the locale of a crime the detective never fully solved or understood—lends lingering mystery and impact to the film's ending. (The film's exploration of unchecked arrogant power becomes timely today as we watch on television the reckless destructiveness of cynical power wielded by the current administration.)

While white contemporary younger directors seem increasingly to push their explorations of the city toward surrealism, black directors deal more forthrightly with its realities, while adjusting the prepared set.

Menace II Society, directed by the Hughes Brothers, pushes the viewer into a world of no exit, and it does so in part by filming Los Angeles through a brownish murk that camouflages the beauty of the city. The violence is not camouflaged; it saturates the film in blood. Even on this muted set, elements of self-reflective performance occur: The killer of a grocery clerk watches raptly the store video tape that recorded his crime. His religious grandparents, just as enthralled watch a Jimmy Stewart movie—perhaps *It's a Wonderful Life*—on their TV screen.

The inspired madness of the *Naked Gun* movies relies largely on surrealizing the action, while leaving the city's "real" background intact. In *Naked Gun 33⅓,* the parody of and homage to Eisenstein's famous "steps" sequence in *Potemkin* gains comic impact when we recognize the Park Plaza Hotel in the mid-Wilshire District.

Katherine Bigelow, in her 1997 *Strange Days,* distorts Los Angeles into burning shadows, twisted silhouettes among Los Angeles landmarks, the Bonaventure Hotel, Broadway downtown.

It is December 31, 1999, the eve of the millennium. Sporadic fires, looting, suggestions of rioting are occurring. (Even these relatively mild intimations assume a humorous aspect when we remember that Los Angeles greeted 2000 with a shrug, perhaps because—I find this endearing—it was the only city to understand that the millennium would not begin until 2001.) A new illicit form of entertainment, "Playback," is now in the hands of black-marketeers, a new pornography that records violent experiences and allows the player to reexperience them, like listening to music with earphones. Recurrently we're seduced into the film's action only to realize that we've really "experienced" "Playback." (In a broad sense, "Playback" suggests the so-called reality shows of today, shows that, however, stop being realistic the moment the camera is aimed.)

There are implications of a collapse of morality. In a dingy club full of costumed revelers, a leggy girl does a sexy song and dance, and an orgy is implied. (Alas, the orgy is even more passive than Kubrick's languorous one in *Eyes Wide Shut.*) Bigelow does not make it clear how all this will bring about the apocalypse, on this particular day; no forecasts of computer failure, no terrorists, no connection to "playback pornography," just Los Angeles as tensile set.

As disparate as the two films are in both content and quality, Curtis Hansen's *L.A. Confidential* opens with a sequence much like that of *L.A. Story;* and as in *Sunset Boulevard,* the narrator turns out dead. The voice of Danny de Vito itemizes a series of L.A. clichés. Unlike Martin's, this litany is delivered with jaunty irony: "Come to L.A.," the voice invites as the camera roams over golden beaches, lush orange groves, a gorgeous landscape. "Life is good, paradise on earth." Yet: How is it possible that in such a city, organized crime can exist?"

It is not only organized crime that exists in this Los Angeles. Corruption saturates every level of power, especially the Los Angeles Police Force—and note that in virtually every one of these films that indictment occurs, an indictment still prevalent.

Early on, the intent of the film's exploration is established: What ethics can survive widespread moral anarchy? There are three cops on the moral spectrum: the police chief is overtly corrupt, another cop has a skewed morality—he draws the line on hitting women; and the third, the good cop, refuses to plant evidence, refuses to shoot even a guilty man in the back, the way Ma got it in *White Heat.* Their ethics will be tested.

As the roams through layers of corruption—racism, planted evidence, beatings, murder—impersonation assumes a major importance in the plot. High-priced prostitutes acquire plastic surgery in order to evoke the stars of fantasy: Rita Hayworth, Veronica Lake. A confusion in the impersonations occurs at the famous Formosa Club, where the good detective encounters petty crook and gigolo Johnny Stompanato with a beautiful blonde, who protests the invasion. The cop retorts: "A hooker cut to look like Lana Turner is still a hooker"—only to be informed that she is Lana Turner.

One cop works as a consultant for a *Dragnet*-like movie, and then we see clips from the actual *Dragnet* series. Location shots look like sets filmed in sepia-tinged colors that suggest the Los Angeles of 1950; occasionally the bright colors of the city are allowed to startle in bright Technicolor.

In this film, the happy ending is rendered with a telling twist: The implicit morality of it is skewed.

David Lynch's *Mulholland Drive* gave banished deconstructionists hope for a . . . comeback, at least for a nudge to queer theorists before they claimed it. Both were emboldened by Lynch himself. "The film is what you see in it," he pronounced about the episodes from a rejected film series pasted together with additional footage.

Roles are constantly reversed: a "monster" is a homeless person, Diane is Betty, there are two Camillas, one of whom, an amnesiac, took Rita Hayworth's name for a time.

At a staged theatrical performance, voices are lip-synched, music canned. Lines like: "Don't play it for real until it gets too real" and "Just like in the movies, pretend you're someone else," constantly remind we're watching a film. A cruel manifestation of self-reflective performance is the filming of indomitable old-time star Anne Miller through a kind lens, until the end, when the camera pounces on her in an unveiled close-up.

"Weird skylines, dangerous parking lots," a voice describes Lynch's Los Angeles. But the skylines look a beautiful. Out of Lynch's jagged forms, the intrepid Los Angeles sunshine bathes the city. Palm trees sprawl majestically. The city glitters at night from a distance as two women, like phantoms, surrender into it from Mulholland Drive.

And along comes Paul Thomas Anderson's *Boogie Nights*. Knights—with a K? Why not?—since it is something of a modern picaresque, and a highly moral one, too. It is a film that could be set only in Los Angeles, the San Fernando Valley, the seat, as it were, of pornography, a most elemental form of performance.

That sense of performance is affirmed even before the film begins. Its star, Mark Wahlberg, once known as Marky Mark, is a one-time homophobe who in this film gets assaulted by gay-bashers.

Here, he plays a legendary porn king à la John Holmes, who was reputed to have had the largest endowment of all time. Scenes from antecedent films are replayed throughout. Mark accepts a best erotic player award, just like Anne Baxter did while getting a somewhat classier "Tony" in Mankiewicz's *All About Eve*. As Mark's character declines, he become Bette Davis as Margo Channing. A "new kid in town," with rivaling endowment, becomes Eve Harrington, lurking in the wings to snatch the Big title away.

Echoing Norma Desmond's protest, "Nobody leaves a star, that's what makes one a star," Mark asserts his challenged place in the constellation of porn: "I'm a star, a star, a big bright star." Upon her return to Paramount Pictures, Norma Desmond haughtily declared, "Without me there would be no Paramount," and Mark asserts his place to his betraying cohorts. "Without me you wouldn't be anywhere."

A scene of dual violence is choreographed. While Mark is being assaulted by gay-bashers, a porn actress beats up a would-be client on another street. The scene of gay-bashing is ritualized into a crucifixion, emphasized by a church in the background; a deep blue Los Angeles sky is somber. The music uniting the alternating sequences is grave, funereal. Later, a wild man on drugs becomes a demented ballet dancer.

A porn entrepreneur trespasses into kiddy porn and is ostracized, then beaten in prison. The husband of a porn queen kills her for indulging in off-screen sex.

This film's ultimate comment on performance occurs at the very end when Wahlberg as Johnny Holmes reveals what is supposed to be his now legendary penis. Instead, it's an obvious prosthesis, a limp, rubbery fake.

I would like to inject a most personal note: I cherish this city so often maligned, a city that despite all the ridicule it is too often the object of, can inspire films like *Chinatown, Sunset Boulevard, L.A. Confidential, Boogie Nights,* and many others, including, of course, *It's Alive, Part One.*

A favorite time of mine occurs at the beach in Santa Monica during late summer. That is when the "blue hour" tints the world in a purplish blue haze created by a conspiracy of haze, clouds, fading sun. Filmmakers often wait for this light to shoot their most memorable scenes. It is a time between dusk and night, a brief, mysterious transition during which, mythology claims, things are at once the clearest and therefore the most ambiguous.

That is how Los Angeles emerges finally in films, clear one moment, ambiguous the next, bold and subtle, always mysterious, as real as movies, as unreal as the city itself.

POSTSCRIPT: This essay was delivered as the keynote address at USC for a conference on Los Angeles and the Cinematic Imagination.

A STAR IS KILLED (2003)

ON THE EVENING of October 30, 1968, Ramon Novarro, once one of Hollywood's greatest romantic idols, now sixty-eight and frail, looking like "a Spanish grandee" in a red and blue robe, opened the door of his Laurel Canyon home and, with all the graciousness of his aristocratic lineage, greeted his guests, a burly young man of twenty-two and a slender one of seventeen, his murderers.

The burly young man had obtained Novarro's telephone number from a previous guest in order to solicit an invitation for himself and his brother. Both understood why they would be invited—both had hustled before. Novarro welcomed such young men. They considered him "an easy touch," "a nice old guy." Only those closest to him knew his guarded secret, that he was homosexual. He was not the only one in Hollywood who kept such a secret. It was necessary self-protection. That, and his rigid Catholicism, created a chafing conflict.

Easy camaraderie developed among the three. Novarro read the older brother's palm and saw a bright future. At the piano, Novarro taught him a song he had composed. The younger brother contributed his own tune. The camaraderie—and the liquor shared steadily with the older brother—made Novarro feel that he was not buying companionship, and it was companionship that he often bought. He frequently passed out, drunk, abdicating any sexual connection. He was a lonely man, his contemporaries dead or in seclusion—Garbo, Fairbanks, Negri. Perhaps remembering their time, Novarro showed the two brothers a photograph of himself, a handsome, muscular young man wearing a toga in the title role of *Ben Hur.* Doesn't look like you, the younger brother said.

Whether coerced by the older brother, or to indicate that he was still a power in Hollywood, Novarro called a film publicist to inform—in agitated words—that he wanted to arrange a meeting for a young man who had star power.

Liquor clouded the sequence of events into the blurred sequence of violence. In the bedroom with Novarro and possibly after a sexual connection—both were naked at a certain point—the burly young man, dressed now, demanded the $5,000 rumored to be hidden in the house. There was no such amount, Novarro insisted truthfully—he never kept large sums in his home. The younger brother—who had been on the telephone mollifying a girl he had beaten up in Chicago—joined the two, adding his own demands for the money.

Novarro's pleading denials aroused rough shoving that escalated into violent pummeling. Bleeding, the frail naked man fell. The brothers yanked him up to strike him down again. One of the brothers danced, twirling a cane like a baton and wearing a glove he had found in a closet.

To avoid Novarro's slipping into unconsciousness, the brothers dragged him to the bathroom, slapping him awake with cold water. Novarro staggered into the bedroom. Collapsing on his knees, he sobbed: "Hail Mary full of grace."

Taking turns, the two aimed the cane at his genitals, his head. They bound him with an electric cord and pounded and struck again. The younger brother scratched the dying man's face. They discarded his mangled body on the bed. Novarro died, choking on his own blood.

The two killers ransacked the house, flinging away photographs of the young star as if rejecting even his past. To suggest that a woman had perpetrated the crime in vengeful violence—and scratched the dead man's face—they wrote on a mirror words that revealed buried motives:

US GIRLS ARE BETTER THAN FAGITS.

Those events are reconstructed from information in *Beyond Paradise: The Life of Ramon Novarro* by André Soares, and from this reviewer's related conversations with the late Jim Kepner, who attended the trial and intended to write a book about the murder. He produced only a condensed account for *The Advocate*.

Along with the killers, Novarro's life was put on trial. It was not rare for violence on nonprominent homosexuals to be left unreported. A declaration by an assailant that his victim made a homosexual pass often guaranteed acquittal. The defense referred to the man who had hidden his homosexuality as "an old queer." The brothers' mother testified that her younger son had written: ". . . he deserved to be killed, he was nothing but an old faggot."

The trial exposed, too, the drab lives of the brothers, who shared a Catholic background with Novarro. Raised in poverty, they were soon on their own, working at menial jobs, stealing, hustling. Squads of other such young men share that background, fleeing to big cities with nothing but their youth to rely on—exploited and exploiting—leading a life made desperate by their knowledge of the brevity of their existence, the brevity of their youth. They are a group not unworthy of compassion.

Any compassion the brothers' dingy existences might have aroused before the crime, was obviated by the savagery of the torture, twenty-two deadly blows. Unrepentant, they blamed each other. Both were found guilty of first-degree murder, sentenced to life in prison. The judge recommended they never be released.

But they were, perhaps because of homophobic attitudes toward Novarro. The younger killer was out six years after his conviction, the older almost nine years after the murder. Both committed more crimes, including, separately, rape. Now old themselves, they remain in prison for crimes unconnected to Novarro's murder.

Soares succeeds in his noble intention: Novarro "created some of the most indelible characterizations of the silent and early sound era. . . . For him to be chiefly remembered today as a perverted elderly homosexual . . . is an injustice to both the complex individual and to the accomplished—and historically important—actor. . . ." The death of Novarro incited brutal lies. The most virulent, which Soares explodes, was invented by a minor filmmaker of erotic movies. In a book of contrived Hollywood scandals, he included a salacious tale that the instrument of murder was an object given to Novarro by Valentino.

Soares roams over Novarro's life—from his privileged Mexican background, his migration into America, his aspirations for the monastic life—on to his emergence as a Latin lover, his hidden romances with men, his faked romances with women.

The allure of the Latin lover faded. At thirty-six, Soares claims, Novarro was a "has-been." But he endured on the stage, returning to films as a character actor, "forever dreaming of a spectacular comeback." That "comeback" occurred when his murder yanked him out of near-obscurity.

The best records of violence—like Norman Mailer's *The Executioner's Song*—take the reader into the very heart of darkness. It is in reporting the crime that Soares's otherwise commendable book misses. His main source about the murder is Kepner's report in *The Advocate*. Court records, he informs without further clarification about this major omission, have been "lost or misplaced." He resorts to reportage that fails to convey the enormous violation involved; and Novarro was doubly violated, by the murder and by the trial that raked over every intimate detail of his hidden sexuality.

Some stars die at the exact time to fulfill their legends: James Dean is forever the rebel; Marilyn Monroe, the quintessential movie star. Marlene Dietrich chose seclusion rather than compromise her legend. Novarro's legend is undeniably tainted by the monstrous ending to his secret life.

Still, the name itself—Ramon Novarro!—evokes the magic of the grand silent-film romances, thus securing his place among the greatest stars of all time. Beyond that, the repressive pressures that made possible the atrocity persist today, keeping famous actors closeted, even homophobic. That gives to the life and death of Novarro an enduring tragic and admonitory relevance.

POSTSCRIPT: I had a hard time writing about this great star's murder. I knew the world the two murderers came from, had experienced it; I would see others like them, young, attractive boys, already on the edge, sentenced to a brief life—"dead" when youth is gone. Those who purchased their bodies purchase new bodies. I heard hustlers sometimes talking with contempt and bravado about their johns; and often, they, the hustlers were abused, abandoned in lonely spots after accepting a ride, exposed to dangers, and exposing others to danger. In the '50s there was a wave of murders of young hustlers. By all accounts Novarro was a kind and generous man to the hustlers he employed, a man who had once been, himself, the object of desire. Ugly circumstances brought him together with his murderers. I wanted not a tinge of sympathy for those two in my essay. I refused to mention their names, link them with the name of the famous star. All sympathy belonged to Novarro, the beautiful fallen star.

A SPIRIT PRESERVED IN *AMBER*

O N MAY 26, a frail woman of eighty-three, once famous, died in New York City, a virtual recluse. News of her death appeared sporadically. I called one newspaper about an obituary. An editor asked, "Kathleen who?"

Kathleen Winsor had died, the author of seven novels, including, in 1944, *Forever Amber*, which in its first week of publication sold a hundred thousand copies and went on to sell millions. Enthusiastically bawdy, the novel was set in Restoration London, then rebounding boisterously from the somber rule of Oliver Cromwell.

Obituaries were largely dismissive, derisive. As if that was all she should be remembered for, even eight-line obituaries evoked the Massachusetts attorney general who brought charges of obscenity by numbering its sexual passages; an adding machine was needed, he said. Since there is no graphic sex in *Forever Amber*, he must have distractedly counted ellipses.

Slightly longer obituaries cited the judge who, dismissing obscenity charges—the book was banned in fourteen states and abused by reviewers as vulgar and trivial—claimed that the novel had put him to sleep. Counting sexual liaisons, not sheep?

In the interim following, several novels aroused censors, none as notoriously as *Forever Amber*. Although four years later Norman Mailer had to coin the word "fug" to ease *The Naked and the Dead* past censors, he and other writers—some of D. H. Lawrence's and Henry Miller's novels were not yet legal here—benefited from Winsor's contribution to the fight. Aside from all that, *Forever Amber* is a grand literary creation.

I heard of it at age thirteen when, with other congregants in the Church of the Immaculate Conception in El Paso, I stood to repeat a decreed vow that I would never read the sinful book. Grateful to God for the introduction, I rushed to read it.

Preternaturally precocious then, and as modest as I am now, I read several long books simultaneously. So it was that while I followed Winsor's glamorous Amber St. Clare from a staid country household to the profligate Court of King Charles II, I also roamed with Molly Bloom through lush memories of fragrant tosses in flower-strewn fields; and I traversed Swann's way to encounter the scandalous Odette; and every now and then I would cast Molly as Amber, and then Odette was Amber and Amber would turn into Molly. Eventually, stubborn Amber refused to become Ma Joad.

Informed by years of research, Winsor, age twenty-five, drew so exuberant a picture of London during the Restoration—"stinking, dirty, noisy, brawling"—that it is difficult to believe she had not been there. She evokes the heat, the advancing flames of the Great Fire. She creates a surreal city during the Great Plague. Predators pillage near-corpses. "Bring out your dead!" echoes along plundered streets.

We sit among raucous theater audiences. In the opulent court of Charles II, we mingle in golden-mirrored halls, all as Amber climbs to the heights as mistress of Charles II. With wry humor, Winsor follows that ascent closely. To upstage everyone else, Amber attends the royal court with breasts exposed. " 'Swounds, madame, this is the greatest display since I was weaned," leers a lord—and I quote from usually reliable memory.

In her sumptuous characterizations, Winsor is in the tradition of Dickens. Mother Red Cap, Black Jack Mallard, Mrs. Maggot— her cast ranges from bawds and pirates to embroidered courtiers and courtesans. Historical figures come to life as vividly as fictive characters. Charles II, cynical, bored, wanders luxuriant gardens with his pampered dogs. Winsor imbues her star-crossed romance with a sense of fateful irony. Amber's love for the haughty Lord Bruce Carlton is impossible because she is lowly born. Only the reader knows that her mother was an aristocrat.

Virtually every one of the Winsor obituaries relegates her work to the realm of "women's fiction." Even Elaine Showalter in an admiring appreciation in the *Guardian* limits the author's scope by identifying readers implicitly only among women. Other writers mention Jacqueline Susann and Grace Metalious as her literary sisters. It is not to demean those significant ladies to uphold that *Forever Amber* belongs with Thackeray's *Vanity Fair,* Defoe's *Moll Flanders,* Margaret Mitchell's *Gone with the Wind*— and with Fielding's famous picaresque novel; Amber is somewhat of a female Tom Jones.

Not only women admired the book. Ring Lardner did; so did Otto Preminger. So did my brother Yvan. Returning from the invasion of Normandy, Yvan, twenty-one then, snatched away my copy. He had started reading it on the ship back to the States but couldn't keep it long enough from other returnees to finish it. When I was in the 101st Airborne Infantry Division in Germany soon after the Korean War, I read it again. It had lost none of its power.

While her primary honor is as a storyteller, Winsor's prose is splendidly robust. It may seem blasphemous to some to say that Winsor was a better writer than Mitchell, who introduces the famous heroine of her undeniably great *Gone with the Wind* with this awful sentence: "Scarlett O'Hara was not beautiful, but men seldom realized it when caught by her charm, as the Tarleton twins were."

Winsor chooses the moments before Amber's aristocratic mother's death to introduce her heroine at birth: "She could hear again, loud and clear, the sound of her daughter's cries. They were repeated over and over, but grew steadily fainter, fading away, until at last she heard them no more." Not spectacular, no, but a kind of resigned viaticum for the child of turbulence.

Many authors acknowledge only sanctified writers as their influences—"And of course Shakespeare"—along with another writer to confound an interviewer (mine is Aphra Behn). Early on, I admired Winsor's Technicolor prose, its possibilities, when effective, when not. I thrilled to her unabashed exploration, with empathy—and necessary humor—of lives disdained as outrageous, and to her storytelling genius.

Perhaps Winsor's stature was minimized because her heroine does not end tragically, like Becky Sharp, Emma Bovary, Moll Flanders, Anna Karenina. Amber is indefatigable to the end. Too, she was created by a woman, and she was lusty. Gentlemen's heroines don't care for sex. Even Scarlett O'Hara tells her bumbling husband, Frank Kennedy, that only men like sex. Unlike Amber, Scarlett marries her suitors, although, as wise old Mammy knew, she would have taken the plunge if Ashley Wilkes hadn't been so prissy. Here's Amber: "Adultery is not a crime, it's an amusement."

Winsor—who was beautiful—may have suffered the curse of the sensational first novel whose reputation is so entrenched that its author can no longer be evaluated beyond it in subsequent work. She wrote more books—*Star Money* (which honed her satirical powers), *The Lovers, Calais, Robert and Arabella, Jacintha* and another massive epic, *Wanderers Eastward, Wanderers West*, in which she displayed again her superb talent to re-create history, here nineteenth-century America.

Consulting the Internet, I stumbled upon another saddening item. A brief note introduces the "Preliminary Inventory" of Winsor's papers, which she donated to the University of Texas at

Austin: "The collection is not fully processed or cataloged; no biographical sketch, descriptions of series, or indexes are available." Included are five drafts of the famous novel and handwritten notes of the author's vast research.

Posterity has a way of correcting literary misjudgments, eventually relegating to derisive footnotes fatuous censorious attorneys general, clownish judges, silly reviewers, uninformed obituary writers. The frail lady who died May 26 was the woman who created Amber St. Clare. Amber survived plague and fire. With equal assurance, her creator triumphs.

POSTSCRIPT: I was pleased by the number of letters agreeing with my appreciation. Ms. Winsor continues to be cherished by many. I hope she knew that.

ON WRITING: THE TERRIBLE THREE RULES (2004)

THE THREE MOST often repeated "Rules of Writing," recited by rote and left uninvestigated and unchallenged in virtually every writing workshop, English course, and composition class, are capable of doing terrible damage to good writing. The Terrible Three are:

1. *Show, Don't Tell.* Major nonsense. Good writing involves "showing"—that is, dramatizing—as well as "telling"—that is, employing exposition. An avoidance of "telling" may convolute and interfere with providing clear motivation (to be exemplified by "showing"). It disallows setting. It obfuscates situation. "It was the best of times, it was the worst of times." In that line Dickens immediately identifies the situation he is now free to develop in *A Tale of Two Cities.* Soon after, dual settings are established. Through exposition: "There were a king with a large jaw and a queen with a plain face on the throne of England; there were a king with a large jaw and a queen with a fair face on the throne of France."

Do we speak of "story-showing"? No. We speak of "story-telling." Many great works of literature are largely exposi-tional, including Swift's *Gulliver's Travels,* Cervantes's *Don Quixote,* and—try this one—Proust's *Remembrance of Things*

Past. In the latter, Proust roams, in exposition, through the inner landscape of the child Marcel's need for his mother's nightly bedtime kiss. Now he can move on to exemplify—"show"—the drama of his foiled attempts. Later, in a passage of sweeping exposition he explores Swann's complex love for Odette and by closely observing its vagaries, renders it universal. Thomas Bernhard's masterpiece, *Concrete,* is all gasping exposition until at the end he opens his narrative into eerie dramatization.

The effect of "scenes"—showing—may be created through refined "telling," as in García Márquez's *One Hundred Years of Solitude,* which is in major part exposition, with very little dialogue, often used as dramatic punctuation: "The earth is round, like an orange." Try to "show" this line of blunt exposition: "Call me Ishmael!" (Still, the famous line that opens Melville's *Moby Dick* is memorable only because of the name Ishmael. Call me Tommy? Call me Sally? Not nearly stirring.)

A good way to add life to exposition, especially to long passages of it, is to pause to capture a dramatic moment, to allow the reader to hear someone speak, see someone move, act—yes, show—since time is the accumulation of moments.

Even in film, the quintessential art of "showing," Ingmar Bergman and other great directors (Kurosawa, Billy Wilder) often use bold exposition. Alma, the nurse, in *Persona* announces, "I am a twenty-four-year-old nurse—" etc. The psychiatrist involved informs us that an older actress went silent during a performance of *Electra* as we see the actress's anguished face. A mysterious male voice tells us that the nurse and the actress were advised by the psychiatrist to go into the country, as we see them moving along a jagged landscape that visually projects (à la Robbe-Grillet) the emotional entanglement they are moving into. In one of the most erotic "scenes" in literature or film, in a long monologue Alma tells the actress—no flashback, no "showing"—about a sexual encounter on the beach.

2. *Write about What You Know.* The moody spinster who left the English moors to travel to London only once in her lifetime fled back to her seclusion to write one of the most passionate love stories of all time. Emily Brontë's *Wuthering Heights* illuminates a love so spectacular that it finds its only safe place within hell, not possible to be contained in a bland heaven.

Many great works of art would be canceled if the author had restricted himself to what he "knows." Think about crime novels—Raymond Chandler, James Cain, Dashiell Hammett. What about Dostoyevsky's *Crime and Punishment*? Stephen Crane never saw war, but he wrote *The Red Badge of Courage*. Purportedly, Vladimir Nabokov was outraged when little girls started popping up at his door one Halloween, inferring that he wrote in *Lolita* about what he knew. Flaubert, asked how he came to understand Emma so well, answered, "Madame Bovary, *c'est moi.*" The good fiction writer relies primarily on imagination, not information, not investigation. Certainly intimate knowledge—plus imagination—have produced many works of grand literature.

The writer doesn't deal with "reality." He deals with verisimilitude. He conjures his own "reality." We would be just as jarred if, along the weary way to California, Ma and Tom Joad encountered crazy old Dorothy skipping along the water-starved earth of Oklahoma as we would be if crazy old Dorothy encountered Ma and Tom Joad trudging along her yellow brick road. In both instances—Steinbeck's *The Grapes of Wrath* and Frank L. Baum's *The Wonderful World of Oz*—it is not, respectively, reality, nor fantasy, but verisimilitude that would be jarred

A better admonition might be: Write about what you feel. Too lofty. Write about what you feel you know. Too elevated. This is it: Write about whatever the hell you want to write about.

3. *Always Have a Sympathetic Character for the Reader to Relate To.* Shakespeare's Macbeth, Lady Macbeth, King Lear, the annoying Hamlet—none grasps our sympathy entirely, at best sporadically; nor does Othello, even if he is black. Albert Camus's *The Stranger*

is no lover of humanity to relate with. In Greek tragedy, just as in popular bestsellers, the most villainous and unsympathetic characters are the ones we remember, including Medea (about whom this writer, however, wrote sympathetically in a novel, proving that Jason was the villain). Ellen Berent in that magnificent underrated "popular novel" *Leave Her to Heaven,* by Ben Ames Williams—no snobbery here—is chilling and unforgettable; she blithely kills everyone who comes close to her husband, including, finally—grasp this!—herself. Blanche DuBois is sympathetic until we imagine her taking up quarters in one's own home (covering all the lights with Chinese lanterns, steaming up the bathroom on a hot day, singing sappy songs as she sprays her assertive perfume everywhere, dousing the air with stray feathers from her boa). Then surely, our sympathy might transfer to villainous Stanley. Willy Loman is often irritating. Lolita is dumb but cunning, and Humbert Humbert is a pervert.

We love hateful, selfish, manipulative characters—Scarlett O'Hara, Rhett Butler, Iago—yes, Dracula. Catherine and Heathcliff are horrors (and still manage—at times—to tear our hearts out). Whom do you sympathize with in any of Kafka's books? Henry James's governess in *The Turn of the Screw* is a driven demon. In Carson McCullers' perfect novel, *Reflections in a Golden Eye,* it is instantly apparent that the author despises every one of her characters, with the possible exception of the horse involved—although she does give him a severe flogging; and so the reader despises them, too, but one reads on.

Despicable, awful, frightening, wicked—but fascinating. That's the key: fascinating. Write about characters, good or evil, who fascinate.

POSTSCRIPT: These three are not the only "rules of writing" that are widely upheld and are deadly to the creative imagination, and they're entrenched in so-called writing courses. In my writing workshops, I emphasize that there is only one rule of writing, and that is this: There are no Rules of Writing.

OUR FRIEND THE COMMA (2004)

NOT EVERYTHING HAS gone haywire in a world that converts this haughtily subtitled book—*The Zero Tolerance Approach to Punctuation*—into a bestseller." (I'll leave it to the reader to discover the meaning of the title.) First in England, now in America, it has perched, proud, aloof, atop massive tomes about war, spies and lying presidents. Witty, smart, passionate, it gives long over-due attention to "the traffic signals of language."

Miss Truss (one longs to call her "Miss Truss" because she evokes the snippy teachers who eventually became our favorites) issues a rallying cry to all devotees of her just cause, "sticklers" who champion correct punctuation: ". . . fight like tigers."

To hearten the troops, she evokes punctuation's noble history, praising heroes, denouncing enemies. In an early English grammar, Richard Mulcaster found even a possible element of survival in the comma, "a small crooked point, which in writing followeth some small branch of the sentence, & in reading warneth vs to rest there, & to help our breth a little."

It wasn't always easy. Bernard Shaw demanded banishing the contractive apostrophe. Umberto Ecco eschewed the semicolon, but recanted, attributing his transgression to a lack of the mark on his typewriter. While warning against "embalming the language," Miss Truss grants only limited absolution for aberrant behavior, "only if you're famous."

Would I be an apostate in Miss Truss's (she insists on three s's) view because I dropped the contractive apostrophe entirely in my first novel? If so, I would explain that I did that, and performed other syntactical tricks—artfully—to suggest the slurred rhythms of rock-n-roll at the time of that novel, and the breathless speech of my protagonists. (I did it so effectively that I was labeled "semi-literate;" and I drew a stern protest from Levi-Straus & Co. for spelling "Levi's" as "levis." Promising not to do so again, I was rewarded with three new pairs of the famous pants.)

Miss Truss celebrates even the seemingly lowly hyphen; she proffers as example of its grandeur the phrase "extra-marital sex," inviting the deduction that if the hyphen is removed, grounds for divorce become a happy sex life.

Bravely, Miss Truss identifies villains, including some copy editors as saboteurs. (In one of my novels, I described the "most beautiful woman in the world" wearing a dress that "adored" her body. The sentence appeared with "adorned" substituted for my thrilling "adored.") She unmasks academics who pretend to understand each other's jargon. She lambastes the clumsy, nasty "instant reviews" that Amazon.com loves to attach like bubble gum to books. And cyber non-language? CU L8r (:-) LOL ("See you later. Smiley face. Laugh out loud."). Letters for words! Emoticoms instead of emotion! (I once returned, unread, a term paper submitted with a one-word note: "Enjoy!" followed by a smiley face.)

Miss Truss is so haughtily right—most of the time—that one exults in finding her wrong, especially since she rushes to thwart such by narrating an incident when she was thought by "gleeful" readers to be wrong but wasn't.

Gleefully, I point out that she disastrously dangles participial modifiers, even, in one such instance, omitting a necessary comma: "Carved in stone . . . in a Florida shopping mall one may see the splendidly apt quotation from Euripides." Did Miss Truss become so instinctively unnerved by the omitted comma after "mall" that she punished herself by casting herself in stone?

Glee overflows! She sends her beloved commas into disarray by frequently misusing "so" as a conjunction. Dear Miss Truss: "So," being an adverb (and an insecure conjunction only when coupled with an implicit or actual "that"), requires either a semicolon to precede it between independent clauses or a period followed by a capital "S" to introduce the resultant sentence. (I draw coveted stars on the margins of assignments when a student punctuates "so" correctly.)

And, oh, oh, Miss Truss, how could you allow the subtitle of your very own book to flaunt the hyphenic ambiguity you rage against! Without the necessary hyphen in "zero-tolerance," one is left to wonder: What is a zero approach? Wait! Did Miss Truss slyly connive to catch lax sticklers?

Despite her dangling modifiers and misused "so's," Miss Truss writes grand sentences that often exemplify the point she's making: "Assuming a sentence rises into the air with the initial capital letter and lands with a soft-ish bump at the full stop, the humble comma can keep the sentence aloft all right, like this, UP, sort-of bouncing, and then falling down, and then UP it goes again. . . ."

"Hope occasionally flares up and dies down again," Miss Truss laments, having seen dangerous signs that much of writing has become clicking and sending. Still: "We must not allow the language to return to the chaotic *scriptio continua* swamp from which it so bravely crawled less than two thousand years ago."

At the end of this splendid book, Miss Truss illustrates the timely relevance of punctuation. She reminds that a document proclaimed in 2003 as the British government's authoritative dossier on the dangers purportedly posed by Iraq was revealed to be a graduate student's twelve-year-old thesis because the fraudulent version reproduced the original paper's incorrectly used commas (while substituting the word "terrorists" for "opposition groups"). It was that fake plagiarized "dossier" that had been used, in part, to justify a disastrous war.

POSTSCRIPT: I was disappointed that Miss Truss did not respond to my article. I would have enjoyed an exchange. I know grammar unassailably, having been taught it in high school by the grand Maude Isaacks, Miss Isaacks.

FRAGMENTS FROM A LITERARY LIFE (2004)

IN APRIL OF 1999, my partner Michael and I travel to England. A first-class journey of grand hotels, chauffeur-guides, grand restaurants. (So different from my much earlier travels hitch-hiking, riding Greyhound buses, eating at lunch counters.)

We are dazzled by the palaces of corrupt royalty, the cathedrals of corrupt prelates, the looming mystery of Stonehenge.

"Where is the setting for *Wuthering Heights*?" I ask our driver-guide, a specialist, we were told, in private literary tours.

He offers to take us there.

The closest we can get to the site he intends is a long, winding distance up a dirt path. Too far to climb. Riskily, our driver maneuvers about dirt roads and finds one that will lead us up—an illegal route. We reach the top of the glorious moors. As we're stepping out, an older man out of the past, wearing a cap, boots emerges threateningly out of the only house within sight. "You can't come up here!" he says threateningly. I suspect he may have a gun.

Michael bravely steps forward, explains to the man that I'm a writer, that I love Emily Brontë, a favorite writer; that we have visited places where, supposedly, she lived, and long to believe we actually touched what she may have touched.

The man says nothing.

Long seconds pass. He looks at us, evenly. Then he points across the moors, way, away, away to what looks like the stony ruins of a large house. "There," he says, "over there. That's where Wutherin' Heights was."

Was it really so? If not, why did the sky suddenly—yes, suddenly, darken, from light to glowering dark, darker? Why did sleet slash at the earth? Why else if not in fitting tribute to the moody writer and the turbulence she captured, physical and psychic?

As quickly as it began, the rain stopped. The man moved back into his habitat. Nearby I gather a bouquet of heather while Michael stands beside me.

Our driver takes us to her gravesite; she's buried inside a church, with her family. Hers is not even the most prominent designation. Kneeling, I place the bouquet of heather on Emily Brontë's grave.

✦

IT'S 1950-SOMETHING, I'm in New York. I have been on a long-night's debacle at someone's apartment, somewhere on the West Side. It's dawning, the New York sky wiped with growing blue light, early morning dusk. I walk across Central Park to get to my rented room and sleep, sleep, sleep.

Am I hallucinating? Who is that man wearing a plaid cap and smoking a pipe and reading a book and sitting alone on a park bench?

A man I have so long and so strongly admired? No. Yes! not quite. I stagger over to him. He doesn't even glance up. He seems entirely at peace. No, it isn't him, can't be.

I walk away and read, during the next few days, that William Faulkner is in town for his play *Requiem for a Nun*. He is, the reporter states, fond of going into the park early morning, to be alone, to read.

✦

I'M . . . WHAT? Twenty-one years old? In San Francisco. No, Carmel. I knock on the door of a strange house, wooden, built like a tower, challenging the ocean, twisted beautiful trees seem to protect it.

"Yes?" a woman answers, staring at my leather jacket, jeans, engineer boots.

"I want to see Robinson Jeffers," I say.

The barest sliver of a smile crosses the serious face. "Mr. Jeffers doesn't see anyone except by appointment."

"May I make an appointment?" I ask.

"Mr. Jeffers doesn't make appointments," she says before the door closes, and I feel the imposing presence, in this jagged house, of that brave, solitary man.

Later that day:

"But," says the man at the tourist storefront in town, "he walks along the coastline with his dog, every morning. You might go there and encounter him."

Yes, yes, I will. I'll spring out before him, identify myself, and . . .

Of course not. The house built like a tower challenging the stormy ocean tells enough of the man's desire for solitude.

✦

IT'S 1960 SOMETHING. I'm cruising Griffith Park in Los Angeles. I've had sex three times but that's not enough. I'm standing on a sandy indention off the main road, waiting to be approached again.

A man drives up. He gets out. "You're . . ."

He's recognized me as the author of *City of Night* and, recently, my second novel, *Numbers*, set in this very park, involving a protagonist who numbers, compulsively, sexual encounters and whose name is Johnny Rio.

"No," I say quickly, certain he's going to ask me if I'm "that writer." For years I continued to guard my privacy, so that I could go on hustling, cruising anonymously.

"I'm sure you are," the man persists. "You're exactly as he described you—"

"What?" He described me? Who does he think I am?

"—in that book," he finishes.

I'm entirely confused. "What book?"

"*Numbers.*"

I'm floundering. "Oh, somebody wrote—"

"His name is John Rechy. Or that's what he calls himself. I don't think anyone would write a book like that under his own name."

I want to laugh out loud. He is very earnest. "I don't know anyone by that name," I tell him.

"He certainly knows you," he says.

I turn away now. This is getting uncomfortable.

"So long, Johnny Rio," the man says.

✦

IN EL PASO, one of many times I returned to my hometown, I become associated with a group from Fort Bliss, the GIs for Peace opposed to the Vietnam War. Noam Chomsky, the renowned linguist and antiwar activist, has been invited to address a rally in support of the enlisted soldiers. I pick him up at the airport, an affable man. I have become involved with body-building and I always welcome an acknowledgment of my success. So, in my car, I make a reference to this endeavor. "Oh," asks Mr. Chomsky, as if trying earnestly to figure out what I have said, "and does it help?"

✦

ON A NIGHT of Sant'Ana winds, those hot sensual desert winds that sweep into Los Angeles—this was back in the early 1980s and about 3 A.M.—along a stretch of alleys behind Melrose Avenue, men congregate intimately in darkened garages. Exiting from such a gathering, I step out into the deeply quiet alley and into a spill of light from a distant street. A man walking toward me halts abruptly on seeing me, applauds loudly—shattering the intense night—and bellows: "Author! Author!"

✦

IN NEW YORK, at a literary reception by Grove Press—the late '60s—a man with a French accent expresses his admiration for my work. Fine, great. But now he's becoming annoying, talking, talking, talking. Irritated, I maneuver to move away. As I'm leaving, he gives me a copy of a paperback book, which I take and pack into my suitcase. In the interim following, I become an appreciator of Robbe-Grillet's theory of subjective objectivity, no double talk, a sound artistic theory I now apply and often discuss with my workshop students. In Los Angeles and unpacking boxes I've left idle, I find the paperback book. There's an inscription, in French: "For John Rechy, some thoughts to be ignored. Alain Robbe-Grillet."

✦

LATER, IN LOS ANGELES, I'm a guest lecturer at UCLA. Late one night, oh, about 2:30 A.M., I'm standing without a shirt, torso oiled, on a corner, hustling or cruising, whichever comes first. A car drives by slowly, the driver peers at me, drives around the block, pauses at my corner and says, "Good evening, Professor Rechy. Are you out for an evening stroll?"

✦

BUT YEARS BEFORE that:

It's 1950-something. I'm hustling Pershing Square. I'm picked up by a man who's staying at the fancy Biltmore Hotel across the street. To avoid floor detectives constantly spying, the man instructs me to go in a back way and meet him in the elevator on a second floor. It works. On the third floor, the door opens and a detective appears. "Get the fuck outta here, I know what you're up to, I can get you arrested," he barks at me. He glares at the man I was going to join in his room. The man pretends not to know me as I step out of the elevator to get out of the hotel.

MANY YEARS LATER, in 1997, I am in the same hotel, in the grand ballroom. It's the yearly awards dinner, and I'm accepting the PEN Lifetime Achievement Award, the first novelist to receive that grand honor; only Billy Wilder, Neil Simon, Betty Friedan have been given it. The place is packed, a literary gala.

Where is the house detective who demanded that I get the fuck out of this lustrous hotel?

HE HUGGED MOMS AND DADS (2004)

A T McDILL Air Force Base in Florida, Bush met privately with the families of ten servicemen killed in the war. According to White House Press Secretary Scott McClellan, quoted in the *Los Angeles Times* of June 17, 2004: "He shared in their grief. He hugged moms and dads."

Hannah Arendt's phrase—"the banality of evil"—had again become monstrously relevant.

Earlier at McDill, the ex-governor of Texas had addressed thousands of troops and their families gathered in a humid hangar. As he faced men and women who might soon die in his disastrous war, he upheld his disproved rationale for the invasion of Iraq; and he lied effectively, having practiced rallying calls during his stint as a college cheerleader.

> I'm the commander—see, I don't need to explain—
> I do not need to explain why I say things. That's the
> interesting thing about being president.
> —GEORGE W. BUSH,
> as quoted in
> Bob Woodward's *Bush at War*

In Iraq, bombs erupted into torches, buildings exploded, heated winds caked spilled blood on the streets, shots rang out without pause; and sacrificial expendable American servicemen, mostly from the ranks of the poor and the ethnic, died. Uncounted, the numbers of Iraqis killed and maimed could only be conjectured.

> And I am an optimistic person. I guess if you want to try to find something to be pessimistic about, you can find it, no matter how hard you look, you know?
> —GEORGE W. BUSH,
> Washington, D.C., June 15, 2004

He stood like Napoleon on an aircraft carrier before a banner that proclaimed MISSION ACCOMPLISHED. This man who had dodged the draft was dressed in a flight suit befitting the proud "war president" he had several times referred to himself as. Although the conflagration in Iraq was then only a bloody prologue, he announced victory.

> I think the American people—I hope the American—
> I don't think, let me—I hope the American people trust me.
> —GEORGE W. BUSH,
> Washington, D.C., December 18, 2002

This was the "war president" who had gone blank for seven minutes of bewildered inaction in a Florida classroom after being told the Twin Towers in New York had been attacked by terrorists. No one had been with him to tell him what to do, what to say. So he held on to the primer he had been reading from to school children, and he waited and waited and waited.

They've seen me make decisions, they've seen me under trying times, they've seen me weep, they've seen me laugh, they've seen me hug.

—GEORGE W. BUSH,
USA Today, August 27, 2004

His lies should have prompted calls for impeachment. Bill Clinton had been impeached for a sexual interlude that harmed no one. Just as they had then, the cowed Democrats, now watching Bush run rampant over civil liberties with a contrived "Patriot Act," stood quietly by like good Germans.

God loves you, and I love you. And you can count on both of us as a powerful message that people who wonder about their future can hear.

—GEORGE W. BUSH,
Los Angeles, California, March 3, 2004

Like a reckless, petulant rich child playing war with toy soldiers given to him by his daddy," he furiously waged his personal war against "Sa-dahm Hoo-sayan," a brutal tyrant, yes, but, more important to Bush, the man who had once threatened his daddy in an attempted assassination, and who, incidentally, controlled abundant oil. Never mind that the Iraqi dictator had once been an ally of the Bush family, and had during a time not too distant been given American weapons to wage his own terrible wars.

The CIA laid out several scenarios and said life could be lousy, life could be OK, life could be better, and they were just guessing as to what the conditions might be like.

—GEORGE W. BUSH,
New York City, September 21, 2004

During the initial violence, Iraq's abundant oil wells had been guarded sternly (while museums and libraries were surrendered to looters). Billions of dollars would be made by American companies restoring what America had destroyed. Vice President Cheney manipulated to grant war contracts, no bidding allowed, to Halliburton Corporation, which he had once headed; and on the front, badly trained, hurriedly trained, untrained, inadequately equipped soldiers continued to fall—soon, over a thousand dead and counting.

> This has been tough weeks in that country.
> —GEORGE W. BUSH,
> Washington, D.C., April 13, 2004

War spawned its repulsive cruelties—the beheading of kidnapped men by Iraqis, the exhibition of headless corpses hanging from poles, the abuse of Iraqi prisoners by Americans, gaunt Iraqis laughingly photographed, hooded, leashed, murdered.

> More Muslims have died at the hands of killers than—
> I say more Muslims—a lot of Muslims have died—I
> don't know the exact count—at Istanbul. Look at
> these different places around the world where there's
> been tremendous death and destruction because
> killers kill.
> —GEORGE W. BUSH,
> Washington, D.C., January 29, 2004

> I hope you leave here and walk out and say, "What did
> he say?"
> —GEORGE W. BUSH,
> Beaverton, Oregon, August 13, 2004

Propaganda churned. Support Our Troops was twisted into supporting the war—and therefore supporting the maiming and dying of men and women on the front lines, the slaughter of Iraqis. The majority of American troops were hardly more than kids, some as young as eighteen. How many cumulative years and decades of life, of possible joy, had Bush stolen from all those men and women on the frontlines, and from their families?

> Obviously, I pray every day there's less casualty.
>
> —GEORGE W. BUSH,
> Fort Hood, Texas, April 11, 2004

In the talks of politicians, there was an eerie silence about the dead and dying men and women. It was if all those deaths were merely "collateral damage," incidental to a larger cause: Bush's terrible illegitimate war. It was as if the dying and destruction were to be taken for granted as necessary, just necessary, only necessary. No photographs were allowed to be shown of the coffins of the American dead returned under the camouflage of night.

> We will make sure our troops have all that is necessary to complete their missions. That's why I went to the Congress last September and proposed fundamental—supplemental funding, which is money for armor and body parts and ammunition and fuel.
>
> —GEORGE W. BUSH,
> Erie, Pennsylvania, September 4, 2004

Billions of dollars available for war in Iraq were unavailable to improve education in America.

Then you wake up at the high school level and find out
that the illiteracy level of our children are appalling.
—GEORGE W. BUSH,
Washington, D.C., January 23, 2004

Millions of Americans lacked insurance, each day facing financial disaster. In pretending to address the problem, the ex-
governor of Texas shifted emphasis away from rich, gouging
insurance companies and onto those who might seek relief from
corporate malpractice.

Too many good docs are getting out of the business.
Too many OB-GYNs aren't able to practice their love
with women all across this country.
—GEORGE W. BUSH,
Poplar Bluff, Missouri, September 6, 2004

Two tyrants, Bush and Hussein, faced each other over a blood-
spattered battleground. Captured, Hussein would be justifiably
tried for war crimes. By having lied to force the country into war,
by having the blood of thousands on his hands, Bush, too,
qualified.

There is no such thing necessarily in a dictatorial
regime of iron-clad absolutely solid evidence. The evidence I had was the best possible evidence that he had
a weapon.

—GEORGE W. BUSH,
Meet the Press, February 8, 2004

And yet millions of Americans supported and support the
lying ex-governor of Texas. Why? September 11 had given him
and his right-wing cadre the opportunity to achieve their

long-determined goal, the seizure of Iraq and its richness. They grabbed that opportunity. A machine of propaganda forced connections, always in the name of patriotism. Yellow ribbons sprouted all over America, flags flew, patriotic pins decorated lapels, all to be read as support for the war. The spurious equation was repeated: The Twin Towers had been destroyed by Bin Laden and his bullies; Bin Laden was an ally of Sadam Hussein; Hussein, the dictator, was the president of Iraq. Iraq had to be attacked. Weapons of mass destruction were there! There was an imminent threat! If war was not taken there, it would be brought here! The message of fear was drummed over and over. The vast populace repeated it, until it was so. Lies became unassailable facts.

My views are one that speaks to freedom.
—GEORGE W. BUSH,
Washington, D.C., January 29, 2004

Ignorant but wily, Bush tapped into the deepest prejudices, always roiling under the surface of America, ancestral fears and grudges. Foreigners—dark foreigners—were lurking at every border, inside every building, waiting to take over the country, its institutions. Those suspicions, that brewing hatred, extended to everything that had struggled to triumph out of the quagmire of prejudice and repression. Women free to own their bodies? Homosexuals claiming rights? The poor demanding help and education?

So what if 80 percent of the country believed Bush was "lying" or "hiding something" or "mostly lying." If he was lying—and, mind you, nobody said he was, the Lord love 'im—it was for a good cause; he was a Christian, right?—and God loved Christians and hated "them." Remember the axis of evil? Never mind that Bush came from wealth, private schools; he talked just like 'em, stumbled over words, acted just like folks, good folks, good Christian white folks, like them.

He opposed birth control, right? Held no truck with fancy experiments to replicate and interfere with the Lord's works. No matter how deep the country sank under the expense of war and Haliburton's thefts, he championed "family values," even a constitutional amendment to deprive them queers of any legitimacy. Didn't he question the need for helping the lazy poor, providing health insurance to the indigent? Maybe not in so many words, no; but they understood him. He spoke their language. He was one of 'em. Sure, American boys were dying, but they were dyin' for patriotism, for love of country, for freedom, for America's safety, for Jesus. So bring 'em on, them heathens! And he had compassion, Pres'dent Bush did, just like them, compassion for bereaved good, patriotic folks.

After all, hadn't he shared their grief, hugged moms and dads? The grotesque banality of evil.

ABOUT THE AUTHOR

JOHN RECHY IS the first novelist to be honored with PEN-USA West's Lifetime Achievement Award. He is also the recipient of the Publishing Triangle's Bill Whitehead Lifetime Achievement Award. He is the author of twelve novels, among them the international bestseller *City of Night*, *The Coming of the Night*, *Numbers*, *Rushes*, *The Miraculous Day of Amalia Gómez*, *Our Lady of Babylon*, and *The Life and Adventures of Lyle Clemens*. He is also the author of the nonfiction bestseller *The Sexual Outlaw*. A National Endowment for the Arts recipient, he has also written several plays. He lives in Los Angeles.

Visit John Rechy on the Web at www.johnrechy.com.